# The H

## &

# Haunting

## of the

# Stanley Hotel

### 2nd Edition

## by

## Rebecca F. Pittman

For my sons and their families.
You are my joy!


And...


For Freelan Oscar Stanley: a visionary extraordinaire.

# Contents

## Part II:  The Haunting

# AKNOWLEDGMENTS

The following people were invaluable in helping me create what I hope you will find to be a comprehensive telling of the wonderful tale that is the history of the Stanley Hotel in Estes Park, Colorado. While there is not enough room in one tome to document all the myriad stories of its creation and hauntings, I have done my utmost to supply you with the hotel's background, latest events, and of course, its on-going dance with the paranormal.

A huge Thank You to the following, in no particular order: Estes Park Museum, Stanley Museum, Estes Park Trail Gazette, Rocky Mountain News, Judge Gary Brown, Susan S. Davis, Ron Lasky, Celeste Lasky, Kirk Fisher, Ron Bueker, Madame Vera, "Scary Mary" Orton, Randy Flanders, Glamourdaze.com, Fred Payne Clatworthy, Colorado Press, COFPhoto.com, Sara Walker, Jack Bullard, Mary Stickland, Chris Hanson, Linda Hostler, Rip Tragle, Trip Advisor, Longmont Times, Fort Collins: The Coloradoan, Greeley Tribune, Loveland Herald, Boulder Daily Camera, Janice Raymond, Movie Man, Dwayne Elmarr, Linda Elmarr, Melton Museum of Antique Automobiles, Denver Business Journal, reliancefiremuseum.com, Stephen King, Bev Vincent, Historic Fall River Hydroplant, Loyd Auerbach, Whaleyhouse.org, Chris Bechard with Alpenglowmedia.com, Marilyn Rudgers, Kris Tennant and Mike Coletta with the Rocky Mountain Ghost Explorers, Denise Brandy, Patrick Andrade with the New York Times, Spiritbearparanormal.com, Linda Grouper, Mike Arnett, Danielle Moniker, Debbie Overton, Beckyphotography.com, David Juliano with The Shadowlands, allwomenstalk.com, and the Denver Post.

For all the intrepid souls who submitted their ghost stories, photos and accounts of their stay at the Stanley Hotel, my heartfelt thanks.

While every consideration was taken to validate stories and photos, the author retains no responsibility for those submitted to her with fraudulent intent.        Rebecca F. Pittman  July, 2015

i

Rebecca F. Pittman

# THE HISTORY

# PROLOGUE

*"Well, if I were going to haunt anyone, this would certainly be the house I'd do it in."* –Lance Schroeder from *The House on Haunted Hill* (1958)

*Estes Park, Colorado: Circa 1909*

*Freelan Oscar (F.O.) Stanley stood on the wide veranda of his sprawling hotel and looked out over the Rocky Mountains. He took a deep breath of the cleansing mountain air and smiled. These jagged precipices were more than just a panoramic view of unparalleled beauty; the Colorado Rockies had saved his life. Diagnosed two years earlier with tuberculosis, the doctors had given him no more than 6-12 months to live. Yet here he stood (at 55 years of age), frail, but alive and well—and hosting the Grand Opening of his latest venture: the Stanley Hotel of Estes Park, Colorado.*

*Sunlight glinted off the water of Lake Estes to his left. He glanced that way; taking in the 9-hole golf course and tennis courts he had created for his summer resort. His appreciative gaze fell over the towering pines, winding drive, and the raw beauty of the 140-acres he had chosen to showcase his vision of an enclave*

4

*of magnificent buildings constituting the hotel grounds. Tonight, music from the Steinway piano in the Music Room, and the soft sound of stringed instruments in the Dining Room, would fill the air. The pristine guest rooms would pulse with people from all over the world as his Stanley Steamer Mountain Buses carried them up the treacherous canyon roads to this very spot. They would tell their friends and family they had turned the key to the first electrically-lit hotel rooms in history.*

*F.O. paused and listened. It was the rumble of car engines. They were arriving! He turned and walked across the freshly painted white boards of the veranda—it was time to alert the staff to be in readiness to greet their distinguished guests. "The Grand Old Man of Estes Park" took one last look at his beloved mountains, straightened a rocking chair, repositioned a Boston fern, and walked through the double doors into the hotel lobby.*

Stanley Hotel in 1909 with Stanley Touring Cars
Photo courtesy of the Stanley Museum

*Within minutes, the lobby was bustling with activity. Hotel stewards rushed to and fro, organizing luggage, and directing guests to the various rooms on the first floor. Women were cautioned that the Pinon Room was for gentlemen only, and were discreetly pointed toward the Parlor, or Music Room, where cushioned chairs were positioned in inviting vignettes. Music could be heard coming from the Dining Room where a pianist and several violinists were serenading the delighted guests. Silver trays laden with cool beverages and delicacies were being passed among the throng by a staff in full livery; their white gloved hands deftly proffering filled crystal stemware.*

Stanley Hotel lobby early 1900s. The staff stands ready to serve.
Photo courtesy of the Stanley Museum

*The sun was beginning to set behind the mountain peaks, sending a prism of pastel hues through the arched windows. Chandeliers sparkled as the first all-electric hotel in the country came to life. Throughout the 100-foot-long lobby guests were chatting excitedly, many looking over the brochure touting the myriad activities offered at the hotel. Some were already making plans for horseback rides or croquet games on the front lawn; a few men had challenged each other to a game of billiards, while still others were teaming up for golf. Children ran gleefully through the polished rooms. Ahead lay a summer of unlimited delights in this strange new mountain setting.*

*With the flourish of an ink pen the hotel registers were signed. Ladies in Gibson-style hairdo's and flowing gowns took the arm of gentlemen in cut-away coats and stovetop hats. With eyes raised to the moon rising through the giant Palladian windows above, the couples swept up the grand staircase and into the history of Freelan Oscar's Stanley Hotel.*

Stanley Hotel Grand Staircase. Photo by Rebecca F. Pittman

### There is Something Odd Here

*As the Lady's Maids and the Gentlemen's Valets unpacked their employer's suitcases in the various guest rooms of the hotel, they felt a slight uneasiness settling in. Inexplicably, they glanced over their shoulders, as if expecting someone to be standing behind them. Trying to dismiss it as only the usual unease in being in a new location, they went about their duties of hanging up gowns, retrieving the jewelry boxes, and turning down the beds.*

*Something fell in the bathroom. A window sash rattled. Did that door just swing shut on its own? What was happening? It seemed their wealthy employers were noticing things as well. The word "atmosphere" began peppering their conversation as the shadows in the hallways outside lengthened.*

*Darkness fell in the Rocky Mountains, cloaking the craggy faces of the wild terrain in sunken shadows and the cast silhouettes of pine trees; their darkened forms appearing as an army of giant's arms and legs thrown out across the valley. An owl hoots nearby. Somewhere an elk bugles in response; its ethereal cry echoing against the rocks.*

*Darkness also seeps into the hallways and corners of the Stanley Hotel. The venue's activity settles down as the upper floors are claimed by paying guests ready to turn in for the evening. The grand hotel's suites mirror the Gilded Age when four poster beds and Boston ferns were the popular décor. Brass skeleton keys placed on beside tables glint in the moonlight streaming in through the eyelet window sheers.*

*The hotel guests take one last surreptitious look about their rooms before settling uneasily beneath the folds of opulent bedspreads. Reluctantly lights are extinguished and ears strain to hear noises that do not belong. In Room 217 the claw foot tub gleams softly through the open doorway, causing an involuntary shudder from the woman watching it from her pillow.*

*The hotel sighs; the night heavy against her boards. Pine boughs sigh along with it as a mountain breeze rushes through them. Something is dancing to phantom music in the Music Room; its iridescent gown sweeping the polished floor. The soft sound of balls falling into leather pockets can be heard coming from the Billiard Room where only moonlight is playing upon the felt-covered tables. The ivories of the piano in the Dining Room are rising and falling beneath unseen fingers—its tune lapping at the dark window glass. A hint of cherry-blend tobacco smoke wafts through the abandoned rooms and dissipates into gleaming walls.*

*A spectral breath raises the hairs on the night clerk's neck as he bends over the day's receipts. He places a warm hand on the spot and shivers.*

*Nighttime has come to the Stanley Hotel.*

## CHAPTER ONE

# THE HOUSE THAT STANLEY BUILT

*"The distance that the dead have gone, Does not at first appear—
Their coming back seems possible, For many an ardent year."*
--Emily Dickinson

The Stanley Hotel was not the first building Freelan Oscar Stanley built in Estes Park. His first creation came from the same drawing board as the famous hotel, but was on a much smaller, and more personal, scale. High on a hill overlooking his beloved Rockies, F.O. built his home, only minutes from the acreage he had selected to build his sprawling mountain retreat. Here, he and Flora would spend their summer days, returning to Newton, Massachusetts for the winter months. There was enough room for visiting friends and family, a garage to house the Stanley Steamer, breathtaking views of the Rocky Mountains, and wildlife that ventured into their yard on a regular basis. Flora could finally stop living the rustic mountain life and decorate her home in the manner to which she was accustomed.

F.O. and Flora were happy with the new home. Based on its location tight against the jagged cliffs of Lumpy Ridge, they decided to call their home…

## "ROCKSIDE"

415 Wonderview Avenue in Estes Park, Colorado. F.O. and Flora Stanley's home. Photo courtesy of Rebecca F. Pittman

# F.O. and Flora Stanley

Freelan Oscar (F.O.) Stanley, and his twin brother, Francis Edgar (F.E.) Stanley, were born in Kingfield, Maine on June 1, 1849. F.O. later married Flora Jane Record Tileston in April 1876.

Flora Stanley had always stood beside her husband and championed all his myriad endeavors, inventions and dreams. The Stanley Hotel was no exception. She took to the title of hotel proprietor with aplomb.

*Flora Stanley walked through the lobby of her new hotel. All-in-all she was pleased with the final result of the gold and burgundy color scheme. It looked rich without being ostentatious. The dark wood of the Smoking and Billiard Rooms were a dramatic contrast to the all-white Lady's Parlor. She entered into this pristine room, looking almost celestial in its pure white walls, and ran a hand along the polished mantel of the fireplace. Her fingers trailed the outline of the ram's head carved there. The deep velvet of the chairs gave the room a sumptuous feeling. The leather club chairs were clustered about a small table while two rocking chairs flanked the room.*

Stanley Hotel Parlor in 1920. A woman is seated reading. The Steinway piano can be seen in the arch. Today this room is called the Music Room. Photo courtesy of the Estes Park Museum.

*It were these quiet moments Flora enjoyed at the hotel; when the guests were down for the night and she could roam the first floor rooms without the ubiquitous chatter of maids asking her questions, or patrons stopping her to engage her in conversation. She reclaimed that which was hers...her space, her designs, her dreams.*

*The melancholy settled over her faster than usual this evening. She felt the familiar tug in her stomach and shifting of her mood. Walking to the tall arched windows of the Parlor she looked out at the dark towering hunks of rock across the field from her. The moon was resting on its side against one of the mountains, its crescent shape reminding her of a Cheshire Cat's lop-sided grin.*

*Her eyes suddenly saw her own reflection in the dark glass and she studied it with the objectiveness a painter might use when sizing up his subject. The hair was piled high in a bun, a few wisps of hair escaping the pins. The nose was not as aquiline as it had been in her youth. It had spread out as the skin began to sag into furrows around her eyes, cheeks and mouth. Absently she pushed the loose skin back toward her ear and for a moment saw the girl she had been.*

*With a deep sigh, Flora turned and walked slowly to her piano where she would spend the late evening hours playing softly. It was 3 o'clock in the morning, and for now, for this blissful moment, the hotel and its secrets belonged solely to her.*

Flora Jane Record Tileston, later Mrs. Freelan Oscar (F.O.) Stanley (1848-1939), was born in Maine and died at her home in Estes Park, Colorado. In *Untitled Poem*, she writes: *The ghostly rap...Call answering ghosts from Memory's hosts I strive to stay in vain,* Flora almost predicts her ethereal appearances, the most documented of all the ghost stories at the Stanley Hotel. At last, her heavy "mortal coil" has been shed, and she can wander the halls and rooms of her beautiful Stanley Hotel, no longer encumbered by the debilitating blindness of her later years. She may have also suffered from what we call today manic-depression, or bi-polar disorder. As a member of the Estes Park community, she was active in what became the Estes Park Women's Club. Curiously, the club's most successful fundraiser was Flora's program: she dressed as a gypsy and told people's fortunes. (*Susan S. Davis, A History and Tour of the Stanley Hotel*)

## Untitled Poem
### by
### Flora J. T. Stanley

Among the leaves,
The sad wind grieves,
The rain falls drearily,
The branches sway.
In a weird way.
The clouds move wearily.


The ghostly rap
And knock and tap
Of branches and wind and rain
Call answering ghosts
From Memory's hosts
I strive to stay in vain.


A Mellow note
From feathered throat
Falls with the falling rain
Above the grief
Of wind and leaf
Drips down the sweet refrain.

So amid the ghosts
Of Memory's hosts

A living hope appear'd
And from her throat
A silv'ry note
Falls with the falling tears.

Oft in the dark
The firefly's spark
Will cheer the traveler's way
And amid the rain
Thy sweet refrain
Sends music throughout the day.

*Flora Stanley first noticed something amiss with her eyesight when she looked across the length of the hotel lobby and found that objects in her peripheral vision were blurry. She blinked several times in succession to clear away the cloudy rim encircling her eyes, but it remained. As the months advanced, it worsened. She hid it from Freelan as much as possible. He had already become irritable with her mood swings and what she thought of as her "dark times." With his no-nonsense Yankee mentality of stalwart perseverance, he had no patience with frailties. While there was no doubt of his devotion to her, she felt at times as though she was a burden to him.*

*It wasn't until she tripped over a chair the maid had moved while cleaning their residence's living room that F.O. noticed something was wrong. He helped lift her from the floor and asked if she was alright. She brushed it off, somewhat irritably, and blamed it on the chair being in an unfamiliar place. When it happened again at the house, and twice at the hotel, F.O. took her to see a doctor. The diagnosis was impending blindness. An operation did little to improve her condition. New rules at their home and at the hotel were now enforced. The furnishings were not to be moved. Simple tricks were put in place to help the proud matriarch of the hotel go about her life with as much independence as possible.*

Flora Stanley in later years

One of the most-tender stories involving F.O. and Flora is the one told of how he would try and help her with social occasions as her eyesight began to fail. Not wanting others to know that she was unable to see them clearly, F.O. assisted her by a very simple scheme they developed. They would sit side by side on the veranda, rocking and talking in their companionable way. If F.O. spotted an acquaintance ascending the stone steps to the hotel, he would whisper to Flora who it was he saw approaching and quickly giving her a few simple traits of their appearance. He might tell her that Mrs. So-and-So was coming up the steps and she was wearing a blue brocade dress with a strand of pearls. Flora would then rise hospitably with her husband, extend her hand in greeting and say something such as, "Why Donna, I love your new pearls. They are lovely."

Before moving to Colorado the Stanley's lived in an elegant home in Newton, Massachusetts where F.O. and his brother F.E. were involved in several businesses, not the least of which was creating Stanley Steamer Motor Cars. Both brothers flourished, the money rolled in, and the future looked promising.

In 1903, F.O. was delivered a sucker punch when he was told by his physician that he was suffering from tuberculosis and could expect to live another 6 months. He was advised to seek the clean mountain air of Colorado in an effort to stave off the illness for as long as possible. In that era Colorado was often heralded as a cure-all for tuberculosis. Manitou Springs, a small hamlet nestled near Colorado Springs, Colorado, built resorts where people suffering with the malady could come to recuperate.

The Stanley's immediately departed for Denver, arriving by train in early 1903. Later that spring F.O. ordered his Stanley Steamer car shipped from Newton. But as summer descended upon Denver, the couple found it too hot and carrying some of the same pollutants as other big cities. His doctor in Denver found them a cabin near the Elkhorn Lodge in Estes Park, and the Stanley's settled in.

Surprisingly, F.O. found his health not only improving but beginning to thrive. He gained almost 30 pounds, and his lungs began to clear. The constant coughing abated and he felt renewed...and ready to launch his next career move. Never one to sit idly by, F.O. began plans to follow the other lodging entrepreneurs who found money in visiting tourists wanting to explore the scenic beauty of the area.

Flora Stanley, who left her stately home in Massachusetts, and followed her man to the outback of the rugged west, had one stipulation. Essentially it was "You can build your hotel, but first you are building me a home I can furnish and regain some sense of refinement." The cabin they had summered in had worn out its rustic welcome.

F.O. bought an 8.4 acre plot only ½ mile from the site where he was to build his hotel. He began construction on a beautiful new home set high on a hill overlooking the mountains. It was designed in the Georgian Revival style by the same architect that would design the Stanley Hotel; in fact it is a miniature replica of the hotel. It was completed shortly after in 1904, with a price tag of $7,000. ($184,210 in 2014.) It is white with a red roof and was used as the Stanley's summer home until F.O.'s death in 1940. He and Flora named it "Rockside."

"Rockside," the Stanley home in Estes Park, Colorado.
Photo by Rebecca F. Pittman

The home was 5,240 square feet. The property contained a two-story garage with a turntable floor that allowed F.O. to rotate the car around so he wouldn't have to ever back up. It was well known that he was not fond of backing his car. The Stanley Steamer also had issues with the backing mechanism—it shot back at full steam! The house had 4 bedrooms within, and 4 bathrooms. It also housed a working Otis elevator. The staircase was an exact replica of the one found in the Stanley Hotel, complete with the 4 twists of balusters found on each step.

Today, the house looks just as it did when F.O. had it built. Many of his furnishings are still there, lovingly preserved.

Grand staircase in Rockside, F.O. Stanley's Estes Park home.
Stanley home interior photos by Kirk Fisher.

The wallpaper in the house (shown here in the photos) was created in 1904 by F.O. It is patented as a Stanley design and is still beautiful today. The dentil crown molding is also original.

Through the closed door to the right of the stairs in the photo are the kitchen and a working Otis elevator. With the exception of a remodel in the kitchen area, a screened-in porch at the front of the house, and an added 4-car garage, the home looks remarkably unchanged.

The original dining room table at Rockside can seat 4-20 people and houses 7 leaves. The floors were milled in Hallowell Park Mill in Rocky Mountain National Park; the wood was from Hidden Valley. The original floors are still in existence.

While touring the home in 2015, this author was privileged to see the original horse-hair cushion in the living room, bell pull, furnishings and F.O.'s billiard table. The home is in pristine shape, thanks to the current owners who have been there 30 years.

Dining Room with original table, breakfront & wall coverings.

Original fireplace w/green glazed Italian tile, brass rail, fan & irons.

Rockside's living room with original fireplace and molding. The Music Room's fireplace at the Stanley Hotel is an exact replica. All interior photos courtesy of Kirk Fisher.

Upstairs landing of Rockside. Mr. Stanley's door is on the right. Flora's is on the left.

F.O. Stanley's room. The bathroom was added in 1914.

In the Victorian era husband and wife had separate rooms. The Stanley's followed suit. The above photo is how F.O.'s room looks today. The tulip-shaped light fixture was very popular in the Gilded Age and was found in most wealthy homes.

Flora Stanley's room with a sitting area and private bath.

Today the house is privately owned and not open to the public. The guest house, which once housed the turntable floor for Mr. Stanley's car, is now outfitted with a bedroom, living room and kitchen. A four-car garage has been added to the property with a storage area above.

One maid lived with the Stanley's. Her room led onto the elevator, even though she was not allowed to use it. She had a back staircase leading to the kitchen, which was customary for servants in that era. The maid's room is a step down from the upstairs hallway and has a private bath and balcony.

We mentioned F.O.'s dislike of backing up his car. According to his brother's granddaughter, Augusta Tapley, backing up wasn't her Uncle's only driving vice.

F.O. Stanley in a 1913 Stanley Steamer
Photo courtesy of the Stanley Museum

"He was called the 'Grand Old Man of Estes Park' and whenever he drove anywhere you got out of the way!" Augusta reported. "They used to have little round things, you were supposed to go around them, you know, and stay to the right to get on the main street. Uncle Freel would just cut right across from the other side of it; he was an absolutely wild driver! He went very fast and he used to see how fast he could go from Denver up to Estes Park, and I'll never forget because he let me drive. One woman who used to go out and stay the summer made it a certain length of time, and he was so pleased that I beat her record, and I was proud I beat it!"

(Augusta Tapley, courtesy of Susan S. Davis, *Stanley Family Reunion*, June 7, 1981, Kingfield, Maine.)

Guests and relatives visiting the home shared stories of the lighthearted fun they had there. There were always games and puzzles, music and laughter. It was said that you had barely entered the door before you were asked to solve a puzzle or spell a difficult word. F.O.'s sister, Chansonetta, often stayed there, taking some of her famous photographs of the inspiring landscape around her.

Flora Stanley had become totally blind while living in the house. She relied heavily on F.O.; although she exerted her independence by making sure the furnishings remained in a fixed position so that she could get around without assistance. She lived with the darkness for eleven years. After suffering a stroke in the hotel lobby, her life was never the same. Flora died in 1939. F.O. died from a heart attack one year later in 1940.

While interviewing the current owner of the F.O. Stanley home in Estes Park, this author was told an unusual story concerning Flora Stanley's death.

A physician had been attending Flora as she lay dying in her bedroom at their home on Wonderview. Mrs. Stanley had been bedridden for some time. F.O. was seated in his study on the second floor, just down the hallway from her room, working on some business papers. The physician stuck his head into where F.O. sat pouring over his work and said softly, "Mr. Stanley? Mrs. Stanley is only moments from death. If you wish to say your Goodbyes, you should come now."

F.O., without barely raising his head, said, "Tell her it's been a good life."

Whether his hesitation at going to her was due to not wanting to see her last moments, or that he had already said his Goodbyes in private earlier, it is hard to say. The stiff-upper lip Yankee mentality was very much a part of his make-up.

The story continued with a bizarre twist. Mrs. Stanley passed away on July 25, 1939. The Stanley's had been in the habit of spending summers in Estes Park and returning to their other home on the east coast to negate dealing with winter in the Rockies. Keeping with that custom, F.O. had Flora placed "on ice" in a vault in Denver until he returned to Maine in the fall, at which point he had her buried at Riverside Cemetery in Kingfield. This story is born out in her obituary that appeared in the Estes Park Trail on July 28, 1939.

## MRS. F. O. STANLEY DIES HERE MONDAY NIGHT

Mrs. F. O. Stanley, 91, wife of the inventor of the Stanley Steamer automobile and builder of the Stanley hotel in Estes Park, died Monday night at the Stanley summer home in Estes Park.

Thirty-six years ago Mrs. Stanley and her husband drove into Estes Park over the toll road from Lyons. It was the first time an automobile had made the trip to the community and was considered a remarkable adventure.

Since that time the Stanleys have made Estes Park their summer home.

The Stanleys had no children. A niece, Miss Dorothy Emmons, Mrs. Stanley's closest relative, arrived in the Park from Boston last weekend, only a few days after Mrs. Stanley became ill.

The body was taken to Denver and placed in a vault until fall, when it will be transferred to Maine for burial there. Funeral services will be held at that time.

Article courtesy of the Estes Park Trail Gazette.
Posted from the Estes Park Trail on July 28, 1939.

# F. O. Stanley Died Wednesday Night in Newton, Massachusetts

Estes Park's "Grand Old Man" is dead!

Ninety-one years of age last June, F. O. Stanley died of a heart ailment at his home in

F. O. Stanley

Newton, Mass., late Wednesday night. The end was not unexpected as he suffered an attack last weekend, and physicians told

relatives that he could live only a few days at the most.

For the past thirty-eight years Stanley has spent the summers in Estes Park, where he built his home, and actively entered into the life of the community.

Stanley was the inventor of the Stanley Steamer, one of the first automobiles, and the inventor of the dry plate process, which revolutionized the photography business.

Stanley was also known for the violins that he made. Musical authorities compare favorably the instruments that he has made with those of the old masters. His interest in music was a lifelong hobby, and each summer for the past few years, a "Stanley night" was held at the Stanley hotel, and Miss Josephine Monahan, who plays one of his violins, and her ensemble would play his favorite selections, and a number of his own original compositions.

Coming to Estes Park in 1903 for his health, Stanley later built the Stanley hotel, drawing the plans himself. Construction began on the large structure in (Continued on Page 7)

Notice of F.O. Stanley's death in the Estes Park Trail on Friday, October 4, 1940. Article courtesy of the Estes Park Trail Gazette.

Graves of F.O. Stanley and Flora T. Stanley. They are buried in Riverside Cemetery in Kingfield, Maine in the Stanley family plot.

F.O. Stanley sitting on the front porch of his beloved "Rockside."
Photo courtesy of Estes Park Museum

My deep appreciation to Judge Gary Brown in allowing me to interview him for this book. He and his wife Kelly have taken such wonderful care of F.O.'s home on Wonderview. Judge Brown is very knowledgeable in all things Stanley and it was a delight to get to know him. Please respect the owner's privacy. The home is on private property and not open to the public.

Chapter Two

# THE STANLEY HOTEL

*"For who can wonder that man should feel a vague belief in tales of disembodied spirits wandering through those places which they once dearly affected, when he himself, scarcely less separated from his old world than they, is forever lingering upon past emotions and bygone times, and hovering, the ghost of his former self, about the places and people that warmed his hearts of old?"*
*--Master Humphrey's Clock,* Charles Dickens

The Stanley Hotel was destined to make its mark on history, whether through the reputation of the remarkable man who built it, or from the spotlight played prominently upon it from a hit book and movie. The international obsession with the paranormal that seems to grow each year peers through the hotel keyholes as well.

Consistently rated in the Top Ten Most-Haunted Places in America, it is usually featured in one of the top two positions. Psychics from around the world have probed its hallways and energy centers, hoping to get a glimpse of something that would validate their belief in another realm. The not-so psychically gifted come here with their own agenda. Some want to see an original Stanley Steamer Motor Car, such as the one residing in the hotel lobby, and to learn more about the man who created it. Others are drawn by the desire to see the room where Stephen King, an internationally recognized author, was inspired to write his bestselling book, *The Shining*. When the book became a blockbuster movie by the same name, the interest in the hotel catapulted. King later returned to the Stanley to film his television mini-series from the book. When *Dumb and Dumber*, the hit comedy, featuring Jim Carrey and Jeff Daniels, also featured the Stanley Hotel in the last third of the movie, the venue's dance with Hollywood continued.

Undoubtedly the hotel's main fascination for visiting guests is the continuing reports that there is something we can't explain going on here. Even non-believers in the ghostly inhabitants are reluctant to say there isn't a feeling of "presence" here, and that some darn odd things keep happening they can't explain.

The Ghost Tours at the hotel offer cards to those who which to write down their experiences and leave them at the tour desk. The "in-box" is piled high. I have stories sent to me at my Facebook page for this book, and others have been told to me through other means. Sorting out the reviews that I can authenticate to the best of my ability is sometimes formidable. It is my desire to relay the underlying history of the hotel, and its cast of characters who have called the Stanley home long after their eulogies were delivered, as well as report on its paranormal activity.

The Stanley Hotel receives a good deal of attention due to the fact there are so many entities reportedly residing within its historic walls. Some psychics have been inside and refused to return due to the sheer avalanche of psychic phenomenon they found here. Though sensing no malice from the inhabitants, they said it was just simply too much and too many to deal with. Most will concede to discovering at least twelve different identities roaming the halls of the hotel complex.

Madame Vera is now a resident psychic at the Stanley Hotel and I can vouch for her authenticity. She told me the spirits at the hotel are people who were happy there—including Flora Stanley, whom she said "welcomed her" on her first day at the hotel.

There were to my knowledge no murders here; no suicides or acts of wanton violence as noted in Mr. King's novel. The only documented death at the hotel seems to be that of a transient woman who crawled into the Concert Hall basement through a window one winter to keep warm. She froze to death and is very active in the basement of that building. Her name is Lucy and we will talk more about her later in the Hauntings section of the book.

The Stanley Hotel rises from the jagged rock as surely as if it had grown there, content to be an addition to the formidable Colorado Rockies and the crumpled mass of Lumpy Ridge. The Twin Owls rock formation is perched atop the Ridge and looks down over the hotel's back courtyard and watchful windows like a talisman against evil.

Beneath the 4-story structure a narrow tunnel is testament to the fact the hotel's foundation is indeed built from chiseled rock. Here and there skeletal tree roots protrude from the jagged stone walls of the tunnel; a passageway used today by hotel employees. At times these members of the hotel staff hear their names whispered from the shadows as they pass a small cave-like entrance branching off into a dead-end of rock, pipes, and utility wires.

The cave in the Stanley Hotel tunnel.
Photo courtesy of Ron Bueker.

The Stanley Hotel boasts 289 rooms, and most are reportedly haunted. While interviewing employees of the Stanley, I was told by more than one front desk clerk that all the rooms are haunted. Based on the plethora of stories sent my way concerning guest experiences at the hotel, I would have to agree. There are those rooms however that seem to be "hot spots" of activity. We will visit them in the Haunting section of the book.

The windows in this historic hotel number 466. Not all who peer from them at breathtaking views of the surrounding mountains are earthbound. The late Lord Dunraven has been seen numerous times looking down from the window of Room 407. Apparitions have also appeared on the other side of the glass—defying the laws of physics—as they float outside, two or more stories above ground.

As for the antique wooden doors of the Stanley Hotel, there are 378. Most behave in an acceptable manner, and remain sensibly shut and bolted, except when inexplicably opened by unseen hands. Room 401 has a frequent problem with the closet door remaining shut, although its latch is perfectly sound. Numerous experiments have been made to see if the door is hung at an odd angle or if the latch is worn, causing the door to pop open from a footfall or vibration. In this case, the door shuts with a distinctive click and cannot be opened without turning the handle a full hard twist. Yet there is film footage capturing the door swaying open, preceded by an audible click as it unfastens itself and swings slowly into the room. Usually this is followed by some type of paranormal activity: an occupant's reading glasses being tossed across the room, jewelry disappearing, or bed covers tugged away. And then, as one watches, the door swings slowly closed; the latch clicking soundly into place.

The guest rooms at the hotel are typically booked to capacity, despite its ghostly reputation…or perhaps because of it. Psychics and ghost hunters continue to come here, hoping for evidence of the afterlife. Unlike the guests who spend a determined amount of time here, obligingly checking out at the agreed upon hour, many of the hotel's inhabitants linger on—floating down hallways, knocking on doors, staging unseen parties and calling out to the staff. Chairs move, items disappear and orbs play languidly in dimly-lit hallways long after the mortal residences retire for the evening. The sound of children playing on the fourth floor is a common occurrence. Many guests have reported hearing laughter and tiny feet running along the hallway when no children are booked into the hotel. The sound of jacks being tossed and rubber balls bouncing along wooden floors can be heard even though the halls have been carpeted for some time now.

Reports of apparitions dressed in attire from a bygone era may not be news. But the continued sightings of F.O. Stanley walking through the lobby and hotel bar area have been seen on too many occasions to dismiss it as folklore. His image bent over a billiard table is also one commonly seen, and he has even joined a tour group or two.

They hang on…these vestiges of yesteryear, as tenaciously as the sparse trees above timberline—an area of the mountains where living things should no longer thrive. It is, in its way, a thumbing of the nose at our foolish inclination to believe all things behave within rigid guidelines or measurable entities.

Theories abound as to why so much paranormal activity is found in one area. I say area, as the ghostly occurrences are not relegated to just the main hotel. The Stanley Hotel complex is actually 35 acres and contains 11 buildings, including the Manor House, Concert Hall, Carriage House, 2 Dormitories for employees, the former Ice House, Laundry, a former Gate House, a new Gate House, and the Manager's House. The basement of the Concert Hall is one area where accounts of paranormal activity are prevalent.

The outdoor swimming pool at the hotel was recently covered over to allow for additional event space. There were at one time tennis courts, a 9-hole golf course, and an air strip associated with the hotel grounds.

# It Begins…

F.O. Stanley's dream of an elite resort hotel rose from the ground in 1909 in Georgian Revival Splendor, securing its place in the contrasting rock and jagged cliff sides of the Colorado Rocky Mountains, 7,500 feet above sea level. The Stanley Hotel, with its red roof and pale mustard yellow siding, began its metamorphosis from bedrock and timbers in 1907 and was completed two years later. It sits on Wonderview Avenue in Estes Park, Colorado. It only takes one look at the surrounding scenery from the hotel veranda to see how Wonderview got its name. Off to the southeast is Lake Estes, bordered by the Rocky Mountains.

View from the front courtyard of the Stanley Hotel of Lake Estes.

As one faces the Stanley Hotel complex you are struck by the architectural planning. Each building, beginning with Carriage House at the far eastern side of the grounds, increases by one level in floors as it goes westward. Thus, the Carriage House is one level, the Concert Hall/Casino boasts two stories, the Manor House has three, and finally the main hotel raises four stories above the ground, not including the garden level basement.

The original Gate House was down at the bottom of the hill when F.O. originally built his hotel. Guests traveled up the dirt road to the complex via his Stanley Steamer Motor Cars.

The Stanley Hotel complex as it was in the early 1900s. The Gate House was down the hill. From left-to-right is the main hotel, Manor House, Concert Hall/Casino & Carriage House. *Estes Park Trail Gazette.*

The main hotel was known as the "summer hotel" as it did not have heat at the time. Stephen King's arrival on the last operating day of the season set his imagination going as to what might happen in a hotel set in the mountains when all the staff and patrons had departed for the winter. The main hotel did not have heat until 1984. It was open to guests from June until mid-September. The fireplaces in the Lobby, Music Room/Parlor, Writing Room, and Smoking Room on the main floor furnished the heat. To accommodate the tourists who were looking for year-round availability, the Manor House was built next to the main building. It is a smaller version of the original hotel and was steam-heated. It opened in 1910.

1909 photo showing the hotel with its original porte cochere.
Photo courtesy of the Stanley Museum

The estimated cost for construction of the hotel ranges between $200,000 and $500,000—both prodigious sums for the turn of the century. Denver architect T. Robert Wiegner was hired to implement Stanley's vision for his grand resort. Frank Kirchoff Lumber Company in Denver was a colleague of Wiegner and was chosen as contractor, with Al Roenfelt as job foreman. C. Byron Hall, who worked with F.O. on completing the North Saint Vrain Road in Estes Park, was hired for the excavation of the hotel site. Stanley now had his dream team and a vision that would place the Stanley Hotel on the map for its opulence and electrical accommodations.

Built upon a cut stone foundation with solid rock lying beneath many portions of the hotel, the four-story structure went up, covered in lap siding and topped with a red-hip roof. The timber was cut and milled locally for the framing and sheathing with much of the finish wood being shipped from Kirchoff's lumber company in Denver. The façade's peaked pediment features box dormers and a two-layer hexagon-shaped bell tower. The hotel takes on a very symmetrical tone with its H-shaped design. Perpendicular wings flank both sides of the 100-foot-long lobby. Six double sets of Doric columns support the roof and adorn the veranda that runs the length of the main floor lobby. A porte cochere once graced the front of the building, serving as a protective roof from the elements as guests were delivered via car to the hotel. It was removed when Flora Stanley decided its massive structure cut the sunlight entering the lobby, leaving it too dark, and restricting the views of the mountain ranges. You can see the Stanley's love of light through the abundance of Palladian and fan-shaped windows throughout the hotel.

It has also been rumored the removal of the porte cochere was more pragmatic and was removed in the 1930s to accommodate larger and more modern buses.

Stanley Hotel with porte cochere and original mustard yellow coloring.
Photo courtesy of the Stanley Museum

When the hotel opened in 1909 it was featured in *Hotel Monthly*. The magazine was effusive in its praise of this modern marvel set high in the Rockies. Room décor was designed to mirror the hotel exterior theme colors of yellow and red. Though the hotel's exterior is now white with the original red roofing, the initial mustard yellow color was used in keeping with the Georgian architectural structure of the time, mirroring the eastern seaboard hotels. No expense was spared to make this western hotel reflect the opulence of its east coast contemporaries. Every detail on the exterior was created with elegance and civility in mind. Swan-neck pediments graced the matching balconies at the end of each wing. The double doors at the entry are framed by leaded-glass windows and topped with a fanlight shape.

Inside, the fine detailing continued in the decorative plaster casting, which included laurel wreaths, urns, and even a ram's head carving on the mantelpiece in the Music Room.

According to *Hotel Monthly*, who ran an 8-page spread on the hotel when it opened, these were some of the highlighted personnel and amenities:

"Mr. Stanley placed the management of his house in the hands of Alfred Lamborn, who formerly kept a hotel in Atlantic City, and of recent years was manager of the Denver Club. The Chief clerk is J.B. Williams; the steward, John Fuller; the head waiter, J.W. Morris; and the hotel chef, Samuel Granger.

"The Hotel opened for business June 20, 1909. The rates, American plan, are $5 a day and upward.

Stanley Hotel in 1909. Number 9 golf hole marker in the foreground, and a row of Stanley Steamer Touring Cars at back.

"The attractions include golf, tennis, bowling, horseback riding, driving, mountain climbing, automobiling, trout fishing, and trails into the wilds for those who love nature." *Hotel Monthly, 1909.*

Women golfing at the Stanley Hotel Golf Course in 1910.
Photo courtesy of the Stanley Museum.

## The Original Layout and Amenities of the Hotel in 1909

The original name chosen for the hotel was either "Hotel Dunraven," or "The Dunraven," or "The New Dunraven." Lord Dunraven was a wealthy gentleman from the United Kingdom who illegally bought up huge sections of land in Estes Park for his own private pursuits. The town was vehement that the hotel would not carry the name of the man who had tried to swindle the valley out from under them. The townsfolk, declaring the hotel should bear the name of its creator—F.O. Stanley—signed a petition. Mr. Stanley finally agreed and the rest is history. You can see the signed animal hide petition in the Estes Park Museum.

The cost to stay at the Stanley Hotel in 1909 would be welcome anywhere in today's economy. A day's stay at the hotel varied from $5.00 to $8.00 per day. One hundred years later, the cost of a room starts at around $145 a night, with the most-requested rooms, such as 217, bringing in a hefty $450 per night.

The original floor plan for the lobby area remains pretty much today as it did in 1909, with a few changes.

The main lobby is 100 feet by 24 feet and was finished in Flora Stanley's favorite colors of red and white. The furniture was mahogany with leather upholstery. It was touted for having all the metropolitan conveniences, including a hydraulic elevator, and telephone exchange.

Stanley Hotel Lobby, 1920 looking east. Photo Stanley Museum

The Writing Room, where the ladies of the Victorian Era would handle correspondence and chat, was to the right of the elevator and is today a full-service Gift Shop at the hotel. It once overlooked a screen porch running the length of the back courtyard. It had a fireplace, individual writing desks, and a library. The fireplace is still in evidence.

The Grand Parlor was also known as the Music Room and measured 40 feet by 40 feet. It was decorated in green and white, with a fireplace and mantel mirroring the one found in F.O. Stanley's living room at home. An alcove housed the beautiful Steinway F.O. ordered for Flora as a gift when the hotel opened. The piano is still there today.

Music Room/Parlor on 1st Floor of the Stanley Hotel.
Photo by Ron Bueker

The Billiard Room had four tables. Women were allowed in this room but only to observe. A long bench against the south wall afforded them a place to sit and admire the male species at play. It is reported F.O. took his prowess as a seasoned billiards player seriously. Many observers who made the unpardonable mistake of laughing at, or teasing, Mr. Stanley about his performance found themselves on the exit side of the door. Today the Billiard Room is used for special events. The original cue rack and balls can be seen still hanging on the west wall of the room.

Original pool ball rack with balls.  Photo by Ron Bueker.

The bench against the north wall where the ladies were invited to sit and observe is there as well.  During the early days of the hotel the bench was left unpadded, as a subtle means to dissuade too many observers. Today, it is padded for comfort.

Observation bench against north wall of Billiards Room.
Photo courtesy of Ron Bueker.

F.O. Stanley playing billiards at the Stanley Hotel.
Photo courtesy of the Stanley Museum

The Smoking Room is today called the Pinon Room. It measures 29 feet by 40 feet and was for gentlemen only. Women were strictly forbidden access to this room. If they wished to view the billiard games in the room to the north of the Smoking Room, they had to leave the Music Room and traverse the East Veranda, passing the Smoking Room door, to where they could then enter through a side door to the Billiard Room. Gentlemen, however, had free reign.

Smoking Room/Pinon Room at the Stanley Hotel with tulip light fixture. Photo courtesy of Ron Bueker

Postcard of a typical Smoking Room in 1910.

View of the Smoking Room/Pinon Room door to the left, and the Music Room/Parlor to the right, looking east from the lobby.

The large Dining Room was 40 feet by 80 feet. It had a terrace to the west where one could sit and view the Rocky Mountains. It was finished in gold and white, with a carpeted floor and commanding views from the windows of Long's Peak. The dining tables were graced with Onondaga (Syracuse) china of neat patterns, silverware from the International Silver Company, and wildflowers that grew in profusion just outside the hotel doors. A Children's Dining Room was found to the north of the Dining Room where the little ones, accompanied by their nannies, would have their meals. Access to the Servant's Dining Room and Kitchen was found to the north of the room as well. A door, leading out onto the South Veranda where high-backed rocking chairs were lined up, lead from the Dining Room on the east side. An orchestra of three pieces—violin, bass viola and piano—was employed for the season. Today the room is called the MacGregor Room as a tribute to the man who helped save Estes Park from the nefarious Lord Dunraven.

Stanley Hotel Dining Room/MacGregor Ballroom circa 1940
Photo courtesy of Estes Park Museum

The Stanley Hotel bedrooms of the early 1900's were luxuriously furnished; the standing furniture of mahogany; the beds brass, with box springs; the floors carpeted; the walls papered; and every room with writing desk, lace curtains, opaque shades, pictures, steam heat, and the connecting rooms with double doors between. The bathrooms had the finest of plumbing and were up-to-date in every respect. There were two sections of public baths on each floor: the men's bathrooms on the west side of the hotel, and the women's to the east.

The Presidential Suite was over-sized, with a connecting room and a private adjoining bathroom. It took up what are today three different guest rooms and their bathrooms. Today that room is Room 217, made famous by Stephen King's occupancy in 1974. A duplicate suite was at the far east side of the floor with the same configuration of rooms. These rooms were later divided up into several separate guest suites.

**\*Please see the Stanley Hotel floor plans in the Appendix section.**

Room 217
Photo courtesy of Randy Flanders

Today the Stanley Hotel's four-story structure casts a formidable shadow over the small hamlet of Estes Park and the vestiges of scenes that have unfolded under its weighty stare for a hundred years. It has undergone many transformations, from bankruptcy proceedings in 1980, to the popular tourist destination it is today. The hotel's annual *Shining Ball* during Halloween weekend brings guests from all over the world. It is also a sought-after wedding venue. On August 8, 2008, the hotel hosted 13 weddings in one weekend to celebrate the triple 8's in the date.

It is no secret that paranormal reality shows are frequent visitors to the Stanley Hotel. Their spotlight on the venue keeps the curious coming from around the globe.

The hotel celebrated its centennial birthday on July 4th, 2009.

Photo of the cake created for the Stanley Hotel centennial celebration on July 4, 2009. Photo by Rebecca F. Pittman.

At the turn of the front door key on June 22, 1909, the hotel's soft opening was official. A group of pharmacists were the first guests of the hotel, with the grand opening falling a few weeks later on July 4th.

Opening day was a hectic one. Stanley Steamer Mountain Wagons made their way up the treacherous winding roads of Big Thompson Canyon. The hotel had arranged for a man in a bear suit to "attack" the passing cars at a certain spot along the designed route. At that point a man armed with a shotgun would dutifully "shoot" the bear that fell down dead, much to the delight, and horror, of the traveling guests. Once the wagon was out of sight, the "bear" made a miraculous recovery and was ready to pounce on the next unsuspecting entourage.

F.O. Stanley was the first to ferry guests from train stations to a hotel. Train stations in Loveland and Lyons, Colorado, would bring guests from all over the country, anxious to spend time at a mountain retreat. The Stanley Steamer Mountain Wagons would load up the luggage, couples, servants and children and begin the 1 ½ - 2 hour trek up the rugged mountain road.

Stanley Steamer Motor Car riding along Big Thompson River as it heads for Estes Park, Colorado. Photo courtesy of Estes Park Museum.

Ladies wearing long gowns with high, stiff collars, broad plumed hats and Victorian-era hairdo's walked elegantly through the cavernous lobby, their long trains sweeping the floor with soft, fluttering sounds. The men wore top hats with dark tailcoats and trousers. Their matching waistcoat buttoned down over a white shirt with winged collars and a white bow tie. Those who had not changed into evening attire could be seen in an occasional bowler hat.

Women in the early 1900's were cinched in with the corsets of the day. Day dresses were typically worn throughout the morning and afternoon hours, still requiring a corset at all times. Tea gowns were changed into within the privacy of their rooms where the dreaded whalebone or iron corset was tossed to the side. The evening gowns were often opulent, with jeweled stomachers and dripping in pearls. The designer of the day was Charles Frederick Worth of England and Paris. Wealthy women made two sojourns a year to Europe to buy their fashions from him, and other sought-after designers, to fill their wardrobes at home for the various "seasons."

Typical women's and men's attire in the early 1900s.
Photos courtesy of Glamourdaze.com

Valets in dark suit coats and trousers, and lady's maids in severe black dresses with white lace colors, managed the luggage, while nannies in shapeless house dresses and aprons did their best to corral children. Little girls in ringlets, pleated skirts and sailor blouses, ran giggling through the massive ballroom; young boys in knickers and striped shirts scurrying after them.

Typical little boy's and little girl's attire in the early 1900s.

The crowds arrived, each peeking into the pristine rooms of the first floor of the rambling hotel. The registration desk ledgers boast the names of the famous, infamous, crowned royalty and inventors of the 20th century, and their footfalls are still heard on the antiquated floorboards and carpeted hallways of the Stanley Hotel today.

The history of Estes Park and the Stanley Hotel are inextricably linked, blending seamlessly into each other's legacy as smoothly as fingers laced in thoughtful repose. F.O. Stanley's infrastructure of power, sewer, water, roads, a clinic, a bank and more laid the foundation for Estes Park. Through the use of the Stanley Steamer Mountain Bus, Estes Park became the first resort community to fetch customers from significant distances by automobile. Automobile tourism was born, along with the first resort hotel to be run completely on electricity. Gaslights were used as back-up in case of electrical failure in the often-turbulent weather conditions of the Rockies.

Estes Park was a tourist destination as early as 1874, long before Rocky Mountain National Park opened in 1913. There was no gold or silver here (as disappointed prospectors soon realized during the gold and silver booms of that era), and ranchers soon gave up on cattle and turned to accommodating the ever-increasing paying boarders.

By 1900 "dude ranches" abounded. They were rustic and appealed to the adventurous spirit of the "town folk" who wanted a taste of "roughing it." Horses, seated with gentlemen and ladies alike, wound their way through pristine mountains and sparkling streams, where herds of elk, big horn ram, and myriad wildlife roamed freely and unfettered. None of the accommodations offered much luxury. Enter F.O. and his wife Flora from back east with a vision for an elegant resort hotel that would fill a hospitality gap.

Estes Park was ripe for the dreams of a wealthy entrepreneur who saw the possibilities that could spring from a setting of unparalleled beauty. He could not have known his hotel would spawn another dream 65 years later when a mystery writer by the name of Stephen King arrived on the Stanley Hotel's sprawling veranda in 1974.

Chapter Three

# THE PERFECT SETTING FOR A GHOST STORY

*"There is more between Heaven and Earth, my dear Horatio, than is dreamt of in thy experience."* --Hamlet, William Shakespeare

Like all things we look forward to with anticipation, the Stanley Hotel makes us wait. It sits, holding court in the center of the towering pines and jagged cliff sides, above the small town of Estes Park, Colorado. You must earn your way there by traversing hairpin turns through the mountain canyons with the crystal waters of Big Thompson canyon leading the way from Loveland along Highway 34. If you travel from Boulder and Lyons along Highway 36 there is still the price of admission as you navigate through the foothills where prospectors once hoped to make their fortunes.

No matter how you find your way to the sprawling veranda of the Stanley Hotel there is always a moment of surrealism when you first see the white cupola that adorns the top of the venue, peering at you from atop the stores and pines of Estes Park. Many first-time guests are surprised to see how closely the hotel sits to the bustling tourist town. They expect the venue to be more remote and unwelcoming as it is depicted in Stanley Kubrick's movie adaptation of Stephen King's book *The Shining*.

A view of the Stanley Hotel over the top of the stores of Estes Park, Colorado. Photo courtesy of Ron Bueker

Estes Park, Colorado sits nestled in a high mountain valley 7,522 feet above sea level. The surrounding peaks range from 8,500 feet to Long's Peak, a popular "14-er" (14,000 feet). Adventurous climbers scale their faces each year.

The first tourists to the Park date back 12,000 years or more. Archaeologists have found remains from the Clovis culture; the first known people to cross the Bering Strait land bridge from Asia into North America. The McKean people, one of the Paleo-Indian cultures, came to the area around 2,000 BC. Ten thousand years ago Ute and Arapahoe Indian tribes summered in Estes and wintered near Grand Lake, Colorado, in the Middle Park. You can still see traces of the trail they used to cross the Continental Divide in Rocky Mountain National Park.

The year 1800 saw hunters, trappers and "mountain men" discovering the bountiful wildlife in Estes Park, especially beaver and bear. Major Stephen H. Long led an organized expedition to "see the

Rockies." As head of the Yellowstone Expedition that set out to document new, undiscovered territories, he stumbled upon the area now known as Estes Park. Long's Peak, the 14,000' centerpiece of the Park, is named for him, though he never scaled the imposing precipice.

The cry of "GOLD!" in 1859 brought Joel Estes and his son, Milton, to the area. Estes had struck it rich in California ten years earlier. The Gold Rush of 1858-1859 brought Colorado to the attention of the nation when the precious mineral was discovered in Cherry Creek and Clear Creek Valley. Prospectors mined those areas and then set their compasses for the hills of adjacent Boulder County in 1859. The gold flashed at Gold Hill and a year later at Jamestown and Ward.

Perhaps Estes Park had a lucky talisman holding sway even back in the early days of the park. Though prospectors tried to plumb its mountains and rivers in the search for gold and silver, the valley yielded nothing promising, thus sparing the Park from the usual scarring devastation of strip mines, marred cliff faces and depleted resources. Even the Intra-Indian wars that once dominated the serenity of Estes Valley left it a pristine, unspoiled landscape. The projectile points of the Arapahoe and Utes in Upper Beaver Meadow are a distant reminder of the turbulence of the 1850s at the mouth of what is now Rocky Mountain National Park.

## THE MAKING OF A TOURIST TOWN

Despite the park's lack of glittering deposits, Joel Estes moved his family there to live in 1860 and erected a makeshift cabin in a beautiful meadow with their thirteen children and a herd of cattle. My hat has always been off to those early settlers and the women who followed their men into the rugged unknown. Today, the "rugged unknown" equates to battling savage shoppers at Outdoor World at the local mall...during the Christmas shopping season.

The Estes family resided in the valley during a turbulent time.

Indian hostilities were rampant, the Union Pacific Railroad was encroaching upon the territory, and newcomers to the valley had to deal with disputes over buffalo, antelope and deer. Any wildlife meandering across Indian emigrating routes was claimed by the Cheyenne and Arapahoe. The Indian warfare lasted until the summer of 1869.

Joel and Patsy Estes. Estes Park was named for him.

Joel Estes and his family weathered the long, relentless winters, the solitude (the nearest neighbor was over 25 miles away), and the unsuccessful search for gold, for six years. He finally decided to leave the valley on April 15, 1866, never to return.

William Byers, the owner and editor of the *Rocky Mountain News,* named the park after Joes Estes in 1864 after visiting the area and lodging with the Estes Family.

Estes Park's beauty, plentiful hunting and the still-pursued promise of glittering minerals, brought hunters, prospectors, campers and the park's first permanent residents. His name was Griffith J. Evans, a Welshman, who came to the area with his family in 1874. Evans added to the ranch Estes had vacated and settled in. It is here the history of offering lodging to tourists visiting the valley really begins.

Photo of the first wagon going up the trail to Estes Park.
Photo courtesy of Fred Payne Clatworthy

Estes Park circa 1908.
Photo courtesy of Fred Payne Clatworthy

Griff and his wife Jane welcomed all who ventured into Estes

Park as a means of breaking up the lonely solitude of the Park, and making extra money through offering lodging, food, hunting trips, and renting out horses. Mr. Evans, seeing the benefit of being the only game in town when it came to providing lodging to the increasing number of people hearing about the opulent wildlife and terrain of Estes Park, made the following announcement to the *Chicago Tribune*: "He and others contemplate putting up a cheap hotel for next season to accommodate visitors who wish a change of air, fresh trout, and restored health." (*Chicago Tribune*, August 18, 1871.)

Longmont's *Colorado Press* announced on April 10, 1872, "Mr. G. J. Evans of Estes Park is fitting up a house preparatory to keeping a hotel this summer. There will undoubtedly be a large influx of visitors to the mountains this season, and if it is known that good hotel accommodations can be had, Estes Park will come in for a large share of them." (*Colorado Press*, April 10, 1872.)

Drawing of Griff Evan's ranch in Estes Park by Isabella Bird

Evans eventually sold his squatter's interest in Estes Park to the

Earl of Dunraven (also known as Lord Dunraven) and went to work for the wealthy Irishman as a foreman. Rumors as to the exact date Evans sold Dunraven his interest, and the dollar amount, vary. Some believe it was February 1873 and the purchase price was somewhere between $5,000 and $10,000. (In today's economy that equates to $98,039 to $196,078, respectively.) Dunraven's agent, Theodore Whyte, also purchased Evan's cattle business, effectively securing Griff Evan's Estes Park operation for Lord Dunraven. Evans took his newfound wealth and purchased St. Vrain Hotel in Longmont, Colorado in 1874, while continuing to call Estes Park home.

On November 7, 1878, the Evans family decided to move back to St. Vrain valley and leave Estes Park behind. Evans sold his remaining 160 acres to Theodore Whyte and the newly formed English Company and departed with an estimated $18,000. (Approximately $352,941 in 2014.) Griff Evans died on July 6, 1900 and was buried in Jamestown, Colorado where he had been living since 1883.

# LORD DUNRAVEN

Windham Thomas Wyndham-Quinn (Lord Dunraven)

Just after Christmas in 1872, a party of English sportsmen visiting Denver decided to try hunting in the mountains above Estes Park. Leading this band of gentlemen was Windham Thomas Wyndham

Quin, also known as the fourth Earl of Dunraven and Mount Earl in the Peerage of Ireland, second Baron Kenry of the United Kingdom, Knight of the Order of St. Patrick, and Companion of the Order of St. Michael and St. George. Aside from being linked to English nobility, the Earl of Dunraven was enormously wealthy. In 1872, at age thirty-one, he already owned forty thousand acres of land and four homes, including Dunraven Castle at Glamorgan. Prior to his Estes Park visit the Earl had traveled widely in Europe, the Middle East, and in Africa. He served in the First Life Guards, was an excellent horseman, and had a nervous energy that led him to become a war correspondent during a conflict in Abyssinia and during the Franco-Prussian War.

Dunraven Castle at Glamorgan, Ireland.

He first came to the United States on his honeymoon in 1869, visiting only the East Coast. In the autumn of 1871 he returned to America, this time to venture into the West. The completion of the transcontinental railroad in 1869 made his trip a bit easier. There he hunted elk in the region of the North Platte River under the guidance of Buffalo Bill and Texas Jack Omohondro. Like other English aristocrats who ventured into the wilderness, the Earl traveled in style, even bringing a personal physician, Dr. George Henry Kingsley. The Earl planned to live an adventurous life. As historian Dave Hicks notes, he "enjoyed a good pipe, good liquor, good food, women and sports. But not necessarily in that order."

Once again, in 1872, the Earl of Dunraven returned to hunt, this time in Nebraska, Wyoming, and in Colorado's South Park. While relaxing among the night spots of Denver, the Earl met Theodore Whyte. Mr. Whyte, then twenty-six years old, had arrived in Colorado during the late 1860s. Originally from Devonshire, England, he had trapped for the Hudson's Bay Company for three years and had tried his hand in the Colorado mines. During some of his earlier rambles, Whyte became familiar with Estes Park. Whyte, much like Isabella Bird and the Earl of Dunraven, represents a then developing English interest in the Rockies. This was a distinctly curious generation of people, investigating regions for adventure or excitement as eagerly as Hayden or Powell explored for science. In *Westward the Briton,* historian Robert Athearn claims that "the state of Colorado drew more of these curious observers than any other western state or territory. So many of them came to visit, and even to stay, that the state has been called 'England beyond the Missouri.'"

"It was sport," the Earl later recalled, "or, as it would be called in the States, hunting—that led me first to visit Estes Park." Theodore Whyte sang the praises of the area, telling the Earl about the abundance of deer, elk, and bear just perfect for "sport." But very little convincing was necessary. Soon the Earl and a few friends were heading into the foothills, following the crude cattle trail leading toward Estes Park. Once there, they stayed with Griff Evans, another of their countrymen and a man eager to please the nobility of his homeland. In the ensuing days, the Earl hunted elk in Black Canyon, along the Fall River, and in the Bear Lake area. "Sport" and the mountains themselves combined to impress this well-traveled man. "Everything is huge and stupendous," he observed. "Nature is formed in a larger mold than in other lands. She is robust and strong, all her actions full of vigor and young life."

William Henry Jackson's photograph of the vast wilderness that was Estes Park in 1873—14 years after Joel Estes first homesteaded there.

The attractions of Estes Park brought the Earl back for a second trip in 1873. Its atmosphere proved addicting. "The air is scented with the sweet-smelling sap of the pines," he wrote, "whose branches welcome many feathered visitors from southern climes; an occasional humming-bird whirrs among the shrubs, trout leap in the creeks, insects buzz in the air; all nature is active and exuberant with life." "The climate is health-giving," he argued, sounding much like a local booster, "unsurpassed (as I believe) anywhere—giving to the jaded spirit, the unstrung nerves and weakened body a stimulant, a tone and vigor so delightful that none can appreciate it except those who have had the good fortune to experience it themselves."

At some point during his visits, the Earl decided he would attempt to acquire ownership of all of Estes Park. Fits of greed, after all, strike at most people; many have had similar desires to possess this land, perhaps wishing to exclude others and control it for selfish purposes. But only the Earl of Dunraven had both the wealth and the will to try to buy it. Only a handful of squatters stood in his way and within a few short years the Earl came close to owning everything.

Assisted by his new friend Theodore Whyte and several Denver bankers and lawyers, the Earl first arranged to have the park legally surveyed. Once that formality was accomplished, the Earl and his agents used a scheme, common among other speculators, exploiting the Homestead Law to their advantage. They found local men in Front Range towns willing—for a price—to stake 160-acre claims throughout the park. More than thirty-five men filed claims using this ploy. Then, Dunraven's "Estes Park Company, Ltd." (or the English Company as it was called locally) proceeded to buy all those parcels at a nominal price, estimated at five dollars per acre. Between 1874 and 1880, the Earl managed to purchase 8,200 acres of land. In addition, the Company controlled another 7,000 acres because of the lay of the land and the ownership of springs and streams.

Exactly what the Earl intended for his Estes Park estate is not clear. The most obvious future for the land was its continued use for ranching. At that time Griff Evans herded about a thousand head of cattle there, some of which belonged to two Denver investors. But Griff Evans, just like a number of other homesteaders, quickly traded his land for English cash. The Earl explained his goal simply: "Herbage was plentiful, and cattle could feed all winter, for the snow never lay. It was an ideal cattle-ranch, and to that purpose we put it."

Whether it was going to be developed as a private hunting preserve for the exclusive use of the Earl and a few of his English friends was a subject for much speculation and popular debate.

Lord Dunraven

Lord Dunraven's official title was impressive. He was not only Viscount Adare between 1850 and 1871; he was the son of the 3rd Earl of Dunraven and Mount-Earl. Lord Dunraven succeeded as 4th Earl of Dunraven and Mount-Earl in the Peerage of Ireland and 2nd Baron Kenry in the Peerage of the United Kingdom on the death of his father in 1871.

After serving some time as a lieutenant in the 1st Life Guards, a cavalry regiment, he became at age twenty-six, a war correspondent for the London newspaper *The Daily Telegraph* and covered the Abyssinian War. Dunraven then became a special correspondent for a "big London daily" during the Franco-Prussian War in 1870-1871. He reported the Siege of Paris, saw the Third Carlist War and war in Turkey, and probably the Russo-Turkish War. Dunraven witnessed both the signing of the Treaty of Versailles, which ended the Franco-

Prussian War in 1871, and later, the signing of the Treaty of Versailles in 1919, an honor no one else had held.

He maintained a famous equestrian farm on his Adare Manor estate and experimented in growing tobacco until his factory burned down in 1916. Upon the foundation of the Irish Free State he became a member of the first Senate in December 1922.

A keen yachtsman, the Earl was the owner and co-owner of the 1893 and 1895 America's Cup yachts *Valkyrie II* and *Valkyrie III*.

As he died without a male heir, the Earldom passed to a cousin, Windham Wyndham-Quin, 5th Earl of Dunraven and Mount-Earl, and the Baronry of Kenry, which had been created for his father, became extinct.

In 1895 he lived at 27 Norfolk Street, then 26 years after his death in 1939 the street was renamed Dunraven Street in his honor.

Lord Dunraven's obsession with acquiring land for his own personal use had already garnered him 40,000 acres in Ireland and Wales. He was Irish-born and Oxford-educated, a world traveler passionate about sailing and hunting. He also crossed paths with the Jack the Ripper case during "Jack's" reign of terror in Whitechapel, England. There will be more on that in the chapter concerning Room 401 and 407.

In Estes Park, Colorado, the Lord was now in control of 8,200 acres of land, and another 7,000 acres through control of the water rights from the rivers flanking his properties. Thanks to a few oversights and misfiled claims, he had let a few parcels of prime property slip through his fingers. Land along the Wind River, including Black Canyon, Will (Moraine Park), and Beavers Meadows were well-watered areas that had been overlooked, along with the property at the base of Long's Peak. The early settlers of 1875 jumped on the "unsecured land" and doggedly held sway despite Dunraven's and Whyte's insidious attempts to oust them. The impact of these men and their families was formidable in the development of Estes Park. Although he operated outside the law, Dunraven was never prosecuted.

# The Ones Who Stayed and Fought

Alexander Quiner MacGregor and wife Clara Heeney

Alexander Quiner MacGregor (1846-1896), for whom the main ballroom in the Stanley hotel is dedicated, was the first settler to arrive and establish a 160-acre claim in the Black Canyon in 1873. (There will be more on Alexander MacGregor in the chapter concerning the MacGregor Room in the hotel.) Alex and his wife Clara homesteaded in the Black Canyon area and were soon joined by Clara's mother, Georgianna Heeney. Mrs. Heeney put forth a preemptive claim of her own on October 5, 1875 and built a log cabin in a wooded section east of the creek. The MacGregors would eventually own 2,931 acres valued at 4.25 million dollars by the time their granddaughter, Muriel, died in 1970.

It wasn't long before tourists came knocking, so Alex constructed a series of log cabins and a dining hall in the beautiful pines to the north of the creek. Estes Park was always destined to cater to the tourist trade. Visitors could also pitch tents. The ever-shrewd MacGregor charged $7.00 a week for room, meals and washing, while stabling a horse ran an extra $.50 a day, sans feed. He also offered long-term leases on his property for those wanting to build their own homes. By 1881, Alex tore down his original ranch house and built a larger, grander version with rooms "fixed up in the latest style." Clara adorned the walls with her original art and played the piano for guests, adding a cultured, feminine aura to the rustic surroundings.

The foundation for a tourist town was laid. The crystal river waters, towering peaks, lush valley and unparalleled beauty of Estes Park called to settlers in 1875.

MacGregor Ranch just north of the Stanley Hotel

Horace Willis Ferguson

The next to heed the call was Horace Willis Ferguson (1826-1912). Horace had heard stories in Denver about an English Lord grabbing up land with "questionable" means in the pristine park in the mountains.

In February of 1874, Ferguson settled near Mary's Lake on land Dunraven had overlooked. In 1875 he built a modest two-room log cabin and in April of that year brought his family from Namaqua. His 16-year-old daughter, Sallie, noted years later that "this was the beginning of our boarding career. Although the summer before one eastern lady had stayed with us sleeping in a tent and having her meals in the kitchen with the family. Visitors from Denver, many eastern states and foreign countries began to come at this time, some for health—many for rest and pleasure. Most of the tourists brought tents and camped on those beautiful rippling streams as the boarding houses or hotels were not sufficiently developed to take care of them. However, within the next two years Elkhorn Lodge, Sprague's Hotel in Moraine Park, Lamb's at the foot of Long's Peak and our resort...as well as the English Hotel, were all caring for visitors. Tents were not so popular. Room and board at these places ranged from $8 to $14 a week and we made money." (Sallie Fergusons' Memoirs)

William E. James (1842-1895) also saw the promise of Estes Park as a lodger's dream. Arriving from upstate New York in 1874, he first visited the park for hunting purposes. His grocery business had fallen on hard times in 1873 and so James left the east coast and brought his small family to Colorado. He built a small, one-room cabin near McCreery Springs, about three miles east of Estes Park. A second cabin was erected a year later on 80 acres in the Black Canyon on a preemptive claim. Georgianna Heeney, MacGregor's mother-in-law, contested the claim and won. James moved to a tract of land on Fall River, slightly west of Dunraven's property and built a humble frame cabin consisting of a living room, dining room, kitchen and two bedrooms. The animosity James felt toward the MacGregor's was slow to die. Years after the land dispute, James would refer to MacGregor as "that pettifogging lawyer." (Memoirs of Eleanor E. Hondius of Elkhorn Lodge, 1964)

James soon succumbed to the ever-increasing demand for lodging. A series of cabins and tent houses were constructed and Elkhorn Lodge was born. It eventually became a resort including 33 cabins and a main lodge. William James' daughter, Eleanor Hondius, later wrote, "Every summer people came to the ranch and begged to be allowed to stay, and each winter another cabin would be built on the ranch to house them. Father and Mother soon found there was more money in caring for summer tourists than in raising cattle." (Memoirs of Eleanor E. Hondius of Elkhorn Lodge, 1964)

Elkhorn Lodge became the largest tourist resort in Estes Park. It is still a favorite among park visitors since 1874. The Lodge was originally named for the giant stack of elk antlers perched outside the main door. Live elk still roam its woods and add their beauty along the street named after James' lodge: Elkhorn Avenue. The lodge is now a National Historic building and has been running continuously for 135 years. It is the oldest guest ranch still operating in the Rocky Mountain region, and the oldest, continuously operating hotel in Colorado. You can find the Elkhorn Lodge at 600 West Elkhorn Avenue, two blocks west of downtown Estes Park.

Elkhorn Lodge. Estes Park, Colorado.

Abner and Alberta Sprague

Abner Sprague (1850-1943) was the next resort builder to take advantage of Estes Park's beauty. On May 9, 1875, Sprague and his partner, Clarence Chubbuck, performed the time-honored ritual of laying four logs end to end to form a cabin's foundation. This constituted a claim, of which they staked out two. Chubbuck was murdered a month later when he accused a man named John Phillips of stealing cattle at a round up near St. Louis on the Big Thompson River.

Abner brought his father back with him in June and together they erected a twenty-four-by-sixteen-foot homestead cabin. By 1881 a dozen additional cabins had been added, a main lodge was constructed housing guest rooms, a dining room and a kitchen. The lodge grew to three stories and a springhouse was added where guests could enjoy cold milk or water from a spring harnessed to do the churning by a makeshift waterwheel.

Abner Sprague's homestead cabin

Abner Sprague later changed the name of the area he lived in from Willow Park to Moraine in 1891 and finally to Moraine Peak in 1902. He made an impact on the park's early life acting as resort owner, surveyor, hunter, prospector, guide, mill operator, locating engineer and a decent historian. For over 60 years he helped in the development of Estes Park, and as a guide, knew its terrain better than most.

Abner Sprague's Resort Lodge. Guests were hauled up by wagon.

Reverend Elkanah Lamb (1832-1915) rounds out the list of prominent settlers who left their mark on early Estes Park. In 1875 he sectioned off land in the Longs Peak Valley at the base of Longs Peak. Lamb originally entered Estes Park in search of gold, leaving Kansas in 1860. After prospecting elsewhere, including Breckenridge, Lamb became an itinerant minister in 1871, for the Church of the United Brethren. He organized churches along the South Platte and in the valleys of the Big and Little Thompson and the Poudre Rivers. In 1875 Lamb brought his wife, Jane, and son Carlyle to the park and built a 12'x14' pole, brush and dirt cabin along with a few other rustic buildings.

It wasn't long before another resort opened its doors to the grateful adventurers who found their way to Estes Park. Longs Peak House, a way station to the peak, consisted of Lamb's additional cabins and remained in the family until 1901 when it was sold to Enos Mills, Sr., who renamed the Lamb resort Longs Peak Inn. The Lambs eventually moved to Fort Collins, Colorado.

Enos Mills (fifth from left), the founder of Rocky Mountain National Park, with F.O. Stanley (to his left) on the park's opening day.

These early settlers, with their diverse backgrounds, rallied together to thwart Theodore Whyte's plan to secure Estes Park on behalf of Lord Dunraven, through some of the most nefarious means of land grabbing the state of Colorado had ever seen.

Lord Dunraven eventually left the area, returning to England, abandoning his interest in Estes Park. He did however manage to build a hunting lodge on Fish Creek Road, just south of Highway 36, and a nearby private cottage. He also built a hunting lodge outside of Glen Haven (now known as Dunraven Glade). The Hotel on Fish Creek Road was named the Estes Park Hotel and was known to the locals as the English Hotel. It burned to the ground in 1911. A large parcel of Dunraven's original land holdings is presently under Lake Estes, a large man-made reservoir, which was completed in 1948. (Ron Lasky, *The Concise History of the Stanley Hotel*, 2005)

The English Hotel in 1877

Lord Dunraven died in June of 1926 at the age of 85. He is buried at St. Nicholas' Church of Ireland in Adar, County Limerick, Ireland.

Burton D. Sanborn began negotiations for the purchase of Dunraven's property; F.O. Stanley who had viewed the area with an eye to opening an elegant hotel venue later joined him. Sanborn and Stanley created the Estes Park Development Company and bought up Dunraven's holdings of 6,600 acres for roughly $80,000. When Sanborn died in 1914, F.O. Stanley acquired title to approximately 1,400 acres in Estes Valley along its northern slopes. The site for the Stanley Hotel was in place, and soon the welcome mat would be out

for all those who wished to stay there—some more permanently than others.

Estes Park in 1903 at the corner of Elkhorn and Moraine Avenues.
Photo courtesy of the Estes Park Trail Gazette.

Chapter Four

# THE STANLEY HOTEL TODAY

*"During the day,*
*I don't believe in ghosts.*
*At night, I'm a little more open-minded."*
*Unknown Author*

When one steps through the double doors of the Stanley Hotel and into the historic lobby, there is a feeling that the hands of a clock have been turned back in time. The architecture, warm colors and overstuffed chairs are a reminder of an era when women gathered to write letters in the soft morning sunlight of the Writing Room (now the Chrysalis Gift Shop) while the men competed against each other in the Billiard Room, bragging of a recent elk they had fallen or touting their conquests in the business world.

It was a time of long tea gowns and bowler hats, of small children in ringlets and sailor suits. Guests played croquet on the courtyard in front of the hotel, spent hours reading and chatting on the veranda, went on trail rides, or partook of billiards, bowling (in the Concert Hall basement), concerts, vaudeville shows, balls, and fine dining. By 1913 the Stanley advertised the resort as a golf destination: "Golf amid such surroundings is the ideal sport, and the links of the Stanley Hotel give every opportunity for 'good golf' as the term is understood by even its most enthusiastic devotees," raved a local newspaper.

# THE FIRST FLOOR

## The Lobby

Stanley Hotel Lobby today. Photo by Ron Bueker

The hundred-foot-long lobby was originally carpeted in Flora Stanley's favorite color scheme of deep red and white. Oversized chairs, upholstered in soft leather were grouped in a square-shaped setting on both ends of the room, their backs to each other, thus giving some privacy to someone seated there reading a local paper or penning a letter. White Rattan rocking chairs were sprinkled throughout, their fresh color mimicking the white walls, pilasters and moldings. The pillars were actually plaster, designed to look like wood. Rich mahogany desks and chair legs added to the opulent feel of the room. Brass light fixtures adorned the ceilings and are still in use today. White beams ran the width of the high ceiling, breaking up the long expanse and humanizing the cavernous room. (See page 5 for photo of original Lobby.)

The first thing you notice upon entering the Lobby is the massive, sweeping staircase that carries your gaze to the soaring Palladian window, flanked by two six-pane windows and a long window seat on the landing to the second floor. "Every four balusters in the railing is a different turning style," reports Susan S. Davis, former curator of The Stanley Museum in Kingfield, Maine. Each of the four styles is a reflection of the Georgian style.

Stanley Hotel Grand Staircase in Lobby. Photo by Ron Bueker.

The entire south-facing wall of the lobby is designed to showcase the views of the mountain ranges outside through the six large windows with fan-shaped tops. The plethora of white Rattan chairs wait just outside these windows where they line the equally long veranda, again, taking full advantage at the unrivaled views of the Rockies. An authentic sleigh used for winter sightseeing at the hotel in the colder months is on display here. Guests are invited to sit, gaze at the breathtaking views and recall the days of simple pleasures.

Front veranda of the hotel with antique sleigh and views of the Rockies. Photos by Ron Bueker.

Two fireplaces, equally spaced from the central stairway, anchor the Lobby's north wall. Picking up the red and white theme of the room, the Colorado red-rock hearths seem to be the only indication that you are inside a hotel set in the West. These fireplaces, and the ones in the Music Room, Writing Room (today the Chrysalis Gift Shop) and Smoking Room (today the Pinon Room) provided the warmth for the summer resort on chilly evenings. Heat was finally introduced to the hotel in 1984 with the Manor House next door receiving the only year-round guests until then.

Stanley Hotel Fireplace on the east end of the Lobby.
Photo by Ron Bueker.

Original Stanley Logo

Stanley Hotel Fireplace on west end of Lobby. The archway to the left leads to the Cascades Restaurant and Whiskey Bar. The arch partially shown to the right is the Registration Desk. R. Bueker.

Men, dressed in snappy uniforms, waited quietly about the room in case a guest required something. The Registration Desk, with its wooden cubbyholes for correspondence and keys, sat in an alcove as it does today, a sweeping arch marking its placement. Every detail shouted refinement and elegance.

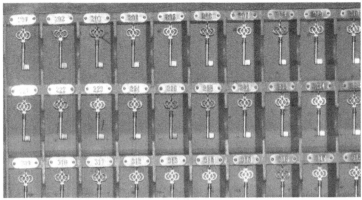

Stanley Hotel keys. Photo by Ron Bueker.

The Registration area showing portraits of F.O. and Flora Stanley above the mail and "keys" cubbyholes. Today the hotel uses electronic key cards. Photo by Ron Bueker.

Visitors to the Lobby today will notice two distinct differences. The opulent carpeting has been replaced by polished wood floors and the once-white interior now sports the dark faux-painted woodwork (faux bois) introduced in an effort to make the area seem more subdued and foreboding for Stephen King's television mini-series, *The Shining*, which was shot at the hotel after King regained the film rights from Warner Brothers in 1996. The walls were painted to look like wood-grained mahogany, a finish carried into most of the first floor rooms used for the television shots, including the ceiling beams. The soft green embossed wallpaper was also put up for the film. A condition was signed that the "wood" would once again be painted white when the interest in *The Shining* died down. I have a feeling the faux bois will be there for some time!

Sara Walker is the owner of the Chrysalis Gift Shop at the Stanley Hotel. She once heard two gentlemen arguing near her shop door as to what wood was used throughout the Lobby.

"It's cherry wood," one man stated emphatically.

"No, it's oak wood," the other exclaimed.

Sara smiled to herself and muttered, "No....it's *Holly*wood."

The oversized leather chairs are still there, though the foursquare seating has been replaced by a more informal grouping. High backed chairs, reminiscent of Dickens, are upholstered in soft shades of green to complement the wallpaper. Area rugs still carry Flora's love of red and cream coloring and the mahogany wood furnishings carry on the original theme.

Stanley Hotel Lobby today. Photo courtesy of COFPhoto.com.

Standing proudly in the Lobby is a Stanley Steamer—a 1906 10 hp Model EX Runabout. It is interesting to note how the steering wheel is on the opposite side from today's American vehicles. A mother-in-law seat for the back could be added to this model. That was an extra $25.00! Originally, this model sold for approximately $700--$800, depending on the extras that were needed. A windshield was an option, undoubtedly coming in handy for any country travel. One intriguing fact about the Stanley Steamer is that the first few models did not have a steering wheel! The vehicle was steered with a tiller! (Ron Lasky, *A Concise History of the Stanley Hotel*)

Stanley Steamer Motor Car in the Lobby of the Stanley Hotel.
Photo by Ron Bueker

"Hanging above the Stanley Steamer at the west end of the Lobby is a large oil painting of F.O. Stanley which was painted from a photograph taken by his sister, Chansonetta, who was a famous photographer. It was taken of him in his violin workshop in Newton, Massachusetts. This portrait of F.O. illustrates his sister's artistic eye and skill. The item, which looks like a tuning fork holding up an unfinished neck of a violin on the bench, is actually the connecting rod of an early 10 hp Stanley Steamer. Chansonetta's effort to accentuate the neck and her choice of a part from a Stanley engine gives us an insight in the story-telling genius behind every picture she composed." (Susan S. Davis, Stanley Museum, Kingfield, Maine.) (As of 2015, the Steamer has been moved to the east of the main entrance into the Lobby.)

Chansonetta was a frequent visitor to her brother's home in Estes Park. Her photography is showcased in the National Museum of American Art at the Smithsonian in Washington D.C.

Chansonetta Stanley Emmons with her camera. Stanley Museum.

Original photograph of F.O. Stanley taken by his sister Chansonetta. You can see the connecting rod from a Stanley Steamer at the left of the photo. Photo courtesy of the Stanley Museum.

Also, at this end of the Lobby, to the right of the MacGregor Room, hangs a photograph of Lord Dunraven. The Lord's ghost is a frequent visitor to the hotel and we will give him his proper place when we talk about the 4th floor. His nefarious plans for acquiring the acreage of Estes Park are legendary and it is perhaps tongue-in-cheek that his portrait hangs next to the room whose namesake was his biggest nemesis during the land grabbing schemes: Alexander MacGregor.

Lord Dunraven's portrait hanging in the Lobby.

Lord Dunraven's portrait hanging next to the MacGregor Ballroom (on left) and the entrance to the Cascades Restaurant (on right).
Photo by Ron Bueker.

The doors leading to the Cascades Bar, Music Room, Pinon Room, Gift Shop and elevator are all on this level. We will deal with them in turn.

Chapter Five

# FIRST FLOOR ROOMS

*"Behind every man now alive stands 30 ghosts, for that is the*
*ration by which the dead outnumber the living."*
*2001: A Space Odyssey. Arthur C. Clarke*

## The 1909 Otis Elevator

In the main Lobby, an attraction to most visitors is the elevator. It is a brass 1909 Otis elevator that originally operated on hydraulics. Water entered a hydraulic ram that would raise the elevator. When the handle in the elevator was pushed down, the elevator would descend and drain the water from the ram into a small pond on the property. Because water is a poor hydraulic fluid, due to its low viscosity, if the elevator had too much weight in it, it would simply "sink" to the basement until the load was lightened—which meant the gentlemen on board would have to alight and allow the ladies to ride upstairs to their floors. The elevator was converted to an electrical cable mechanism in 1935. However, this improvement required that the housing for cable operations be located on top of the hotel. A cupola, similar to those already on the roof, had to be built. To the dismay of many—especially architects—this destroyed the symmetrical design of the hotel. In the spring of 2005, the elevator was totally refurbished electrically and mechanically while still maintaining its original charm. (Ron Lasky, *A Concise History of the Stanley Hotel*, 2nd Edition.)

Otis elevator in Stanley Hotel Lobby. The door to the Chrysalis Gift Shop is on the right. Photo by Rebecca F. Pittman

Original Elevator Conveyance Handle inside the Elevator.
Photo by Rebecca F. Pittman

The elevator featured prominently in Stephen King's book, *The Shining,* and later in his film versions of the book. It has been the site of many ghostly occurrences in the hotel.

## Chrysalis Gift Shop

Today's Chrysalis Gift Shop used to be the Lady's Writing Room. It was fashionable in those days for women to keep journals, write letters and cards, and in Flora Stanley's case, to write articles often published in magazines of the day. When the men were off on sporting expeditions, or otherwise together, the women might stay inside in the morning or afternoon to write. (Susan S. Davis, *A History and Tour of the Stanley Hotel*)

Inside the Chrysalis Gift Shop at the Stanley Hotel. You can see the
windows and door that originally looked out over the back veranda and
courtyard. Today they are an addition to the Shop offering myriad delights.
Photo courtesy of Inspirock.com

The Writing Room once looked out onto the back patio through
large Palladian windows. There is a fireplace adorning the north wall,
exactly opposite to the fireplace in the main Lobby. The room has
since been expanded twice: once, to accommodate the gift shop
merchandise and dressing room, and then again to add an office for
the gift shop owner along with additional storage room. The fan
windows of this office overlook the Billiard Room that rests on the
other side of the wall.

The Chrysalis Gift Shop offers an eclectic blend of upscale
clothing, home décor, items documenting the Stanley Hotel's history
as well as a section dedicated to *The Shining* phenomenon. There
are duplicate plaques of Room 217 (both profitable and pragmatic as
guests kept removing the room plaque next to the door where
Stephen King stayed when inspired to write the hit book), DVD's,
books, glassware and other memorabilia for the movie enthusiast.
Books about Estes Park, the Rockies and the Stanley Steamer are also
found here, along with elegant jewelry, works of art, postcards and

quaint accent pieces. An enchanting display of puppets and toys adorn one wall, while objects of whimsy are scattered throughout. The eclectic blend of merchandise is truly wonderful.

Otis elevator and Chrysalis Gift Shop on Lobby floor.
Photo by Rebecca F. Pittman

## The Kitchen

The Stanley Hotel kitchen is a large one, with old wooden stairs leading down to the newer employee dining area. John Cullen of the Grand Heritage Hotel Group renovated the dining area, expanding the tunnel on the garden level and turning it into a bright, cherry area filled with tables, beverage machines, a salad bar area and serving counters. There are numerous well-thumbed paperbacks lining the windows that look out onto the west side of the building toward the Executive Offices.

Employee Dining Area at end of tunnel running beneath the hotel.

The cooking staff at the hotel is top-notch. Their unique menu has garnered praise and a faithful following of those in search of elk, buffalo, fresh trout and prime rib. The fare offered is very unique and the plated presentation is absolutely amazing. It rivaled anything a fancy restaurant in New York could serve up.

The beverage area door accesses the back of the Whiskey Bar in the Cascades Restaurant. Stories of glasses suddenly falling from shelves and the ice machine sounding as if someone is scooping out ice, and dropping it into crystal or ice buckets, have been reported from this area when the room is empty of staff. Many of the servers have heard music echoing from the several doors that lead from the kitchen area into the MacGregor Room.

The floors are hardboard and old, the rooms decidedly turn of the century, yet the menu is rich in elegance and unusual fare.

When the hotel first opened *Hotel Monthly* praised the new kitchen for its use of electricity; something that was still a fledgling convenience in the early 1900s.

"The kitchen of the Hotel Stanley is out of the ordinary. In describing the kitchen it is well to bear in mind that, not alone is the roasting, frying, broiling and toasting done by electricity, but that all the hot water and steam is produced by electricity generated by water power. Also it is well to bear in mind that the articles of kitchen equipment are, as a rule, but slightly changed in appearance from those we are accustomed to see; for the skill of the inventor has adapted electrical energy to serve the cookers in their old forms, except that he has done away with coal, wood, charcoal, ashes, gas and hot steam pipes, and made the kitchen a more comfortable room for the workers."

The genius of F.O. Stanley went far beyond the advanced services of his new kitchen, as we will see later.

From the menu at the Stanley Hotel today.

## The Reception Desk

The front registration desk at the hotel sits just inside the Lobby to the left of the grand staircase. It hasn't changed much since it was built in 1909. There are wooden cubbyholes behind the warm wood counter, once used for door keys, now mainly for correspondence as the Hotel has kept up with our technologically savvy world and today uses electronic keys.

Two small portraits flank the cubbyhole area: F.O. Stanley to the left and Flora Stanley to the right. It is from this position that Mrs. Stanley's photograph was said to fly off the wall and land on an offensive stain the film crew had created while filming the TV version of *The Shining*.

Registration desk at the Stanley Hotel. Note the laurel wreaths on the molding. The laurel wreath denotes victory and accomplishment. Photo by Ron Bueker.

Behind the desk to the left is a door leading to the office. It is here that the Stanley Hotel safe once sat. Today you can see that safe on the Garden Level, or Basement, floor. Other doors leading from the desk area go out into the hallways near the Grand Staircase and the Cascade Restaurants. They are kept locked at all times; although it is rumored ghosts have rattled the doorknobs, or knocked, on more than one occasion.

Original Stanley Hotel safe found on the Garden Level/Basement Level of
the Hotel. Photo by Ron Bueker.

# The Music Room/Parlor

The entrance to the Music Room is through the pocket doors at the
far east side of the hotel Lobby. Its south wall is completely encased in
large windows showcasing the view of the Rockies and other mountain
ranges that surround the hotel in protective enclaves. After the
weighty feeling of brown mahogany and heavy leather chairs that
permeate the large Lobby, it is a refreshing change to step into the
Music Room with its original crisp white walls and fireplace

mantelpiece. Your eye is immediately drawn across the hardwood floor to the music alcove built into the east wall. Here Flora Stanley's beloved Steinway sits today as it did a century ago.

Flora Stanley's magnificent Steinway piano in the Music Room.
Photo by Rebecca F. Pittman.

The Steinway grand piano that graces the small stage in the alcove was F.O. Stanley's gift to his wife Flora on the opening of the Stanley Hotel, June 22, 1909.

This room is the site of the Stanley Hotel's best known and best documented haunting. To this day, people hear, or see, Flora Stanley at her piano, or most recently, near the piano. We will cover the strange paranormal activity in this room in the next section of the book called The Hauntings.

The Music Room, perhaps the most beautiful room in the hotel, depicts the Stanley family. Even in their private homes in Newton, Massachusetts, their music rooms were elegantly appointed, often the largest as well as the most stunning rooms in their homes. Interest in music was not uncommon in the day, but the Stanley's took it further than most, from building fine violins, to owning the best pianos, studying voice, even composing music. The Concert Hall (originally called the Casino, meaning entertainment, not gambling), one of the four primary buildings of the hotel, was designed for music, and in fact is the only other space on the property with the same amount of architectural detailing. It is a sure sign of F.O. Stanley's artistic investment in music, and thus in these spaces. It is also reflective of the main hotel's Music Room with its pristine white walls, ceiling moldings and appointments.

Music Room with its many windows. The door to the left leads out onto the veranda where women would walk in order to bypass the off-limits Smoking Room and enter the Billiard Room to its north.
Photo by Jerry Cordhall

In the early 1970s, the Stanley Hotel was in the most rundown condition of its history. People were literally backing up to the building and taking furniture away by the truckload in a ruthless example of looting. The Steinway piano was moved into hiding by its owners for its protection. It returned in 1976 when Frank Normali finalized his purchase of the hotel. Most of the stories of hearing it played started after that. We have chosen to interpret it as a statement by Flora that she is glad to have her piano back. The music is often Strauss; Flora's favorite composer. There is also the strong smell of roses in the room, known to be Flora's favorite flower, and perhaps perfume.

The incredible views of the Rockies through the Music Room windows. Photo by Ron Bueker.

The seven-and-one-half-foot Steinway was brought up to Estes Park by ox cart and was personally played and tuned by John Philip Sousa from 1930 to 1934. Each time Sousa tuned the piano he etched his initials and the date of the tuning on the inside of the piano. When the piano was restored in Denver years later, the technician proudly announced that he had been able to "remove all those chicken scratchings from the interior." Fortunately, the hotel has a picture of the "chicken scratchings" for posterity.

Many famous people have played Flora's piano, or been accompanied by it. Caruso, Lily Pons, Joan Baez, Bob Dylan and

Marian Anderson are just a few. Today the Music Room hosts concerts, weddings, receptions, and conferences.

Many years ago, a master painter and his crew removed many layers of paint from the Music Room's walls, ceilings and the carved woodwork. Directly over the fireplace was an intricately carved panel with a large "ball" in the center of it. It wasn't until the painters painstakingly chipped away at the "ball" that the ram's head was found under the layers of paint. (Susan S. Davis, *A History and Tour of the Stanley Hotel*)

The fireplace in the Music Room. Note the same swan neck pediments that

grace the front of the hotel. This fireplace is an exact replica of the one found in F.O. Stanley's personal home.
Photo by Ron Bueker.

A close-up of the ram's head medallion on the Music Room fireplace that
was once buried beneath layers of paint.
Photo by Ron Bueker.

# The Pinon Room/Smoking Room

On the east side of the Lobby you will find the swinging doors to
the Pinon Room. It is interesting that these are the only swinging
doors in the hotel leading to public areas. The other major rooms on
the Lobby floor are accessed by pocket doors, with the exception of
the Cascades Restaurant, which have beautiful etched glass doors
which open outward.

The Pinon Room was originally called The Smoking Room,
thought to have been a drinking and smoking room for men only
until Prohibition in 1918. It was designated for such purposes for
the first 36 years of the hotel's operation. F.O. and his twin brother,
F.E. were young members of the temperance movement in Maine.
At the impressionable age of 12 they had watched a partner in their
father's general store business drink the business into debt. It took

their father, Solomon almost 10 years to pay off the bills. It was well known that F.O. did not approve of drinking, smoking or gambling, but as an astute businessman, he realized that many of his guests would require an establishment offering such amenities.

East Lobby looking toward Music Room door on right, and the Pinon Room swinging doors on the left. Photo by Ron Bueker.

The early 1900's smacked of the Victorian segregation that men and women had become accustomed to. At the Stanley Hotel this was apparent in the areas designated for the males and females. Primarily the women used the Writing Parlor and Music Room to congregate, write letters and articles, and discuss the fads of the day. Next door to the Music Room was the Pinon Room, where the men would sit before the large stone fireplace and read the news of the day, relax and exchange viewpoints. The women were not allowed in this room. If they wished to watch the men play billiards, which took place in the room adjoining the Pinon Room, they had to exit from the Music Room onto the balcony and follow it past the Pinon Room doors to enter the balcony door leading into the Billiard Room. Here they were encouraged to take a seat on the padded bench that runs the length of the south wall and admire the adroit skill of the stronger gender.

Does this mean the ladies were without their libations and eccentricities? Well, according to Patricia M., the hotel's public relations manager many years ago, she was let in on the "inside scoop." While she was giving a tour a of the Pinon Room to a group that included a very elderly lady in a wheelchair, Patricia told the attendees about women not being allowed to drink alcohol at the Stanley Hotel in the 1900's. The woman in the wheelchair piped up and announced she had been a guest at the Stanley Hotel when F.O. was there, and said, "Oh, but my dear, all of the ladies had flasks in their purses!"

Original Mirrored Bar in Pinon Room. Photo by Ron Bueker.

Roe Emery was an owner of the hotel from 1929-1945. He took the original mirrored bar cabinet that is still there today and turned it into a soda fountain for the children visiting the hotel. After Prohibition, this was the only bar at the Stanley until 1946 when the back porch was razed, and the Dunraven Grille (now the Cascades Restaurant) was added to the main hotel. The bar with the mirror was used as the bar in ABC's mini-series *The Shining* in which the crazed caretaker Jack Torrance sees the ghosts of the old Hotel reflected in the mirror. (Susan S. Davis, *A History and Tour of the Stanley Hotel*)

The bar is a beautiful piece, with burled wood and rich detailing. The original brass foot-rail disappeared when the hotel fell into disrepair.

Unlike the Lobby, most of the wood in the Pinon Room and Billiard Room is real. The light from the original lighting fixtures glows richly in the deep luster of the pinon, mahogany and dark green oak paneling and trim. It is decidedly a masculine room, dominated by a massive fireplace in large stone blocks. The rock is local and the fireplace is reportedly the largest keystone fireplace still in use in Colorado. This author can verify that it puts out an enormous amount of heat as I have been in the room when the fire is lit!

Pinon Room fireplace. The small wood square above the mantel covers a swastika. Photo by Rebecca F. Pittman.

Above the fireplace mantel there are four corners, each covered with a wooden square. Two of these have aspen leaves mounted on them. If one looks carefully, it is obvious that the aspen leaves have been placed on top of some other carving or decoration. That "decoration" was a swastika. Before the swastika was covered, some visitors who observed it wanted to know if Stanley was a supporter of the National Socialist Party of Germany—the Nazi Party. Certainly he was not! So, several years ago the Stanley Hotel covered the swastikas with the aspen leaves. Actually the swastika was not a Nazi invention at all. Early white traders in the late 1800's encouraged the Navajo Indians to use the swastika, the thunderbird, arrows, and other previously non-Indian designs because of the salability to the white man. So the swastika was wildly popular in Navajo jewelry and rugs at the turn of the century. It did not fall into disfavor among Americans until it was adopted by the Nazi Party in 1920—well after F.O. incorporated his fireplace design. (Ron Lasky, *A Concise History of the Stanley Hotel*)

The Pinon Room has several sets of doors leading out onto the balcony, which overlooks the parking lot and a breathtaking view of Lake Estes. This is a favorite location for guests who wish to have a ringside seat for the fireworks display on the 4th of July as it erupts over the lake and falls like fireflies into the pine trees.

An original piano of the hotel sits between the Music Room & Pinon Room doors.

# The Billiard Room

The Stanley Hotel Billiard Room retains the masculine feel of wood-paneled walls and beamed ceilings. F.O. Stanley might be amused to see the room used today for elegant weddings and corporate banquets. Yet, his stamp is still there in the in the wood bench along the south wall where women sat to watch his prowess on the pool table, and in the billiard ball rack on the west wall. Large antique mirrors reflect the light from the fixtures and east-facing windows, giving the space a feeling of warmth.

Billiard Room facing west. The large transom windows on the left now overlook the Gift Shop. They once looked out onto the back veranda and courtyard. Photo by Ron Bueker.

The room originally had four billiard tables. One of them was discovered a few years ago behind a locked door at the hotel. It was perhaps hidden away, just like Flora's beloved Steinway, during the period the hotel was languishing and people were making off with the furnishings.

The floor was originally made of corkboard. Today it is carpeted in a motif that matches much of the hotel flooring. The large transom windows on the west wall now overlook the Gift Shop Office on the other side, where once they viewed the back courtyard.

French doors give out onto the veranda that wraps the east side of the building. The views of Lake Estes from here are incredibly lovely.

Susan Davis headed the Stanley Museum when it was once housed in the hotel basement. She is also involved with the Stanley Museum in Maine. Susan has written a wonderful book about the Stanley family and hotel. She was kind enough to share some of these remembrances for this publication.

"It was typical in those days to have billiard tables in the home, which allowed the family members—especially children—to play without having to go to public places of possible disrepute. F.O.'s grandniece, Augusta Tapley (his twin brother's granddaughter), tells the story of having to learn to play when she came to visit in the early 1930s so that her Grand-Uncle would have someone to play with on the billiard table at his home in Estes Park.

"Augusta became so proficient that she occasionally beat "Uncle Freel." Except for her Uncle Raymond, she and other members of the family knew better than to beat Uncle Freel too many times.

"The Stanley's loved games of all kinds, from word and board games to cards. They enjoyed bridge so much they reputedly shut the curtains in their homes on Sunday in order to play. Relatives remember playing games—word games, board games, puzzles, etc.— within minutes of entering F.E. or F.O.'s home for a visit." (Susan S. Davis, *A History and Tour of the Stanley Hotel*)

# The MacGregor Ballroom

At the far west end of the Lobby you will find the hotel's largest event area. The MacGregor Room plays host to lavish wedding receptions, large corporate meetings, the popular Sunday Champagne Brunch and of course, the Stanley's annual galas: *The Shining* Halloween Ball and the New Year's Eve Ball. The Estes Park High School Prom is also an annual event.

MacGregor Ballroom set for a special event. Photo by Ron Bueker.

With the addition of the Stanley Film Festival, held each May since 2013 at the hotel, the ballroom, and many other spaces, is packed to capacity. It is a horror film festival showcasing independent horror films, including features, shorts and special events with guest filmmakers. The festival also hosts a student film competition titled The Stanley Dean's Cup. The walls of the ancient hotel throb with music from several bands, while happy attendees are offered everything from shaves to dancing the night away. In 2015 actor Elijah Wood made an appearance and acted as guest DJ.

This author spoke with Candace Carnahan, the Catering and Sales Manager of the Stanley Hotel and asked her about their annual events. She said there were several that were favorites and tended to garner a faithful following each year. Candace told me they have the 4th of July fireworks every year with a view of the fireworks over the lake, entertainment, food and drink. *The Shining* Halloween Ball is a huge event for the Hotel and they have people from all over the world attending; some returning each year just for the event. Candace said the Hotel offers Christmas, Thanksgiving and Mother's Day Brunches, which are also hugely popular, and a Sunday Brunch, which runs year round. Then of course, the New Year's Eve Gala offers food, entertainment, champagne at midnight and party favors. At the time I spoke with her about the New Year's Eve Gala, she said they were sold out with only one guest room at the hotel remaining.

Candace went on to tell me they hosted 150 weddings in 2009 as well, not an unusual number of nuptials for any year at the stunning mountain resort.

*The Shining* **Halloween Ball** is a sought-after ticket. People from around the world attend this opulent gala, dressed in everything from gangsters to characters from the Wizard of Oz. Every era is represented as pirates, can-can girls and even a Michael Jackson look-alike parade merrily through the sold-out event. ,

I attended the ball in 2009 while researching this book. The hotel spared no expense in turning the area into a thrill-seeker's paradise. Giant cobwebs, spiders and other theatrical decorations adorned each archway in the giant ballroom. The tables were draped in black and purple with antique candleholders topped with glass sconces, their soft candlelight flickering throughout the room. A giant drop-down screen showing Stephen King's movie *The Shining* hung above the large stage, acting as the perfect backdrop for the ball that bears its name. A photo op was set up in the northwest corner of the room with a replica of the door from 217 used in the mini-series version of *The Shining*.

Here you can pose while peering through the large hole in the door that Jack Torrance had taken an axe to and recreate the "Herrrrre'ssssss   Johnny!" sequence from the movie. There was also a claw foot tub with a decomposing female resting inside it, one green leg thrown over the side.

Denise and Lisa Froehlich won a prize at the *Shining* Halloween Ball for their portrayal of the twins from the movie. *Estes Park Trail Gazette.*

Shawn DuBois won for the "Scariest Costume" for her creation of the "Axe Wife" at one Shining Ball. Photo courtesy of *Estes Park Trail Gazette.*

There were costume contests, dancing and a riotous good time. An antique typewriter was also set up in the Lobby on a period-piece desk with pages spilling from it—the words "All work and no play make Jack a dull boy" typed in eerie repetition. Fall colors and neon-lighted pumpkins adorned the Lobby while life-size Halloween figures of ghouls and ghostly butlers posed throughout the festive area.

One of the continuing hits of the *Shining* Halloween Ball is the appearance of "Jack." Jack has been named the top Jack Nicholson impersonator in the world and has a recurring stage show in Las Vegas. I first met Jack while writing the first edition of this book in 2010. He has since appeared at my book signings in Colorado and draws a tremendous crowd.

Jack Bullard, world renowned Jack Nicholson impersonator.
www.jacknicholsonimpersonator.com

The MacGregor Room was originally the main dining hall. It served guests on the American Plan—three meals a day. Before its allocation for special events only, it served hotel clientele and the public a standard, often gourmet, a la carte menu. (Susan S. Davis, *A History and Tour of the Stanley Hotel*)

When the hotel was having some roof repair done a few years ago above the Cascade Restaurant, the MacGregor Room was once again returned to its original purpose for fine dining. I overheard a number of guests commenting how happy they were to be once again enjoying the room with its original light fixtures and breathtaking views of the Rockies while feasting on the Stanley's sumptuous fare.

An extension was built onto the room to enlarge the seating capacity. It is not clear when it took place. The area was at one time the west patio. Looking toward the west from the entrance door, one can see a wall with arches dividing the room. These arches were once part of the original outside wall—possibly part of Palladian windows as are found throughout the room. The views from this area overlook the buildings to the west of the complex, towering pines and of course, the backdrop of the majestic Rockies.

MacGregor looking west. The arches were once the wall overlooking the west patio. Photo Rebecca F. Pittman

In 1996, Stephen King came back to the Stanley Hotel for five months to film the ABC Mini-Series of his hit book, *The Shining*. Never happy with the film adaptation done originally from his novel, King could now shoot the movie his way. As executive producer and screenwriter for Lakeside Productions, King was able to include images and scenes not in the original film, including the hedge animals that come to life and the exploding boiler. For this film, the MacGregor Room was used for the famous ball scene. An extension of the original piano proscenium was built to accommodate the large orchestra used in this scene. Stephen King made his cameo appearance here in the TV mini-series. The stage is still there today, though the film crew offered to dismantle it after production. A piano rests on one side of the weathered platform and it is used extensively for weddings, galas and meetings.

MacGregor Ballroom stage where King made his cameo appearance for the TV mini-series of *The Shining*. Photo Rebecca F. Pittman

The main entrance into the MacGregor Room is through double pocket doors, a fixture of the Georgian Revival period. Other doors lead from the room into the Cascade Restaurant, kitchen and storage areas.

Adorning the arch above the stage alcove is a beautiful vase and leaf motif designed by F.O. and lovingly restored over the years. The pilasters and plaster covered steel beams still sport the faux bois look, rather than the correct white of the building's architectural style.

MacGregor Ballroom entrance. Photo Ron Bueker.

The MacGregor Room was named for attorney, Alexander MacGregor (1846-1896), who settled in Estes Park in 1874 and established a ranch in an area called the Black Canyon—not far from the Twin Owls rock formation. He is known for foiling Lord Dunraven's attempt to buy up land in Estes Valley and allegedly turn it into a private hunting reserve for himself and his friends from Europe.

Apparently MacGregor's name over the doorway to the formal dining room is in appreciation.

## The Whiskey Bar and Cascade Restaurant

The Cascades Restaurant was originally called the Dunraven Bar and Grille when it was constructed in 1946 as a smaller dining room and bar area. It sits next to the MacGregor Room and is accessed by two towering etched-glass doors. The mountain and leaf motif on these doors is representative of the beauty that lies just outside the windows that surround the upper level of the restaurant. Matching etched-glass dividers cut to resemble rolling mountain ranges adorn the half-wall that separates the bar from the fine dining area. Large pillars painted in faux bois to match the mahogany colors of the Lobby support the copper Victorian-style ceiling.

Entrance to the Cascades Restaurant and Whiskey Bar. Photo Ron Bueker.

The Whiskey Bar offers thirsty guests almost 600 whiskey choices, from the common blends to top shelf servings in the three digit price range. The Whiskey University offered at the Stanley Hotel offers knowledgeable staff who will guide you through whiskey tastings and enlighten you on the fine art of distilling.

The Whiskey Bar at the Stanley Hotel. Photo by Ron Bueker.

A very famous guest once sat at this bar while filming a scene from *Dumb and Dumber*. The last quarter of the movie was shot at the Stanley when it was transformed into the "Hotel Danbury" for the film. Shots of Jim Carrey at the bar were shot in this room. The main hotel staircase was used, as was the outside of the Manor House (now The Lodge) for the Lamborghini scene. The snow scenes were filmed at Copper Mountain, Colorado.

Jim Carrey at the Whiskey Bar during shooting of Dumb and Dumber Movie. It was called the Dunraven at that time.

Jim Carrey did one of his funniest scenes from the movie when he sat at the hotel bar and listened ad nauseum to a female guest who went on and on about her boyfriend. Mr. Carrey played Lloyd Christmas and was seated next to an under-cover FBI agent named Beth. After she had rattled on for hours, she finally says:

Beth: "So I told myself, Beth...you just got to run girl and oh you know what the klutz did next?"

Lloyd: "No and I DON'T CARRRRRRRRRRRRRRRREEEEEEEE!"

As Lloyd is leaving the bar in one of the shots, he stops and notices an old newspaper clipping hanging on the wall describing America's historic landing on the moon. He looks at the photo and caption and exclaims, "No way! That's *great!*" (chuckling) *"WE'VE LANDED ON THE MOON!"*

Jim Carrey reacting to "Man Lands on the Moon" clipping.

One of the most important features of the Cascades Restaurant and Bar is the dining chairs. These are one of the few remaining original furnishings from when the hotel was built a hundred years ago. The tabletops in the bar area are crowned with hammered copper, beautifully reflecting the candlelight from the small glass candleholders. The paneled walls also cast a warm glow.

On the upper level of the restaurant you will find a private alcove called the Wine Room. The back wall is covered with wine cabinets, their glass doors mirroring the warmth of the room. The walls are done in a soft faux finishing emulating Old World Tuscany. A single table resides there for private parties.

The Whiskey Bar area with etched glass dividing panels for the Cascade Restaurant. Photo by Ron Bueker

There is an eclectic offering on the menu at the Whiskey Bar—from elk burgers to Tuna Tar Tar. The door to the west of this area leads to the outdoor courtyard.

The back of the bar has two exits, one door leading into the MacGregor Room to facilitate alcoholic beverage service, and another leading into the kitchen area via the soft drink and ice department.

Many of the ghost stories pertaining to F.O. Stanley are from the bar area of the hotel. These and other stories will be covered in the Haunting section of this book.

Cascades Restaurant. Photo courtesy of the *Estes Park Trail Gazette*.

The Dunraven Bar and Grille, when built in 1946 was added onto the hotel replacing what was originally the back porch. Today, as the Cascades Restaurant, it sports a large patio for outdoor dining and a beautiful waterfall that empties into a rocked pond. There is also a fire pit for cool evenings and festive summer gatherings.

Stanley Hotel back courtyard with waterfall.
Photo courtesy of the *Estes Park Trail Gazette*.

Chapter Six

# THE GARDEN LEVEL/BASEMENT

The Garden Level of the Stanley Hotel is accessed from the parking lot to the east, and the stairs leading down behind the main staircase in the Lobby. Guests toting heavy suitcases find it much easier to have the bellboy, or one of the hardy people in their group, carry, or cart, the luggage through the Steamer's Café from the parking lot entrance. The antique Otis elevator awaits them, just to the right of the staircase leading to the main floor and Lobby.

## The Steamer's Cafe

With an obvious nod to the Stanley Steamer Motor Car, the Steamer's Café is a casual deli-style offering at the hotel, where patrons can grab a quick bite. Many have found it a great place to obtain the necessities for a picnic in the Rockies, or to await a tour of the hotel from the room just to the west.

As far back as the original opening of the hotel a small dining area has been featured on this level. The door leading from the parking lot is also used during major renovations at the hotel that impede entrance through the main doors.

The Steamer's Cafe offers pastries, sandwiches, soft drinks, juice, coffee, tea and an assortment of souvenirs and snacks. A cozy eating area, complete with tables, chairs and overstuffed couches, welcome guests to come and sit for a while. As a nod to technology, there is an Internet area with two complimentary computers for guest usage.

Sandwich display at Steamer's Café. Photo by Ron Bueker.

The Steamer's Café at the Stanley Hotel on the Garden Level.
Photo by Ron Bueker

As you leave the Steamer's Café you will come to a cozy seating area where you can sit while waiting for the Ghost Tours to begin.

Photo by Ron Bueker.

# The Ghost Tour Office

Ghost Tour area with hotel movie posters and short film.
Photo by Ron Bueker.

The Ghost Tour Office is just outside the Steamer's Cafe. Here people book different tours depending on their interest. There is also a short film concerning the tours and showing images of some of the more famous guest rooms on the upper floors of the hotel. Several tours are offered here:

**The Stanley Hotel Tour**: During this 90-minute walking tour around the Stanley Hotel property guests will be privy to the history of the hotel, past and present. Besides learning about F.O. and Flora Stanley, attendees will be able to view the remodeled Ice House harboring Stanley Steamer Cars, do a walk-through of the hotel, hear about the paranormal history, and view the underground tunnel.

**The Stanley History Experience:** This 45-minute tour goes into F.O. Stanley's impact on Estes Park, the hotel's beginnings, its original layout and much more. The Archive Room houses many artifacts from the 1900's when the hotel opened. Here you can see some of the china used in the hotel's dining, an original billiard table, photos, furnishing, remnants of the hotel's exterior, and more.

**Night Ghost Tour:** Up for a 90-minute nighttime paranormal experience? This tour will enlighten you as to what constitutes paranormal activity and the type that is haunting the hotel today. The tour includes visits to the hot spots of paranormal activity on the hotel property, with the exception of the guest rooms. This is in deference to the guests who have booked those rooms.

**Stanley Paranormal Investigations:** These Ghost Hunts are the ultimate in the paranormal offerings at the hotel. Delving into some of the hotel's most-haunted areas, you will have first-hand experience to see what a real paranormal investigator goes through in search of things that go bump in the night. You must be 18 years or older to participate. Dates for these adventures are posted the 15th of each month for the following month's investigations.

**Ghost Stories:** Wanting something the entire family can enjoy? Gather around for the Stanley Hotel Ghost Stories where you will hear about the hotel's haunted rooms and some of the tales of paranormal activity centered on them. This one is for all ages.

From the history of the Stanley Steamer Motor Car to the hotel's beginnings, from F.O. and Flora to Stephen King, and the ghostly goings-on, there is a tour for everyone.

## The Doll House

As you exit the Ghost Tour Office, you will see to your immediate left the "doll house" version of the Stanley Hotel used in the TV mini-series, *The Shining*. In the film, the playhouse sat out front in the snow and was the source of a few scary moments for young Danny, the small boy in the film who has the gift (or curse, depending on how you look at it) of "the shining." While playing with the doll house, the hedge animals come to life and advance toward him. There was a duplicate of this playhouse, but it burned completely in the final filming of the TV version of the film.

The doll house used in the TV mini-series of *The Shining* shot at the Stanley Hotel. Photo by Ron Bueker.

Across from the playhouse are the 1909 Otis elevator and the staircase to the upper floor. As you continue down the hallway outside the Steamer's Cafe, you will see an overlooked door to your right. It has a plaque that reads "F.O. Stanley, Proprietor."

Adorning the walls of this hallway are old black-and-white photographs capturing moments of the hotel from ages past. F.O. is featured prominently as are photographs of the hotel's interior in the early 1900s.

If you continue down the hallway on the Garden Level you will see the Men's and Lady's Restrooms on your left. Between these rooms is a large glass-enclosed collage of photographs from *The Shining* (both the original movie directed by Stanley Kubric, and the TV mini-series filmed in 1996) and *Dumb and Dumber*, the two movies shot at the hotel. Contrary to popular belief, the original movie of *The Shining*, starring Jack Nicholson was not filmed at the Stanley. We will talk more about that later.

## The Archives Room

Are you interested in the Stanley Hotel history? The Archives Room houses memorabilia from the hotel's early days and the Stanley Steamer history. There are displays of the beautiful china used at the hotel, an original billiard table used in the Billiard Room during F.O.'s time, historic photographs, samples of the original wallpaper and trim, as well as floor plans and blueprints.

To the west of this room, at the end of the hall, is the hotel's latest treasure, Madame Vera.

## Madame Vera

Madame Vera has been known for years as the beloved psychic of Estes Park. She had her office in the Park Theater Mall until it burned to the ground shortly before Halloween, 2009. The Stanley Hotel offered to set her up at the hotel and guests are thrilled to have her there.

When this author talked to her about the fire, she sat back in her chair and looked off into space for a moment, and then she said, "You know, on October 11th, I was at a wedding at Mary's Lake Lodge here in Estes Park. Smoke started coming through the air vents. The alarms went off, and suddenly the big door blew open. We couldn't find any source of a fire there. One week later the fire hit the Park Theater Mall where my office was. I think what happened at Mary's Lake Lodge was a warning that a fire was coming. I had been having anxiety for months about something bad coming." She shook her hands as if to ward of the shivers. "It was really bad...I just knew something really awful was going to happen."

Then she smiled and told me she was very happy at the hotel and that everyone had welcomed her, including Flora Stanley's spirit.

Madame Vera's office is warm and suffused with antique lamps, beautiful scarves, and old-world artifacts that capture and radiate her gifts for seeing into worlds to which most of us would love to be privy. Next to her desk is a basket filled with toys for the spirit children of the hotel.

Madame Vera does readings for the public at very reasonable prices. I found her to be incredibly accurate when she did a reading for me and I was truly amazed by some of the facts she knew about a few of my relatives who had passed away the year before. She is warm, gracious and very humble. We had an instant report, as we are both hovering around 6 feet tall. I teased her that we should start a volleyball team!

## The Tunnel

Outside her door, and to the north, is the ominous entrance to the underground tunnel that is actually part of the original foundation of the hotel. When the hotel was first built, the tunnel was only a small area, used during the original construction when beams were laid across the rugged rock. It was expanded to allow employees entrance and egress as they traveled between their outside dormitories and into the Garden Level of the hotel. Its chiseled rock and protruding tree limbs are indeed an eerie addition to this historic hotel. A small tunnel runs a short distance to the right as it branches off from the main hollowed rock hallway. The room that houses the hotel's telephone computer system is found in this tunnel.

The tunnel and small cave beneath the Stanley Hotel.
Photo by Ron Bueker.

Frank and Judith Normali, former owners of the hotel, dug out and expanded the tunnel in the early 1980s. All visible timbers were cut from the Hidden Valley area sawmill run by the Griffith family for F.O. In building the foundation, only enough rock and debris were removed to create the level space necessary for the Hotel utility lines, and to lay floor joists. Two tree trunks are still visible in the rock. A smaller tunnel servicing utility lines gives a sense of the size of the rest of the tunnel before it was dug out. It is for the use of staff only and can be viewed on official tours.

If you continue along through the tunnel, the smell of earth encapsulating you, you eventually come out into a brightly lit area that is the dining hall for the employees. John Cullen, the hotel's owner, expanded the tunnel and added to it to give the employees a welcoming place to eat and relax. The old wooden steps from this area lead up into the kitchen. There is also an office here for housekeeping.

Finally, large doors to the west open to the outside where employees can walk to their dorm rooms if they are living on the property. There are two buildings, the North Dorm and the South Dorm sitting just north of the building housing the Engineering Department. We will cover these in our section on the out buildings of the property.

Chapter Seven

# THE UPPER FLOORS/GUEST ROOMS

*"When people believed the earth was flat, the idea of a round world scared them silly. Then they found out how the round world works. It's the same with the world of the supernatural. Until we know how it works, we'll continue to carry around this unnecessary burden of fear."* (Dr. John Markway from the 1963 movie, *The Haunting,* based on Shirley Jackson's novel, *The Haunting of Hill House*)

At the top of the main staircase leading from the Lobby to the first landing you will find a long padded bench nestled beneath the large Palladian window. Looking down one sees the front doors of the hotel, and looking up…the notorious second floor of the Stanley Hotel. The walls in this staircase area are adorned with ornamental mirrors and portraits of the people responsible for the hotel's creation: F.O. and Flora Stanley. There are other historic notables peering from portraits and keeping an eye on the guests as they ascend to the 2nd floor of this haunted hotel.

First stairway landing with historic photos and mirrors.
Photo by Ron Bueker

Without a doubt the second floor of the Stanley Hotel receives the most attention when it comes to ghost stories, even though the 4th floor purports the most-haunted rooms. It is largely due to the notoriety Stephen King brought to Room 217 when he booked into the Stanley Hotel in 1974 and began his fascination with this historic site. There is a special section later in the book about *The Shining* and how Mr. King came to choose the Stanley Hotel.

## The 2nd Floor

As you climb the main staircase and step onto the 2nd floor landing, you will see the Dunraven Room directly in front of you. This room is used for conferences and has also been recruited as the headquarters for paranormal research teams as they go about investigating the hotel. You will have seen the Ghost Hunters using this room as their headquarters when they filmed a segment at the hotel. Currently, it also houses a resident Tarot Card reader.

1st landing leading up to 2nd floor and Dunraven at the top center.
Photo by Ron Bueker

If you turn right and continue down the hall you will pass several rooms with haunted reputations. At the end of the hall on your right is the fire hose that featured so prominently in Mr. King's book, and later his two movies based on *The Shining*.

Fire hose spigot on 2nd floor landing. Photo by Ron Bueker

An antique writing desk, one of the few remaining original pieces from the hotel's opening is found at this end of the hall. The cubbyholes used for storing stationary and envelopes are visible, as is the inkwell receptacle.

Original writing desk on 2nd floor hallway.  Photo by Ron Bueker

## The 2nd Floor West Staircase/The Vortex

To the left of this desk is what is called the vortex of the hotel. The winding staircase that climbs in a clockwise rotation as it winds its way to the third and fourth floors is the epicenter of energy at the hotel. It was on the landing going up to the 3rd Floor that this author had an encounter with Sarah, the ghost of a 14-year-old nanny who frequents that area. Many people who stand on the 2nd Floor directly beneath the opening of the staircase as it twists and turns its way upwards, feel a little light-headed. Some have said they feel nauseous if they stand there, and some have reported a "rushing" feeling.

Mary Orton (Scary Mary), lead tour guide at the hotel, points out that the spirits who gravitate to this hotel are not just guests of by-gone days. She believes there was a hefty Native American heritage in this valley and they are here as well as others who were never at the hotel.

The 2ⁿᵈ floor vortex. Photo by Ron Bueker

"On April 18, 2004, Elizabeth and John W. of Aurora, Colorado, stayed at the Stanley Hotel for their honeymoon, checking out the next day. Elizabeth had had previous experiences with supernatural forces, but nothing as bad as what happened this time. She talked her husband into walking the evening Ghost Tour of the hotel. The tour was going fine and she was learning a lot when they approached the west end stair well on level Two. The tour guide, her husband and three other people, walked across a spot where Elizabeth stopped.

"As she stopped, several of the tour guests heard what sounded like the pop heard when someone experiences static shock. The guests and guide turned around to see what happened and reported that Elizabeth's hair was standing straight up as if she had touched a static orb. She felt as though she had walked through a bubble that was popped by cold air. As the tour ended, she started to get a very painful headache that started making her sick. The next day after taking stuff to the car, she talked her husband into going back to the spot again. As they approached the spot, John walked through and Elizabeth followed where she was again popped with a static shock." (Susan S. Davis, *Stanley Ghost Stories*)

Directly across from the staircase and below the old-fashioned fire hose attachment is a modern-day encasement housing a fire extinguisher. It is a rectangular metal box with a glass face.

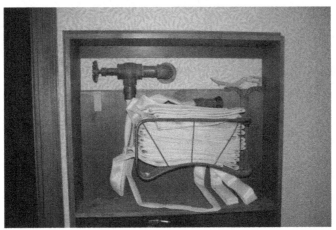

Fire hose encased in glass on 2nd floor hallway. Photo by Ron Bueker

During a private tour Scary Mary was conducting for a wedding party, she stopped by the staircase with her tour group and was talking about the vortex when suddenly the glass face on the fire extinguisher burst, glass shooting out into the startled group. No one was hurt, but there was absolutely no explanation for the explosion. The group was standing several feet away from the box so no one had tampered with it. The eerie thing is that just before it happened, a young boy in a wheelchair had been watching his reflection in the polished glass.

Just before the short hallway leading to Room 217 is a linen closet sitting close to the stairs. It has its original brass handle. Strange lights have been known to play up and down this door and across this brass knob. People standing with their back to the door and one hand resting on the handle have seen small cluster of colored lights crawl up their arm and torso. No explanation has been found for the phenomenon. This author experienced it personally.

Linen closet door near stairs. Room 217 on the right.
Photo by Rebecca F. Pittman

Room 217 from hallway. Photo by Ron Bueker

# Room 217

*"Ghosts make the papers along with celebrities every day of the week."* (Dr. John Markway, *The Haunting,* a movie based on Shirley Jackson's book, *The Haunting of Hill House)*

Room 217 is not the only room of distinction on the 2<sup>nd</sup> floor of the Stanley Hotel, although it is the most requested. While author Stephen King may have put the nefarious room on the map, it is claimed to be haunted by someone who laid claim to the room long before the writer was born.

In June of 1911, the all-electric hotel had a power outage due to a storm that put the Stanley power plant out of commission. The hotel went to its backup acetylene system. The wall lamps at that time were both electric and gas—a pragmatic solution for a still burgeoning concept of electric lighting, especially in the Rocky Mountains.

Elizabeth Wilson, a chambermaid at the hotel, had entered Room 217 to light a lamp. However, unbeknownst to her, the gas had been on for some time. When she attempted to light the lamp the gas was ignited and she was blown out of the room, literally. The ceiling and several heavy steel girders fell. The blast blew her through the floor and into the MacGregor Room below where she broke both her ankles.

Amazingly, she survived the impact that took off the hotel's exterior to the entire southwest end. Four busboys were also injured but there were no fatalities. The hotel's facade did not fare as well. Estimates of up to $60,000 for repairs were given.

Mr. Stanley, who was devastated at her fall, paid all of her medical expenses and put her up in one of the rooms as she healed, while he held her job open for her. She remained a loyal employee until her death in 1951 at the age of 90. She died peacefully in her sleep.

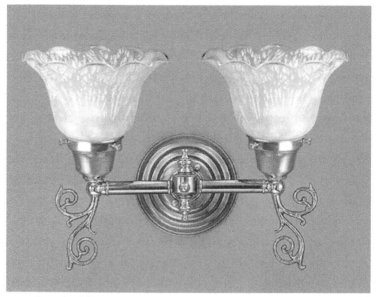

A gas & electrical light fixture. The gas element is found in the center.

Room 217. Photo by Mary Stickland.

Many famous people have stayed in Room 217, including Teddy Roosevelt, the "Unsinkable" Molly Brown, Emperor Hirohito of Japan, Jim Carrey and, of course, Stephen King, among others.

Stories of Mrs. Wilson's presence still circulate around Room 217. It is said that she is a tad judgmental of those who stay in the room. If you tend to be messy, she has been known to toss clothes about and try to rearrange the bed linens—whether you are in them or not! If she likes you, and you are taking good care of her domain, she will lovingly unpack for you and put your clothes into the dresser drawers.

Most of the guests staying in 217 see Mrs. Wilson in the form of a large vertical purple bar that appears in their digital camera viewfinders when they are preparing to take a picture of the room. No matter where I stand in the room, the purple bar always appears, most frequently in front of the settee that sits in front of the 4-poster bed.

Claw foot tub in bathroom of Room 217. Photo Rebecca F. Pittman

One has only to step into the bathroom to be transported to another era. The claw foot tub was said to be an inspiration for Mr. King for *The Shining* as it appeared to him as a place someone might die, or already had! Curtains hanging from rings surround the tub, giving it an even more secluded and spooky feeling. The floor is reminiscent of another time; its white-and-black tile calling forth memories from the 1920s.

The bathroom also houses reports of paranormal activity, presumably from Mrs. Wilson. Lights turn on and off, the faucets shoot forth water under their own volition, and the door opens and closes as she goes about her housekeeping.

There was a rumor that Stephen King returned to the room after roaming the halls of the hotel and found his and his wife's clothes put away. They had left their suitcases unpacked while they toured the hotel.

There is another story that upon occasion a black "hole" is seen in the carpeted floor of the room at the exact location where Mrs. Wilson was blown into the ballroom below. Guests of the room have set up video cameras, their lens aimed at the location just outside the bathroom door and to the left (west), hoping to capture the elusive spreading stain.

Room 217 is a beautiful room, complete with a 4-poster bed, opulent writing desk, tall dresser and a glassed door bookcase filled with Stephen King's books and DVD's. A large Boston firm erupts from its standing vase near the east window, giving the room the charm of a bygone Victorian era. The white lace and velvet curtains give way to a commanding view of the mountains and the hotel swimming pool. An overstuffed chair invites you curl up with one of Mr. King's thrillers.

As mentioned earlier, Room 217 was originally a three suite clustering of rooms with adjoining bathrooms used for visiting presidents, royalty and other famous guests. That area now comprises several separate rooms with their own bathrooms.

Room 217 writing desk. Photo by Rebecca F. Pittman

View from the balcony window of Room 217. Photo by Linda Hostler.

Books by Stephen King offered for reading in Room 217.
Photo by Chris Hanson.

The oval brass room number plaque in the hallway next to the entrance to the room has been stolen so many times, that you can see pry marks beneath it. Souvenir plaques for Room 217 are sold in the Chrysalis Gift Shop in the Lobby, both as a great piece of memorabilia, and pragmatically, to help reduce the need to pilfer the one that adorns the wall outside the room.

Room 217 wall number showing pry marks from enthusiastic souvenir collectors. Photo by Rebecca F. Pittman.

Room 217. Photo by Rip Tragle

The long H-shaped hallways are lined with embossed taupe-colored wallpaper riding above the wainscoting that runs the length of the 2$^{nd}$ story. If you are attentive you can feel the difference in the flooring beneath your feet, indicating where the boards were redone at some point. It left a slight ledge to the otherwise even flooring. This may be the site of the reconstruction after the explosion in Room 217 took out a good portion of this area on the 2nd floor.

2<sup>nd</sup> floor hallway looking east.  Photo by Ron Bueker.

While there are other rooms on the 2<sup>nd</sup> floor that have garnered their own reputations, it is for paranormal activity, which we will cover in our Haunting section of the book.  We will also take a closer look at the Housekeeper's Stairs, located down the west hallway on this floor, toward the rear of the hotel.  Many stories of paranormal activity are centered on this steep staircase.  Let's move to the 3<sup>rd</sup> Floor.

Chapter Eight

# THE 3ᴿᴰ & 4ᵀᴴ FLOORS

*"There are nights when the wolves are silent and only the moon*

*howls." George Carlin*

The 3rd Floor of the Stanley Hotel looks much like the 2nd. It has long hallways that end in turns leading to more long hallways that culminate in outside doors leading to the wooden exterior staircases.

3rd floor hallway. Photo by Ron Bueker

At these crossroads sit original writing desks that once adorned the hotel when it was new. I love picturing the men and women of the early 1900s sitting there, exchanging pleasantries of the day, as they dipped pens in inkwells and scribbled off notes to friends and relatives in other states and other countries.

One gets a feeling of vertigo at times when looking down these long, uninterrupted hallways, tall doors flashing by like railroad cars as you make your way along the carpeted passageways. At night, when everyone is sleeping and the boards creak lightly in the mountain breeze, the hotel settles in with a heavy, collective sigh. The burgundy and gold carpeting that lies in unbroken lengths along the meandering halls, releases the countless footprints that have pressed into its pliant weave during the day. The stairways wrap the entrances to the floors with long and winding arms and the myriad windows blink in the waning moonlight.

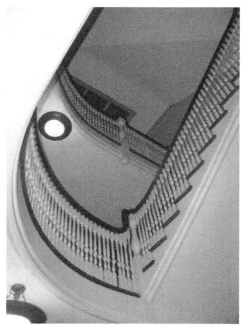

3rd floor staircase looking up to 4th floor. Photo by Ron Bueker.

Although the reports for the 3<sup>rd</sup> Floor do not rival those of the 2<sup>nd</sup> and 4<sup>th</sup>, it carries its own dubious notoriety. We will cover the myriad ghost stories associated with the 3<sup>rd</sup> and 4<sup>th</sup> floors in the Haunting section of this book.

## The 4<sup>th</sup> Floor

The 4<sup>th</sup> Floor of the Stanley Hotel was originally designated as the area for the private staff of visiting families and the children. In those days families traveled with valets, maids and nannies. When visiting a resort, such as the Stanley Hotel, they would stay for extended periods of time, a caravan of luggage and servants following the elegant ladies and their gentlemen up the stone steps to the waiting lobby.

Nanny with children in the 1900s

Families were not as they are today where children are encouraged to sit at the table and engage in conversation or attend social events. The mantra "Children should be seen and not heard" was probably penned in this era of the late 1800s and early 1900s. They even had their own windowless dining area in a small corner of the hotel kitchen while their parents dined on sumptuous fare in the MacGregor Room, attended to by waiting staff for their every need. When not eating, the children were usually ensconced on the 4th Floor with their nannies, playing hide and seek, jacks, bouncing balls and interacting in role playing as children do.

The 4th Floor was rather stuffy, hot and cramped when the hotel was celebrating its birth. Chambermaids, valets, nannies and children all shared the area. Outdoor activities that didn't interrupt the adults were a much coveted past time. In those days, children tended to rely on governesses and nannies for their discipline and nurturing. Mother and Father were often a remote presence. It brings to mind the popular movie *Mary Poppins.*

It is perhaps that so much time was spent here in the form of play and interaction among a large set of people, that so many stories of spirits lingering on is told. The floor itself is unremarkable, looking very much like its two sister floors beneath it. Lovely taupe-colored brocade wallpaper adorns the walls, and the same color theme of carpeting can be seen rolling forth like a manicured fairway.

4th floor hallway. Photo by Ron Bueker

Bell Tower trap door with REDRUM written on it.

The one distinction is a small set of stairs across from the elevator that lead up into darkness. This is the steep wooden stairway to the bell tower. A trap door sits at the top of the steps and is always locked. It is this tower that can be seen from the roadways of Estes Park and crowns the hotel in landmark tradition. Sometime in the summer of 2009, someone climbed to the trap door and wrote the word "REDRUM" on the wood panel. It is of course in reference to Stephen King's book, *The Shining*. For whatever reason, the hotel has allowed it to stay. It cannot be seen without shining a flashlight, or, one's cell phone light, high above your head.

It is here on this floor that the ghost of Lord Dunraven holds sway; his cherry tobacco smoke wafting down hallways as he strides confidently through the halls founded on the property that he once owned and had, at one time, envisioned as his own resort and private hunting reserve. Stories of his appearances in the 4th floor rooms, pinching fannies, and pilfering jewelry abound. As a notorious lady's man, it is also said he has no affinity for the men who check into his guest rooms on that floor. He has caused them angst on more than one occasion.

Room 401 on 4th floor with portrait of Lord Dunraven near the room he is said to haunt the most. The elevator is at the right. Photo courtesy of Trip Advisor.

Room 401 was originally the Nanny's Lounge when the hotel was first built. You can see where the small balcony off the room used to be. It is now enclosed and offers a patio table and two chairs for the guests of the room to relax and enjoy the view of Lumpy Ridge. Today it is frequently booked as a Bridal Suite. In the fall of 2009, it underwent a complete renovation. Many wondered if that would increase the ghostly activity in the room, though heaven knows it receives enough as it is! It is this room where guests report the closet door swinging open on its own volition, followed by some kind of paranormal activity. Other stories of missing items, running faucets and flying objects are also written about this room.

# Lord Dunraven and the Jack the Ripper Connection

Lord Dunraven was part of an elite Free Mason Lodge called The Savage Club. The Savage Club had been founded in 1857 by a "little band of authors, journalists and artists" to provide an informal but private venue for members of London's Bohemia. The Prince of Wales became an honorary member of the Club and, appreciating its informal atmosphere, took a great interest in the affairs of the Club.

Lord Dunraven (Viscount Adare) joined an elite group of journalists in the Club. He was at that time the Provincial Grand Master of Oxfordshire. He was well ensconced in England during the Jack the Ripper rampage and no doubt, with his journalistic instincts was much involved in the surmises of the day as to whom the madman could be. One of the theories put forth was that it was in actuality none other than Albert Edward, Prince of Wales.

Lord Dunraven and the Savage Club came under notice when it was proposed that they were in some way involved in a concealment of the true identity of Jack the Ripper. The theory was that the Jack the Ripper killings were undertaken by freemasons in order to keep secret the clandestine marriage of Prince Albert Victor to a former East End prostitute. Her "area" happened to be White Chapel where the killings of five prostitutes were taking place.

Jack the Ripper's identity remains a mystery today.

Jack the Ripper. Courtesy of www.thedungeons.com

Chapter Nine

# THE MANOR HOUSE/THE LODGE

*"There are an infinite number of universes existing side by side and through which our consciousnesses constantly pass. In these universes, all possibilities exist. You are alive in some, long dead in others, and never existed in still others. Many of our "ghosts" could indeed be visions of people going about their business in a parallel universe or another time—or both." Paul F. Eno, Faces at the Window*

Manor House/The Lodge at the Stanley Hotel. Photo by Ron Bueker

The Manor House on the Stanley Hotel complex has been called by many names, including the "Little Stanley", and, the "winter hotel." It is now known as The Lodge at the Stanley Hotel. The main hotel, which began as a summer resort only, had no heat. Construction on the Manor House, with year-round heating, was begun only months after the Stanley opened in 1909 to unimagined success. It is an identical replica of the larger hotel, designed in the same Georgian Revival architectural theme. It has 33 rooms, all with private baths and lovely sitting areas on each of the three levels.

If you look at the location of the Concert Hall (originally called the "Casino"), which opened its doors to coincide with the opening of the main hotel in 1909, you can see that Mr. Stanley had probably envisioned opening a second hotel all along. A large space was left between the main hotel and the Concert Hall, leaving room for expansion.

Ad from June 20, 1924. The Manor House and Stanley Hotel were called the Stanley Hotels collectively. *Estes Park Trail Gazette.*

Stone Lion at entrance to Manor House/The Lodge.
Photo Ron Bueker.

In 1916, Stanley did expand, extending the East Wings on both buildings and putting an extension on the Carriage House.

The Manor House housed the bachelors in the 1900s as F.O. did not think it suitable for the single men to be roomed in the main hotel with the single ladies and married couples. The main floor is a smaller replica of the main hotel and houses a Library, Ranch Room (the companion Billiard Room to the Pinon Room in the main hotel), a ballroom (similar to the MacGregor but on a smaller scale), and a Lobby; complete with piano. There are three fireplaces on the main level, found in the Ballroom, Library and Ranch Room.

In the 1980s the Manor House was in total disrepair. The hotel's owner at the time, Frank Normali, had it completely gutted and refurbished in 1992.

Although the Manor House is about a third the size of the main hotel, the amenities are just as plentiful. There is a kitchen here, dining area, parlor, library, billiard room and lavish suites.

Today, The Lodge at The Stanley is the newly-remodeled 40-room boutique hotel sitting steps away from The Stanley Hotel to the east. Previously known as The Manor House, The Lodge features a variety of amenities including beautiful updated rooms, a complimentary breakfast, and all the extras found throughout the Stanley complex. With one fine distinction:

The Lodge is dog friendly. With the Preferred Pooch Program at The Lodge, your four-legged friend will be just as pampered as you are. The package comes with a plush dog bed and feeding dishes, and homemade peanut butter and banana dog biscuits. As for walking your best friend, the Rockies are right outside the door. The Vet of the Rockies is also close at hand. There is a 50 pound weight restriction for pets and one dog per room.

The Library in The Lodge has not only an ethereal feeling to it, but of all the rooms at either of the hotel buildings, it has, to me, a haunted feeling to it. Perhaps it is the wooden paddle fans that sit within the fan-shaped windows in the room, or the large stone fireplace. The wallpaper and carpeting are subdued and the light fixtures let off a soft glow that never quite makes the room feel illuminated enough to dispel the feeling of isolation. The glass-fronted bookcases house a selection of well-thumbed books. The room has a decidedly masculine feeling to it. Today it is used for conferences and small gatherings. It is usually void of furnishings to allow for easy table set-up for events.

The Lodge Library Room. Photo by Ron Bueker.

The Ranch Room with its antlers and beamed ceilings.
Photos by Ron Bueker.

The Ranch Room. Note the mirrors and back hall resembling the Billiard Room at the main hotel. Photo Ron Bueker.

The Ranch Room sits next door to the Library. They are arm-in-arm, much like the Pinon and Billiards Rooms of the main hotel. This room was used for billiards, and again, has a very masculine feeling with its antlers and stone, though I didn't find it as "atmospheric" as the Library. It too is used for meetings and small gatherings.

The dining hall sits to the west of the main doors. Windows with breathtaking views flank two sides of the room. A large fireplace with Stanley's trademark designs of vases and wreaths dominates the north wall. This room is all in whites and cream colors and it is a refreshing change from the darker event rooms across the Lobby from it. Today, as the dining room for The Lodge, it is known as Manor Hall and serves a Continental Breakfast to those rooming there.

The Lodge Dining Room/Ballroom. Photo by Ron Bueker.

The Lodge Grand Staircase. Photo by Ron Bueker.

The grand staircase again mirrors its larger counterpart in the main hotel, sweeping up to large Palladian windows that overlook the back courtyard and the crumpled face of Lumpy Ridge. When you reach the second landing, there are comfortable overstuffed chairs welcoming you to a host of suites. There is a more unhurried, casual feeling to the Lodge than the hectic bustle of the main hotel. The tours at the Stanley Hotel host an average of 500 people a day in peak season.

The Lodge Room 1302. Photo courtesy of Janice Raymond.

Room 1302 has the dubious honor of being the most-haunted room in The Lodge. The alcove to the back of this photo shows the small table and chairs featured in an episode of the *Ghost Hunters*. In this feature the table "jumped" while the chair to the left slammed into the wall.

The rooms in The Lodge are beautifully appointed, with the same breathtaking views of the Rockies. The bathrooms are enormous with large Jacuzzi tubs and views of the pines and walkways. There is a courtyard in the rear of the building, and steps leading to a convenient parking lot.

This author stayed in Suite 1301 for a week while researching the hotel and doing some faux painting for the first edition of this book written in 2010. The faux bois (fake wood) painting that had been done throughout the main level of the Stanley Hotel had some dings and scratches from various pieces of luggage hitting the walls during the elapsed time from when the area had been painted to look more subdued and "spooky" for Stephen King's mini-series shooting of *The Shining* at the hotel. I have been a muralist and faux painter for over 35 years and it was an honor to have the opportunity to update the impressive fake wood look of the main floor while gathering information for this book.

The 3rd Floor landing has a cozy sitting area with soft couches and high-backed chairs. An elevator transports you to each of these areas. To the west of this seating area are two large suites: Room 1301 and 1302. They have their own private area with overstuffed chairs and a coffee table sitting just outside their doors.

Entrance to the Parlor Salon and Spa in the Manor House basement.

The basement area of The Lodge is now home to The Parlor Salon and Spa, a lavish treatment center offering everything in the way of rejuvenation. It caters to all who are in search of decadent pampering. The private spa rooms are plush with low lighting, mood music and soft scents. You can have your hair styled or your nails done. Facials, massages, spray tanning, anti-age therapies, henna tattoos, aromatherapy and other temptations are all there for the weary traveler. There are bridal packages and even a couple's retreat, complete with fireplace.

The Manor House (as it was called at the time) made its Hollywood debut as the Danbury Hotel in *Dumb and Dumber*, starring Jim Carrey and Jeff Daniels. It was here the two stars climbed the stone steps and into the Stanley Hotel archives.

Jim Carrey and Jeff Daniels on steps of the Manor House. Photos courtesy of *Movie Man*.

Jim Carrey in front of the Manor House with a Lamborghini.

Chapter Ten

# THE CONCERT HALL/CASINO

*"Courage is fear that has said its prayers."* Dorothy Bernard, actress

Concert Hall at the Stanley Hotel. Photo by Dwayne Elmarr.

The second building to the east of the main hotel is the Concert Hall, called "The Casino" by F.O. Stanley. It was completed in 1909 along with the main hotel. In addition to concerts, the Casino also once hosted elegant dances with impressive guest lists—*de riguer* for a truly "grand resort hotel."

In the basement, two bowling alleys provided another one of F.O.'s favorite forms of recreation. The Stanley Museum has one of his bowling balls, made of lignum vitae, in its Estes Park collection.

F.O. himself laid out the site of the building on September 30, 1908. By October 9, ground had been broken and by mid-month the foundation was complete. The framing of the Casino was well along when a "hard wind" toppled the entire structure on November 19. The damage was quickly repaired and the building completed in time for the June 22, 1909, soft opening of the hotel. (Susan S. Davis, *A History and Tour of the Stanley Hotel*)

Concert area at the Concert Hall. Photo by Ron Bueker

The Concert Hall has played host to an impressive ensemble of performing artists, in part due to its perfect acoustics. Included in the Who's Who of talented musicians and singers are Bob Dylan, Barbra Streisand, Wayne Newton, Joan Baez, Enrico Caruso, Johnny Cash, Mitch Miller, John Philip Sousa, Tony Bennett, Marian Anderson, Frankie Lane, John Fodor, Les Paul, Lawrence Welk and Lily Pons. This is by no means a full reporting of the amazing musical genius's that graced the Concert Hall stage. One has only to walk beneath its soaring ceiling to imagine being wrapped in the swelling cacophony of music that continues to fill this beautiful room.

Concert Hall stage & close-up (below) of ceiling lights. Ron Bueker.

166

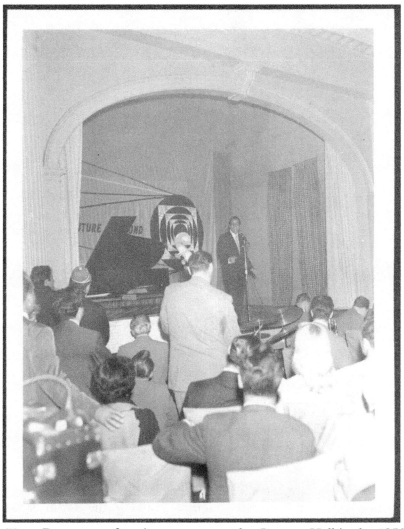

Tony Bennett performing on stage at the Concert Hall in the 1950's.
Photo courtesy of the Estes Park Museum.

Today the Concert Hall continues to showcase international, as well as local talent. The acoustics have been touted as some of the finest in the country.

Close-up of Tony Bennett at the Concert Hall.
Photo courtesy of the Estes Park Museum

Like the Music Room in the main hotel, the Concert Hall is pristine white, its interior columns flanking the room in short intervals. The stage dominates the east wall, nestled into a massive arch. There is a balcony at the back of the hall where spotlights and chairs sit today, but I like to look up at it and picture F.O. and Flora there, with the selected VIP guest of the day sitting happily beside them while they overlook the filled hall below. There portraits flank the stage on each side.

At the left of the stage area, up behind the curtains, obscured from view, is a small room with a very old upright piano sitting there. The ivories are chipped and yellowed. This was area used for storing equipment. At the opposite side of the stage is a staircase leading down to the hall and eventually to the basement. Here the honored performer of the day would make their entrance and exit and utilize the dressing rooms.

J.T. Thompson, head engineer at the hotel was kind enough to show me around during the creation of the first edition of this book. As we were crossing the weathered boards of the stage, I stopped and asked what the trap door was for. He turned and looked down at the rusted iron ring that acted as a handle and said, "I don't know...let's find out!" He tugged on it and the wooden door finally rose. Beneath it was some very old-looking lumber, a few scraps of insulation and some dirt. It went back a ways but I couldn't see it in the dark.

Close-up of stage trap door. Photo by Ron Bueker.

The basement, which was once a bowling alley, is accessed by two sets of stairs: one flight is to your right as you enter the main doors, and the other goes down from the stage area. Today the area is used for receptions, meetings and banquets. There is a small kitchen here with a pass-thru window and a carpeted area for small gatherings. There are two dressing areas, used for bridal parties or performing artist's needs. These have make-up mirrors with large Hollywood-style bulbs. A few extra rooms for storage, and public bathrooms, and that about completes the Concert Hall, well, not quite. The basement of this building is also a hot spot for paranormal activity. Please consult the section of the book called The Hauntings.

# Grand Concert by "Skovgaard"

## THE DANISH VIOLINIST

### Under the auspices of the Estes Park Music and Study Club at the

# STANLEY CASINO

**Monday Evening**
**June 18th**
**8 o'clock sharp**
TICKETS $1.00

SKOVGAARD
THE DANISH VIOLINIST

**Monday Evening**
**June 18th**
**8 o'clock sharp**
TICKETS $1.00

Skovgaard's Hand Insured for $50,000

$50,000

$13,000 "STRAD"

### PROGRAMME

AXEL SKOVGAARD, Violinist    ALICE McCLUNG SKOVGAARD, Pianist

Advertisement in the *Estes Park Trail*, June 8, 1923 for the upcoming performance of the world-famous "Skovgaard" whose hand was insured for $50,000. He appeared at the Stanley Casino on June 18th, 1923. Article courtesy of the *Estes Park Trail Gazette*.

170

Over the years, many celebrities from different arenas in the spotlight have visited and performed at the Stanley Hotel. This list is by no means comprehensive, but it does show the range of personalities who enjoyed F.O. Stanley's resort:

President Theodore Roosevelt
Crown Prince Naruhito of Japan
Empress Michiko of Japan
Emperor Akihito of Japan
Chief Justice Harlan Fiske Stone
Author Stephen King
Astronaut Scott Carpenter
Titanic Survivor the "Unsinkable" Molly Brown
Violinist John Fodor
Folksinger Boy Dylan
Bandleader Lawrence Welk
Composer John Philip Sousa
Folksinger Joan Baez
Opera Singer Marian Anderson
Opera Singer Enrico Caruso
Continued on next page...

Guitarist Les Paul
Country Singer Johnny Cash
Actor Elliott Gould
Actor Melvin Van Peebles
Actor Jim Carrey
Actor Jeff Daniels
Actress Lauren Holly
Actor Stephen Weber
Actress Rebecca DeMornay
Actor Wallace Berry
Actress Gene Tierney
Actor Pat Hingle
Actor Gary Burghoff (Radar of M.A.S.H. Fame)
Dr. Jonas Salk (inventor of polio vaccine)
Evangelist Billy Graham
Harvey Firestone (Rubber Tire Magnate)
News Commentator Lowell Thomas
The J.C. Penney's
Dr. William Mayo
Jane Adams of Chicago's Hull House

**TV and Movies:**
Ghost Hunters (Sci-Fi Channel)
Ghost Adventures (Travel Channel)
"Haunted History—The Rockies"—2001 (History
Channel)
"Historic Hotels of the Rocky Mountain West" –1991-
1992 (PBS Video)
"Haunted Hotels"—2001 (Travel Channel)
"Dumb and Dumber" –1994
"The Shining Mini-Series" – 1997
and many more.

Chapter Eleven

# THE CARRIAGE HOUSE

*"I'm here, because you believe I'm here. Keep on believing and I'll always be real to you."*
*Capt. Gregg in The Ghost and Mrs. Muir, by Phillip Dunne and Joseph L. Mankiewicz*

Carriage House at the Stanley Hotel. Photo by Dwayne Elmarr.

The third building to the east of the main hotel is the Carriage House, completed in 1909 as well, and built specifically for Stanley Steamers.

F.O. designed the famous nine- and twelve-passenger Stanley Mountain Wagons to bring his hotel guests up from train stations in the foothills—Lyons, Loveland and Longmont—or "the valley," as it was known locally. On June 16, 1908, the same month the Lyons Road was finished, F.O. Stanley incorporated the Estes Park Transportation Company (not be confused with the "Loveland-Estes Park Transportation Company" run by the Osborn's starting in 1907). F.O.'s auto stage line was in operation by July of 1908, a year before he opened his hotel. (Susan S. Davis, *A History and Tour of the Stanley Hotel*)

Stanley Steamer coming up the mountain to the hotel. Photo courtesy of Fred Payne Clatworthy.

As guests eventually arrived in their own vehicles, accommodations in the Carriage House were made for those vehicles as well. Since the

174

days of the Stanley Steamers, the building has been used variously for staff housing and storage. In the 1950s it was made over into a motel unit in an attempt to meet the needs of the modern traveling public. The front of the building today still shows the door configuration of the erstwhile motel.

Considering F.O.'s investment in Estes Park and Colorado infrastructure, in the Stanley Hotel and Stanley Steamers to facilitate travel, it is fair to say F.O. Stanley ushered automobile tourism into the western United States. (Susan S. Davis, *A History and Tour of the Stanley Hotel*)

1915 Stanley Steamer Mountain Wagon. Photo courtesy of the Melton Museum of Antique Automobiles in Norwalk, Connecticut

The Carriage House today is undergoing some changes. It is used primarily for storage and visitors are rarely allowed inside. There are current plans to renovate it and turn it into a lavish Stanley Museum, touting the accomplishments of the man who built the hotel and helped his twin brother in the design of the Stanley Steamer Motor Car and other wonderful inventions.

For Stephen King's TV mini-series of *The Shining*, the Carriage House was once more brought into use, housing the infamous 'snow cat' that was needed to transport hapless victims down the 'sidewinder' if things should go...um...awry at the hotel in the dead of winter.

The Carriage House was featured on *Ghost Adventures* where several areas of paranormal activity were featured.

Chapter Twelve

# THE OTHER OUT BUILDINGS

*"The oldest and strongest emotion of mankind is fear, and the oldest and strongest kind of fear is fear of the unknown." H.P. Lovecraft*

Besides the four main buildings, there are six more out buildings on this 35-acre complex. These buildings and their purposes have changed over the years, with the exception of the two dormitory dwellings.

Originally there was a 9-hole golf course on the grounds, an air strip for two planes giving sight-seeing flights over the Rockies, an outdoor swimming pool (removed in 2014), pet cemetery for the beloved pets of the hotel owners, an ice pond, and a barn and stables.

The original gate house was moved from farther down the road when the complex was much larger. It now sits just west of the main hotel and is used as a private guest house called the Presidential Suite. A small gate house with guard arm sits on the east side of the complex, just below the Carriage House and most hotel traffic enters here into the main parking lot.

Estes Park Village is to the south, as is Highway 34 and 36.

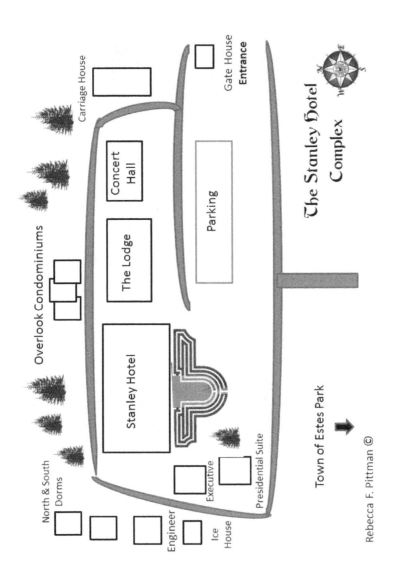

Stanley Hotel Complex

# The Former Gate House/Presidential Suite

The Former Gate House/Presidential Suite on the west side of the complex. Photo by Rebecca F. Pittman.

The former Gate House sits to the west and slightly south of the main hotel. It was originally located on Elkhorn Avenue, flanked by two stone pillars with gates. It was a majestic setting heralding the entrance from Elkhorn Avenue and up the hill to the stately hotel. It was originally located well below the hotel, near today's intersection of US Routes 34 and 36, roughly where the Egg and I, and West Star Bank sit today. The road wound up through the meadow behind and to the east of the current location of the Safeway supermarket in Stanley Village. It was a regal entrance to where the Stanley Hotel sat waiting in kingly splendor. In 1909, the hotel was considered "simply palatial, equaling anything of its size in the world," according to the *Rocky Mountain News*. Today it would seem modest in size compared to some of the mind-blowing resorts that commandeer entire city blocks and vast country sides.

As the town encroached upon the wooded acreage, the Gate House was moved in the late 1930's and relocated to its current position just outside the main hotel. At that time it was remodeled into ten rooms and five baths and was used for employees. Later it was used as the General Manager's home or occasionally for employee housing. Today it is the Presidential Suite and acts as a prestigious retreat for VIPS or those willing to cover the hefty price tag that goes with the luxurious lodging.

Reports of hauntings in this building, as well as some of the other out buildings, will be covered in our Haunting section at the back of the book.

## The Former Manager's House/Executive Offices

Former Manager's House/Executive Offices.
Photo by Rebecca F. Pittman

As you look north from the former Gate House, you will see the former Manager's House. It is directly west of the tunnel entrance that leads into the hotel. This building was originally designed to act as

180

housing for the hotel General Manager. In 1938, it was renovated to provide baths for each room. Today the historic structure is home to the Stanley Hotel Executive Offices. The views of the Rockies from the large windows wrapping the General Manager's Office on the top floor would be distracting to say the least.

The Executive Secretary's office is located to the left, just inside the door. A long, steep staircase greets you as you step inside the foyer. Offices here belong to much of the executive staff, including the General Manager, Head of Operations, Sales and Catering, etc.

## The North and South Dormitories

North and South Dormitories on west side of complex.
Photos by Ron Bueker.

Directly north and to the west of the Executive Offices you will find two large buildings whose purpose is to house the hotel's employees who don't live nearby. These are the original structures that were built in 1908 to house the summer, and now, winter help. In recent years I have noticed an influx of divergent ethnicities. From

Russia to England, South America to Pakistan, the staff at the hotel adds to its richness and newly acquired heritage.

As one might imagine the two dorms offer housing in a manner F.O. would have approved of: the men in one, the ladies in the other. Originally it housed the black staff in one building and the white staff in the other. These employees dart across the back parking lot, past the Executive Offices and into the tunnel entrance as they travel to and from the hotel; the tunnel acting as a short-cut that allows them to circumvent the main entrance at the front. The tunnel leads to the employee dining area and up the stairs to the kitchen, or through the earthen passageway and into the Garden Level of the hotel, where Madame Vera's Office is today.

## The Former Laundry/Engineering Building

Engineering building that was once the Laundry House.
Photo by Ron Bueker.

Just below the South Dormitory is the former Laundry House. In 1909 electrically heated boilers supplied the hot water for the hotel.

The original washers and dryers can still be seen there today, though the hotel's owner, Roe Emery, constructed an electrically generated steam facility for the Stanley's laundry in the building just north of the Executive Offices in 1935. Today the former Laundry House is home to the hotel's engineering staff, its walls covered with shelving housing everything from paints, solvents and varnishes, to wood working tools, power drills and ladders. There are planked partitions here that reminded me of a barn and stables, though I am told it was not this building but the former Ice House that had been used periodically as a small stable for the hotel.

## The Former Ice House

Former Ice House/Stables and Corral. Photo Ron Bueker.

Just south of the former Laundry House is a small building whose original purpose was to store large blocks of ice cut from the nearby ice pond and rivers and lakes of Estes Park. The ice was used to keep food fresh in the food storage areas and not for drinking purposes as it had not been filtered of impurities.

This small structure was also used for a time to house a coal-fired steam boiler. A 30-foot tall smoke stack rose from it, emitting smoke that carried over the roof of the hotel. The corral fence next to it evidences it also doubled as a small stable.

## The Current Gate House

Current Gate House at the entrance to the Stanley Hotel. One of the local elk is headed toward the guard arm. Photo by Rebecca F. Pittman

Today's Gate House is located at the main entrance to the hotel on the east side of the property. It is a small structure with a guard arm that rises and closes to allow guests entry onto the property. A guard there usually asks you if you are staying at the hotel or attending a special event. If you are merely sightseeing, there is a $3.00 charge. You are given a token that can be exchanged in the Cascades Restaurant for $3.00 worth of drinks, so it evens out. In the winter months, the Gate House is usually unattended with the exception of large special events going on inside the complex.

The road just past the guard arm rises into the main parking lot. You will pass the Carriage House on your right as you near the Concert Hall, Manor House and finally the main hotel. There is parking here as well as in the back of the Manor House and main hotel with walkways and steps leading down to the back patios of both buildings. You can also enter the Cascades Restaurant from the rear parking area.

## The Overlook Condominiums

Overlook Condominiums at the Stanley Hotel. Photo by Ron Bueker.

The Overlook Condominiums at the Stanley Hotel are the upscale version of hospitality offered at this ever-growing complex. These units feature hot tubs, garages, full kitchens, marble floors, and many other amenities.

The units range from one-bedroom (790 sf) that sleep four, spacious 2-bedroom units (1,200 sf) that sleep six, and spacious three- and four-bedroom units (over 2,400 sf) that sleep from eight to ten people. These larger condos offer family rooms and dining areas, with plenty of room to relax and enjoy the Rocky Mountains.

## The Ice Pond

Down the hill and just west of the Pet Cemetery you will see a stone retaining wall. This wall acted as a dam to house the water needed for ice in the winter months. The pond was fed by water trickling down from the large boulders above it and doubled as a swimming area in the summer, much to the delight of the vacationing children. Ice was harvested here and used for food preservation. Straw and sawdust helped to insulate it.

The ice was then brought in and packed the refrigerator. Here meat, fish and other perishable foods were kept cool for the guests and staff.

Beautifully landscaped walkways lead from the west side of the complex where the pond and out buildings sit, to the main hotel.

Stanley Hotel walkways. Photo by Ron Bueker.

## The Pet Cemetery

The Stanley Hotel was not only home to two-legged bipeds, but also their beloved 4-legged variety. The Pet Cemetery is testament to the love felt for these pets as they were lovingly buried in a special section of ground near the pond. Stone markers, engraved with their names and dates of their mortal journey, were placed there. It has since been moved.

Stanley Hotel Pet Cemetery at the far west edge of the property. It has been recently moved. Photo by Rebecca F. Pittman.

Stephen King penned a book by the name of *Pet Cemetery*. It was written in 1983 and nominated for a World Fantasy Award in 1984. Whether the Stanley's pet cemetery was an inspiration for that book is not known.

## The Front Patio Area

Stanley Steamers used to deliver guests to the hotel under the Porte Cochere, the large semi-circular patio acting as a turn-around area for the lengthy Mountain Wagons. There is a long, low wall here, tall lampposts rising from it in precise intervals. At the center of this wall is a large, brass disk. F.O. placed the pedestal here to help guests identify the myriad mountain ranges within view. The peaks of the Snowy Range rose up before them, most of which define the Continental Divide and are now proud residents of the Rocky Mountain National Park whose official entrance is only minutes up the road to the west. The brass disk marks over a 180-degree sweep of the towering peaks, indicating the distance, elevation and direction of the mountains, as well as that of nearby towns. Though worn, the details of F.O.'s favorite views are still intact and still educate those who stand at the disk and trace the faces of the Colorado peaks.

Turnaround patio in front of the Stanley Hotel today.
Photo by Ron Bueker.

The patio overlooks the area where a large outdoor swimming pool and tennis courts were once located. Today, no longer a vehicle drop-off spot, it acts as an outdoor area for summer weddings, special events and festivals, including the much-attended 4th of July celebration which offers live music, food and games annually. The patio commands a breathtaking view of the fireworks shot off over Lake Estes below. Tables and chairs are placed in advantageous settings, allowing access to the food booths and the sound stage where entertainment is offered throughout the day. Guests of the hotel also grab the choice viewing locations found along the balconies of the main hotel and the Manor House; their seats jealously guarded until the fireworks begin at roughly 9:30 in the evening. The show is impressive, rivaling the larger cities of Colorado and usually runs about 35 minutes with a finale that echoes throughout the Rockies. I have often wondered what the elk, deer, rams and bear must think of it all. Some probably have a heart attack fearing the cacophony of booms is a herd of hunters opening fire!

The lawns below the Stanley area are filled with picnickers nestled happily onto blankets, their baskets and beverages near at hand. The only challenge to this nostalgic setting is avoiding deer and elk droppings, so choose your site carefully.

Fireworks over Lake Estes. Photo by *Estes Park Trail Gazette.*

April 27, 1945 ad in the *Estes Park Trail* newspaper advertising the Stanley Hotel when Roe Emery was owner.

Photo courtesy of the *Estes Park Trail Gazette.*

Chapter Thirteen

# THE ORIGINAL OUTDOOR AMENITIES

*"The lawn is pressed by unseen feet, and ghosts return gently at twilight, gently go at dawn, The sad intangible who grieve and yearn..." T.S. Eliot, To Walter de la Mare*

F.O. Stanley made sure his summer guests were surrounded with ample outdoor activities while staying at his opulent hotel. Every recreation he could think of was offered beneath the benevolent stare of the surrounding mountains.

While the obvious past times of trout fishing, hiking, bird watching and tracking the numerous "critters" frequenting the mountains outside F.O.'s back door were high on the list, so were some of his favorite offerings.

## The Stanley Livery

The Stanley Livery and Stables was managed by Elijah (Lige) Rivers and was located on Elkhorn Avenue across the street from the original location of the Gate House. Although F.O. Stanley originally owned the property, it was sold by The Stanley Corporation to Elijah Rivers in 1927. F.O. Stanley frequently gave Lige money—reportedly $50 at a time—so that the children who wanted to ride the horses, but did not have the money, would not be denied the opportunity. In later years, the stable was housed in the Ice House. (Ron Lasky, *A Concise History of the Stanley Hotel, 2nd Edition*)

Ad for the Stanley Livery, June 27, 1924. *Estes Park Trail Gazette.*

# Golf and Airplanes

The game of golf made its way westward from its birthplace in St. Andrews, Scotland. Thought to be a game of refinement and skill, it appealed to the people of the early 1900s who sought to put forth an air of gentility and mental acumen.

Teeing up on the Stanley Hotel Golf Range in the 1900s. Photo courtesy of the *Estes Park Trail Gazette.*

F.O. Stanley built a nine-hole golf course on the hotel grounds shortly after building his dream hotel. Lord Dunraven had beaten him to it years earlier when he constructed a nine-hole course in 1877 alongside Fish Creek. F.O., along with two other investors, purchased the land where Dunraven's course had originally been and built an 18-hole course in 1917 that still exists today. An airport runway was constructed there in 1944, downsizing the course back to nine holes. But in 1957, the Estes Park Recreation District had purchased the airport land, and once again, initiated an 18-hole course. Today it is a manicured paradise for golfers and their biggest fans...the elk of Estes Park.

Estes Park Golf Course with elk roaming freely…and a warning sign.

At one time a small airstrip was located not far from the hotel, offering guests a bird's eye view of Estes Park and the Rockies. Unfortunately, while wonderfully inventive, it was not pragmatic for the turbulent and changing weather of the mountains. After only a few maiden flights, the small prop plane hit some bad wind gusts and nearly crashed, scaring its female passenger nearly to death. The airstrip was canceled, one of the few ideas F.O. had that was not a resounding success!

1910 aeroplane over the mountains.

Wright 1910 Model B aeroplane.

Chapter Fourteen

# WHAT'S NEW AT THE STANLEY?

*"When you've exhausted the rational, left unexplained the reasonable, you are in the company of something beyond our current understanding of how life works. That's the paranormal."*
*-Rebecca F. Pittman-*

## The Stanley Hotel Maze

To say the impact of Stephen King's book and hit movie *The Shining* has had a profound impact on the Stanley Hotel is an understatement.

After the release of Stanley Kubrick's dark thriller, *The Shining*, the hotel was inundated with the curious and thrill seekers, hoping for a glimpse of the "atmosphere" that inspired horror writer Stephen King to pen his bestseller. Many thought the movie was shot at the Stanley Hotel. While the TV mini-series of the same name was filmed there, the original movie was shot in Oregon.

The movie had many iconic moments, one of which was the

famous maze segments. The staff at the hotel was asked continuously "Where's the Maze?" Well, now, in the summer of 2015, that question will be answered: "Right here."

Jack Nicholson in The Shining with the hedge maze.

In the fall of 2014 a contest was announced. Entries from around the world were being accepted to create a hedge maze design to be installed on the front property of the Stanley Hotel. It would cover 61,500 sq. ft., and, in true Colorado spirit, would be comprised of 1,600 to 2,000 Alpine Currant hedge bushes. The deadline for entry was January 31, 2015.

The contestants were supplied with a template (see next page) and the designs were restricted to the use of hedge and path only. The template showed the entrance and exit points that must be observed. The maze was to remain inside the lines indicated on the template. The size and width of the path was to be utilized and a PDF or EPS file submitted for consideration. Maze template designers were provided. They had to design their maze within a designated gray area, using the entrance and exit points.

The contest was a popular one. Over 300 designs from over 40 states and 30 countries were submitted. The winning design was put forth by Mairim Standing from New York City, and a CSU alumnus, Dan Skinner, finished in the top seven.

The designs were reviewed by an expert panel of judges that included CSU Assistant Professor of Landscape Architecture Kelly Curl. Curl has judged contests like these before, although few sites have captured the popular imagination like the Stanley Hotel.

CSU Professor of Landscape Architecture Merlyn Paulson also helped with the judging when Curl was unable to attend the final session when the winner was picked from the final 20 that Curl helped select. Other judges included: Stanley owner John Cullen; Midge Knerr (Stanley Hotel Lodge Inn Keeper); Town of Estes Park Mayor Pro Tem Wendy Koenig; Tom Botelho, Exec. Dir., Denver Film Society; Harriette Woodard (Estes Park); and, Cydney Springer, Estes Park local artist.

Mairim Standing will have her name featured on a plaque adorning the new maze.

The installation of the maze at the Stanley Hotel was in celebration of the Grand Heritage Hotel Group's 20-year anniversary of acquiring the property. This is the longest-running ownership of the hotel, including that of its creator, F.O. Stanley.

Landscapers laying out the hedge maze in May, 2015. Ron Bueker.

The Stanley Hotel Maze after initial planting of hedges. Ron Bueker.

# STANLEY STEAM CAR MUSEUM

Stanley Steamer Motor Car coming up Big Thompson Canyon in 1909. Photo courtesy of Fred Payne Clatworthy.

The Stanley Steam Car Museum will initially feature historic fire engines with tour rides around Estes Park, Colorado and the surrounding area. Phase II of the museum will include multiple Stanley Steam Cars ranging from two-passenger production models, an 8-passenger Stanley Mountain Wagon and even a steamer Fire Engine. The museum will be housed at the historic Stanley Hotel in the Carriage house on the east end of the Stanley Hotel property and may include other Stanley history currently offered in the Archives Room located in the hotel basement.

Stanley Steamer Fire Engine in front of Stanley Hotel. Photo courtesy of reliancefiremuseum.org.

Other projects are on the Stanley Hotel drawing board as the famous complex continues to evolve beneath the sun-drenched skies of Colorado.

**The Ownership Legacy of the
Stanley Hotel**

**1909-1926**: F.O. Stanley—Owner

**1926-1929**: The Stanley Corporation (G. Fred Bond, Erna Bond, & James Shaw, Owners)

**1929-1930:** F.O. Stanley-Owner

**1930-1946:** Roe Emery-Owner (Estes Park Hotel Company)

**1946-1966:** Abbell Management Co. (Abbell Hotel Co, Maxwell Abbell, Principal Owner)

**1966-1969:** Stanley Hotel Inc. (Dr. Maurice Albertson-Principal Owner)

**1969-1970:** Richard Holechek, Charles F. Hanson, and Carol Hanson Pick-Owners)

**1970-1972:** Dr. Maurice Albertson-Owner

**1972-1973:** Stanley Property Trust (Bill Wagner, Jim Wagner, Bob Wagner & Leon Fedderson- Owners)

**1973-1975:** Leon Fedderson-Owner

**1975—1976:** Leon Fedderson & Frank Normali- Owners

**1976-1979:** Frank Normali-Owner

**1979-1980:** James Quincy-Owner

**1980-1982:** Bankruptcy Proceedings

**1982-1995:** Frank Normali-Owner

**1995-present:** Grand Heritage Hotel Group (John Cullen-Principal Owner)

Chapter Fifteen

# THE SHINING & THE STANLEY HOTEL

*"I wondered what would happen if you had a little boy who was sort of a receptor, or maybe even a psychic amplifier. And I wanted a little kid with his family and put them somewhere cut off, where spooky things would happen. I sort of wanted it to be Disney World---Goofy's coming to kill you..."* Stephen King on his idea for *The Shining.*

Author Stephen Edwin King was born on September 21, 1947, in Portland, Maine. King is recognized as one of the most famous and successful horror writers of all time. Over the years, King became known for his frightening and critically-acclaimed titles. His books have sold more than 350 million copies worldwide and have been adapted into numerous successful films.

His parents, Donald and Nellie Ruth Pillsbury King, split up when he was very young, and he and his brother David divided their time between Indiana and Connecticut for several years. King later moved back to Maine with his mother and brother. There he graduated from Lisbon Falls High School in 1966. King stayed close to home for college, attending the University of Maine at Orono. There he wrote for the school's newspaper and served in its student government.

King published his first short story while in college, which appeared in *Startling Mystery Stories*. After graduating with a degree in English in 1970, he tried to find a position as a teacher, but he had no luck at first. King took a job in a laundry and continued to write stories in his spare time until late 1971, when he began working as an English teacher at Hampden Academy.

## Let the Horror Begin

While making novels about sewer-dwelling monsters and vicious, rabid dogs—as seen in *IT* and *Cujo*, respectively—King published several books as Richard Bachman. The four early novels—*Rage* (1977), *The Long Walk* (1979), *Roadwork* (1981) and *The Running Man* (1982)—were published under another name because of King's concern that the public wouldn't accept more than one book from an author within a year. He came up with the alias after seeing a novel by Richard Stark on his desk—which it turned out was a pseudonym used by Donald Westlake—and coupling it with what he heard playing on his record player at the time, which was "You Ain't Seen Nothin' Yet," by Bachman Turner Overdrive.

In 1973, King sold his first novel, *Carrie*, the tale of a tormented teen who gets her revenge. The book became a huge success after it was published the following year, allowing him to devote himself to writing full time. It later adapted for the big screen with Sissy Spacek as the character. More popular novels soon followed, including *Salem's Lot* (1975), *The Shining* (1976), *Firestarter* (1980), *Cujo* (1981) and *IT* (1986).

Although many of King's works were adapted into film or television—*Firestarter* became a film in 1984, starring Drew Barrymore; *Cujo* became a film in 1983; and *It* became a miniseries in 1990, starring Tim Curry—*The Shining*, which was released on film in 1980 starred Jack Nicholson, became a classic horror thriller.

For much his career, King wrote novels and stories at a breakneck speed. He published several books per year for much of the 1980s and '90s. As with his earlier works, his compelling and thrilling tales continued to be used as the basis of numerous feature and television films. Actress Kathy Bates and actor James Caan starred in the critically and commercially successful adaptation of *Misery* in 1990. Four years later, *The Shawshank Redemption*, based on one of his stories, became another smash hit.

## Later Work

King continued to produce fascinating works. He has worked in television, writing for *The Dead Zone* series (based on his own novel) and for *Stephen King's Kingdom Hospital* series, amongst other projects. King has remained one of the most popular writers with his later work. In 2011, he published *11/22/63*, a novel involving time travel as part of an effort to stop the assassination of President John F. Kennedy. King also wrote the novel *Joyland* (2013), a pulp-fiction style thriller that takes readers on a journey to uncovering who's behind an unsolved murder. He also surprised audiences by releasing *Doctor Sleep*, a sequel to his popular sophomore novel *The Shining*, in 2013. The novel became No. 1 on the *New York Time*s best seller list in October 2013.

## On the Home Front

King and his novelist wife divide their time between Florida and Maine. They have three children: Naomi Rachel, a reverend; Joseph Hillstrom, who writes under the pen name Joe Hill and is a lauded horror-fiction writer in his own right; and Owen Phillip, whose first collection of stories was published in 2005.

Outside of writing, King is a music fan. He even sometimes plays guitar and sings in a band called Rock Bottom Remainders with fellow literary stars Dave Barry and Amy Tan. The group has performed a number of times over the years to raise money for charity.

Stephen King at his home in Bangor, Maine

Stephen King's home on Casey Key near Sarasota, Florida.

## *The Shining* and the Stanley Hotel

There are hundreds of stories circulating as to just what part the Stanley Hotel played in inspiring horror-writer, Stephen King's best-selling book and movie, and TV mini-series, all entitled *The Shining*. Many of the reports are erroneous. I hope the following chapter will help illuminate the real ghosts in the closets.

Stephen King, after struggling for years in menial jobs, such as working at a laundry, and teaching at the Hampden Academy in Maine for $6,400 a year, was beginning to see light at the end of the literary tunnel. He was selling stories to Men's magazines and trying to land a home for a novel about a bullied teenage girl with telekinetic powers. The novel was *Carrie*. After several revisions, Doubleday bought the novel for a $2500 advance against royalties. Though it wasn't much, the paperback rights, sold to Signet, netted him $200,000, half of the $400,000 purchase price, which he split with Doubleday.

Thrilled to be published at last in such a prestigious forum, King next went to work on a book that was originally entitled Second *Coming*. It was later re-titled *Salem's Lot,* the paperback rights bringing in a hefty $500,000, which he again split with Doubleday.

In early 1974, not long after selling both *Carrie* and *Salem's Lot* (both set in his home state of Maine), Stephen King wanted a change of scenery for his next novel. Randomly picking Boulder out of an atlas, King packed up his wife (novelist Tabitha King) and their kids and moved to Colorado. After trying out a few ideas (one of which was *Darkshine*, about a psychic little boy in a haunted amusement park), none of which worked, King and his wife decided to take a little vacation away from the children. At the behest of a friend, they decided to check out The Stanley Hotel in Estes Park, near the base of Rocky Mountain National Park. Checking in on Halloween weekend 1974, King and his wife were nearly turned away. It was the last day of the season, the hotel was closing down for the winter, the credit card slips had been packed away and the place was nearly deserted. King paid cash and he and Tabitha checked into room 217.

The Stanley Hotel in Estes Park, Colorado. Photo *EPTrailGazette*.

That night, after eating in the massive-yet-empty main dining room, and going back to their room through long, eerily deserted corridors, Tabitha turned in, but Steve decided to do further investigation. He ended up as the sole customer in the rustic Colorado Lounge, where he was served drinks by a bartender named Grady. Returning to 217 – after briefly getting lost in the maze of hallways – King went to the bathroom, noticed the antique clawfoot tub, pulled back the shower curtain and ... *What if somebody died here?* King thought.

Says King: "That night I dreamed of my three-year-old son running through the corridors, looking back over his shoulder, eyes wide, screaming. He was being chased by a fire-hose. I woke up with a tremendous jerk, sweating all over, within an inch of falling out of bed. I got up, lit a cigarette, sat in a chair looking out the window at the Rockies, and by the time the cigarette was done, I had the bones of the book firmly set in my mind. It was like God had put me there to hear that and see those things."

"The empty hotel struck King as the archetypal setting for a ghost story. He encountered many of *The Shining's* iconic images as he wandered the corridors. The claw foot tub looked like someone could die in it—or already had. Later, he dreamed of his young son, Joe, screaming as a fire hose chased him down the hotel's endless hallways. By the end of the night, King had the story outline mapped out in his head." (Bev Vincent, *The Stephen King Illustrated Companion*, Fall River Press, 2009)

There are many rumors that King and his wife came back from dinner that evening to find their packed bags, which they had slung onto the bed, unpacked, and all their things put neatly away into drawers. Those type of stories have often been attributed to the ghost of Mrs. Wilson, who was the hapless housekeeper blown through the flooring of 217 during a gas explosion. If anything paranormal did occur during King's stay at the Stanley Hotel, he is not saying. He does attribute a lot of his inspiration for the story plot of *The Shining* to the hotel's "atmosphere."

"Stephen King had been trying for several years to put together a story where a family is trapped in an amusement park where terrors await around every corner. He'd been playing with an idea and "wondered what would happen if you had a little boy who was sort of a receptor, or maybe even a psychic amplifier. And I wanted a little kid with his family and put them somewhere cut off, where spooky things would happen. I sort of wanted it to be Disney World---Goofy's coming to kill you..." (George Beahm, *The Stephen King Story: A Literary Profile. Andrews and McMeel, 1992*)

The working title for the book was *Darkshine*, but the premise was not workable. What would keep the family from merely escaping the park, albeit a bit tattered and marred? Enter the Stanley Hotel in a blizzard, keeping its inhabitants virtually snowbound and captive to all those things that go bump in the night.

The Stanley Hotel was not the only inspiration for *The Shining*. Images from Edgar Allan Poe's *The Fall of the House of Usher* and *The Masque of the Red Death*, along with a nod to Shirley Jackson's *The Haunting of Hill House* and *The Sundial*, all found an underlying role in the book. In the book, *The Sundial*, you find the Halloran house, which in *The Shining* became the name of the hotel chef, Dick Halloran.

"While working in Baltimore in July of 2009, I toured Edgar Allan's Poe's home there and was informed that Stephen King, along with Michael Jackson, were regular visitors to the dwelling of the

Actor Scatman Crothers as Dick Halloran in the film *The Shining*.

Since their rental house in Boulder was rather small, King leased office space in a boardinghouse where he could look out the window at the Flatiron Mountains. He remembers that, once he started working on the book, he entered a zone where everything he wrote worked. He averaged 3,000 words per day, and the first draft required the least rewriting of all of his early books. (Bev Vincent, *The Stephen King Illustrated Companion, Fall River Press, 2009*)

Writing the book was not all glory for the author. Memories of the poverty he had endured while living in a trailer in Hermon, Maine, isolated and afraid of what the future might hold for a man whose dreams seemed to be always out of reach and struggling to find the next dollar for himself and his family, sat at his elbow as he typed away on the manuscript about a man, out of work, struggling to become a respected writer and accepting the only job offered to him; that of a caretaker for an isolated hotel cut off from the world when white cloaked the resort in unrelenting captivity.

King was already a heavy drinker by this point in his life. Struggling to support his family while trying to break through as a writer had taken its toll, as did his mother's death. In interviews, he confessed to feeling rage toward his family—and guilt over the anger—but he often didn't make a direct connection between himself and Jack Torrance until after he became sober. (Bev Vincent, *The Stephen King Illustrated Companion, Fall River Press, 2009*)

In an interview from 1983, King said: "Sometimes you confess. You always hide what you're confessing to. That's one of the reasons why you make up the story. When I wrote *The Shining*, for instance, the protagonist is a man who has broken his son's arm, who has a history of child beating, who is beaten himself. And as a young father, I was horrified by my occasional feelings of real antagonism toward my children. *Won't you ever stop? Won't you ever go to bed?* And time has given me the idea that probably there are a lot of young fathers and young mothers both who feel very angry, who have angry feelings toward their children. But as somebody who has been raised with the idea that *Father Knows Best* and Ward Cleaver on *Leave It To Beaver,* and all this stuff, I would think to myself, *Oh, if he doesn't shut up, if he doesn't shut up* ... So when I wrote this book I wrote a lot of that down and tried to get it out of my system, but it was also a confession. Yes, there are times when I felt very angry toward my children and have even felt as though I could hurt them. Well, my kids are older now, and they're all super. I don't think I've laid a hand on [them] in probably seven years, but there was a time ..."

King was also struggling with alcohol and drug abuse at the time, but has been sober since the late 1980s.

By the late 70s, King was already a brand name. Brian DePalma helped put him on the map with his excellent film adaptation of *Carrie* in 1976. Three years later, Tobe Hooper also did a good job with the TV mini-series of *Salem's Lot.* It wasn't until 1980, however, that King received the ultimate push into the literary stratosphere, when visionary director Stanley Kubrick adapted and directed his ode to family dysfunction and spooky hotels.

Using both Pinewood Studios and Elstree Studios in England, the sets for the Overlook Hotel were the largest constructed at that time – including full recreations of the hotel's exteriors and interiors. A few exterior shots were done at Timberline Lodge on Mount Hood in Oregon – notable because the hedge maze is missing (the book used hedge animals). The Timberline Lodge asked Kubrick to change the number of diabolical Room 217 of King's novel to 237, so customers wouldn't be afraid to stay in the real room 217. (They needn't have worried). Room 217 at the Stanley Hotel is the most-requested room, often booked a year or more in advance.

Though the film (starring Jack Nicholson as conflicted caretaker Jack Torrance) has since achieved cult status, at the time of its release, it got a very mixed reception. Critics and King fans agreed that while the film was a technical marvel, it lacked the heart and emotional complexities of the novel. Nicholson's Torrance goes so crazy so quick there is no time to empathize with anyone in the story.

Stephen King originally wanted to call the book *The Shine*, after John Lennon's song, *Instant Karma*. The chorus of the song is *"We all shine on—like the moon and the stars and the son..."* Doubleday thought the word shine might be offensive to some people of African American descent as it had once been a nickname for black shoeshine boys. King settled for *The Shining*, but felt it was "rather unwieldy and thudding."

"King was once asked if he had ever written anything really scary that kept him up all night. Once again, he referred to *The Shining*. "Yeah. Not very often, though, because a lot of the time, you feel like you've got it in the palm of your hand...But sometimes I think it gets out. The worst was the tub thing in *The Shining*...It wasn't too bad when I wrote it; all at once it was just there... But on the rewrite, as I got closer to that point, I would say to myself, eight days to the tub, then six days to the tub. And then one day it was *the tub today!* When I went down to the typewriter that day I felt frightened and my heart was beating too fast and I felt the way you do when you have to make a big presentation, or when something's going to happen. And I was scared. I did the best job I could with it, but I was glad when it was over." (Stephen King. *Secret Windows: Essays and Fiction on the Craft of Writing.* New York: Book of the Month Club, 2000.)

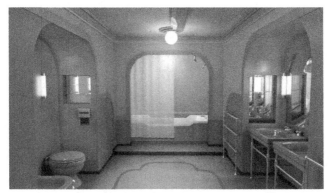

The bathtub from Kubrick's *The Shining*.

Before Doubleday released the book in January 1977, Warner Brothers bought the rights, with Stanley Kubrick and Jack Nicholson in mind. The movie arrived two and a half years later, in June 1979. Although King liked what the director had done, it did not stay true to his book. It wasn't King's book; it was Kubrick's movie.

Although King wanted the movie to be shot at the Stanley Hotel, Kubrick determined that it could not be filmed there. His reasons were that there was not enough snow and the town encroached on the hotel too closely for the distance shots.

Timberline Lodge at Mt. Hood, Oregon.

Not long after the release of Kubrick's film, King opined: "Stanley Kubrick's version of *The Shining* is a lot tougher for me to evaluate, because I'm still profoundly ambivalent about the whole thing. I'd admired Kubrick for a long time and had great expectations for the project, but I was deeply disappointed in the end result. Parts of the film are chilling, charged with a relentlessly claustrophobic terror, but others fall flat ... Not that religion has to be involved in horror, but a visceral skeptic such as Kubrick just couldn't grasp the sheer inhuman evil of The Overlook Hotel. So he looked, instead, for evil in the characters and made the film into a domestic tragedy with only vaguely supernatural overtones. That was the basic flaw: because he couldn't believe, he couldn't make the film believable to others. What's basically wrong with Kubrick's version of *The Shining* is that it's a film by a man who thinks too much and feels too little; and that's why, for all its virtuoso effects, it never gets you by the throat and hangs on the way real horror should. I'd like to remake *The Shining* someday, maybe even direct it if anybody will give me enough rope to hang myself with ..."

"Nearly two decades after Kubrick's version, ABC television – who had great success with other King miniseries, *IT* and *The Stand* – asked King what he wanted to do next. King didn't think twice. Adapting the novel himself this time and utilizing the same production team from ABC's *The Stand* (including director Mick Garris), *Stephen King's The Shining* began production in mid-1996 and aired in the spring of 1997. Largely filmed at the Stanley Hotel in Estes Park (returning its karmic debt after nearly a quarter century), the three-part miniseries starred Steven Weber as Jack, Rebecca DeMornay as Wendy and Courtland Mead as Danny. Reviews were again mixed, but there are those (including myself) who champion this as a much more faithful adaptation. Steven Weber (TV's *Wings)* is so good in this role – especially when Jack goes completely over the edge – he nearly makes one forget Nicholson's iconic performance. Rebecca DeMornay is also excellent, making Wendy Torrance a much stronger, more emotionally rounded character than Shelly Duvall in Kubrick's version. The opening scene around the massive, sweating boiler of The Overlook (which must be regularly *dumped* to maintain its integrity), is a brilliant metaphor for the anger management fable which follows. (The Wordslinger.com)

Boiler from *The Shining*

"In 1995, Stephen King and ABC teamed up to create a three-segment mini-series of *The Shining*, filmed at the Stanley Hotel and in studios in Denver. The timing was perfect for the hotel, King got to come back to the Stanley and ABC got a ready-made set—almost. The ABC producer walked into the white plaster Georgian Colonial Lobby of the Stanley and, declaring that 'this would NOT do,' ordered it changed to its current fake-wood look (faux bois, meaning fake wood in French). In fact the only wood in the entire Lobby and MacGregor Room is that of the door and window frames, easily seen on close examination.

"The Stanley Hotel ownership changed through a bankruptcy action in May 1995. The new owners welcomed the use of the hotel for a movie while it gathered itself to embark later on what turned into a multi-million dollar renovation (upgrades are still taking place). Thus, ABC had remarkable free rein in changing things to suit its needs. Who would mind new paint and interior decorations the owners didn't need to fund?" (Susan S. Davis, *A History and Tour of the Stanley Hotel*)

King was totally involved in his TV mini-series, from the production, the script and even a cameo appearance as band director at the Ball.

Stephen King cameo from *The Shining* on the stage of the MacGregor Room at the Stanley Hotel.

*The Shining's* book disclaimer reads:

**Some of the most beautiful resort hotels in the world are located in Colorado, but the hotel in these pages is based on none of them. The Overlook and the people associated with it exist wholly within the author's imagination.**

*The Shining* became King's first hardcover bestseller, reaching number eight on the New York Times list and selling roughly 50,000 copies. To this day, it is almost universally acknowledged as a modern classic that will probably be one of the seminal works that King will be remembered for in generations to come. (Bev Vincent, *The Stephen King Illustrated Companion*, Fall River Press, 2009)

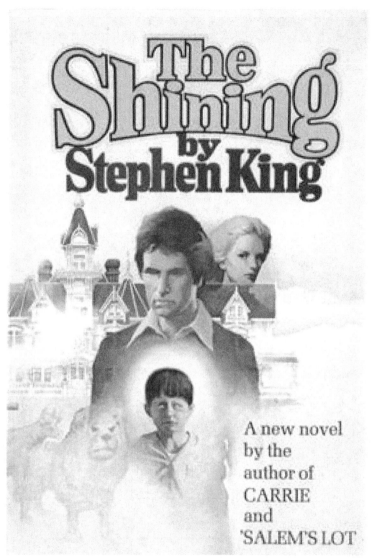

Original cover for *The Shining*.

While the mini-series is not as well-known as the Kubrick movie, it has a faithful following. Photos of its stars, Stephen Webber and Rebecca DeMornay, along with King's bandleader role, can be seen in a display case in Garden Level of the hotel.

Car scenes from the movie (top) and the TV mini-series (bottom) of
*The Shining.*

## *The Shining* Shines On

It appears that Stephen King's beloved novel *The Shining* is all the rage at the moment. King has released his sequel novel *Doctor Sleep* and the *Shining*-centric documentary *Room 237* recently hit theaters. It now appears that the story is headed to the big screen once again by way of a prequel. Glen Mazzara—who previously took over for Frank Daramont as showrunner on AMC's *The Walking Dead*—before running into creative differences halfway through the most recent season—has been tapped to write the screenplay for the Warner Brothers prequel film *The Overlook Hotel*.

Word first broke that Warner Bros. was considering a prequel to *The Shining* last summer, when it was reported that writer/producers Laeta Kalogridis (*Shutter Island*) and James Vanderbilt (*Zodiac*) were developing the film alongside producing partner Bradley Fischer (*Black Swan*). It appears that the trio has settled on a story that they believe warrants a full film, as Deadline now reports that Glen Mazzara has been hired to pen the screenplay for *The Overlook Hotel*. (*Deadline*, 2013)

No further details for the film are given, but it's reasonable to assume that the story will involve the haunted goings-on at the titular hotel prior to the Torrance's arrival. Kubrick's adaptation of *The Shining* is a masterpiece so Mazzara certainly has some big shoes to fill, but it'll be interesting to see if he strikes a tone similar to Kubrick's film or if his take falls more in line with King's original novel.

## The sequel to *The Shining*: *Dr. Sleep*

"Being scared is like sex," Stephen King says. "There's nothing like your first time."

For a lot of readers, King's 1977 horror novel *The Shining* may have been their first fictional scare. "An awful lot of the people who read *The Shining* were like 14 years old, they were at summer camp, they read it under the covers with a flashlight on," King tells NPR's David Greene.

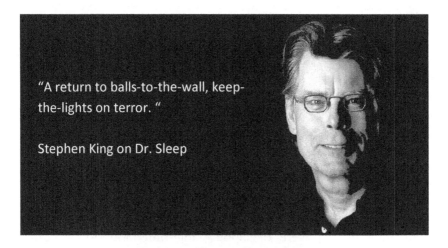

"A return to balls-to-the-wall, keep-the-lights on terror. "

Stephen King on Dr. Sleep

Book cover for King's *Dr. Sleep.*

Now, nearly four decades after The Shining was released, King picks up Danny's story as an adult in the novel's sequel, *Doctor Sleep*. King says that "revisiting such a celebrated horror story was no small challenge."

"I wanted to revisit Danny and see what he was like as a grown-up. I think that we all have this ... desire to reconnect with friends from when we were younger — you know, that's the whole basis of high school and college reunions. So, I was also wanting to re-meet some of the people I knew from *The Shining*. I also wanted to investigate this whole idea about, can we rise above our parents? Can we rise above the mistakes that our parents made or the character flaws that our parents had?

"As a writer, I've always been confrontational. I've never been cool, I've never been calculating. My idea is to come up to you, grab you by the lapels and say: I have this story. I want to tell it to you, and when you hear it, you're not going to want to cook dinner, you're not going to want to clean the house, you're not going to want to go to your job. You're just going to want to read this story and care about what comes next."

Stephen King has been ridiculed at times for his prolific outpouring of novels. To this statement, he retorts:

"A lot of people have suggested that the stuff that I do may be second-class because there's so much of it. My response to that is: I'm going to quit and be dead for a long time. This is the time that I've got, and I want to use it to the max. I really want to try and mine everything that I've got.

"There are plenty of people who have got lots of talent. This world is lousy with talent. The idea is to work that talent and try to get to be the best person that you can, given the limits of the talent that God gave you — or fate, or genetics or whatever name you want to put on it."

"I'm very interested in the actual act of dying, which is the last great human action that we have in our lives. It's the one event in our lives that no one can describe adequately because nobody comes back to talk about it."

"My feeling is, death is the great mystery, and it's the final act in our lives, and it deserves, if anything ever does, the kind of treatment that a guy like me can give it — which is speculative and imaginative."    - Stephen King

Chapter Sixteen

# The Estes Park and Stanley Museums

Estes Park, Colorado is replete with organizations determined to preserve her myriad history. The Stanley Hotel offers its Archives Room and the Stanley Steam Car Museum; the Estes Park Museum offers a plethora of historic artifacts, gifts and books; and the Historic Fall River Power Plant now houses many artifacts from the Stanley Museum in Kingsfield, Maine. Here is a brief overview of the Estes Park offerings outside the Stanley Hotel:

## Estes Park Museum

## Estes Park Museum, Colorado

200 Fourth Street
Estes Park, CO 80517
970-586-6256
www.estes.org/museum
Located at Fourth Street and Highway 36.

**Admission is free.**

**May – October Hours**
Monday – Saturday, 10 a.m. – 5 p.m.
Sunday  1 – 5 p.m.

**The need for a museum was recognized in 1962** when the National Park Service decided to raze Stead's Ranch, an 1876 homestead and guest ranch located at Moraine Park in Rocky Mountain National Park. In response, concerned Estes Park citizens organized to preserve its historical items. They formed the Estes Park Area Historical Museum, Inc., a non-profit organization established to preserve and interpret the pioneer history of Estes Park. This group later became the Estes Park Museum Friends & Foundation, Inc.

In 1966, the Museum was constructed with volunteer labor on public land donated by the Town of Estes Park. The very basic building was called the "Morgue" for its windowless, cinderblock construction, but it provided exhibit and storage space. Since then, the Museum has undergone four expansions and now includes a gift shop and meeting room.

In 1985, the circa-1900 Cobb-Macdonald cabin, located behind the Macdonald Book Shop on Elkhorn Avenue, was acquired and moved to its present site behind the main Museum building. In 1987, the original 1915 headquarters for Rocky Mountain National Park was brought to the site.

Since 1992, the Museum has been a department of the Town of Estes Park. In July 2002, twenty years after it had been heavily damaged in the Lawn Lake Flood, the newly-restored 1909 Historic Fall River Hydroplant on Fish Hatchery Road was opened by the Museum as an interpretive center. In 2004, the Museum's name was shortened to the "Estes Park Museum." Today the Museum house a collection of 25,000 items related to Estes Park history, and is recognized as a leading local history museum in Colorado.

The Museum's mission is to "collect, interpret and preserve local history, as well as present exhibits, programs and events, for the education and benefit of residents and visitors of all ages."

The Estes Park Museum manages the Historic Fall River Hydroplant, which F.O. Stanley built in 1909. It was the first power plant in Estes Park and was originally intended to power the Stanley Hotel; however it quickly became the town's source of electricity. The plant stayed in operation till it was damaged by the Lawn Lake Flood of 1982. Today the museum manages and interprets the plants historical relationship to Estes Park. Additionally, the museum cares for a number of artifacts and archival items related to the Stanley family. Recently the museum acquired a number of objects from the Stanley Museum located in Kingfield, Maine, who used to operate a sister museum in Estes Park.

## Historic Fall River Hydroplant

Freelan Oscar Stanley earned a fortune by making water useful. With his brother Francis Edgar (they were known as F.O. and F.E.)

he co-invented the Stanley Steamer automobile. Shunning unreliable and unproven internal combustion technology, they harnessed water to power their popular horseless carriages. Their company sold 170 Stanley Steamers in 1902 for six hundred dollars apiece. They sold twice that number the following year. However, poor health dampened F.O.'s spirits. Diagnosed with tuberculosis, Stanley's weight fell to 118 pounds and his doctor warned him that he faced certain death if he stayed in New England. Following thousands of other health seekers, he moved to Colorado where the altitude and dry climate restored his health. Smitten by the scenery and business prospects, Stanley decided to stay. He bought property in the burgeoning resort community of Estes Park, built a permanent summer home, and applied his proven entrepreneurial skills to developing a hotel.

Stanley viewed water as the essential building component for his development. He told friends that he wanted to build the world's first fully electrified hotel in the world. To realize this goal, he-along with several other investors-established the Estes Park Light and Power Company in 1908. The company's hydroplant would provide electricity to the hotel and, eventually, to the town itself. Newspapers in cities that stood to benefit from increased travel to Estes Park gushed about the plan. When construction commenced in 1908, the *Longmont Times Call* wrote:

Mr. Stanley, the man who is transposing Estes Park from a wilderness into a modern city, is pushing improvements in the park. The big hotel will be lighted with electricity... He is putting in a power plant at a cost of $20,000 from which the town will also be lighted. ...When the [tourist] season opens next summer, visitors will hardly know the town. F. O. Stanley is certainly all right.

Built three miles northwest of Estes Park, the one-story, concrete-floored 28 X 26-foot frame building housed a turbine and a 200-kilowatt generator. The turbine was driven by water siphoned from nearby Cascade Lake via a twenty-inch steel intake pipe. An operator's cottage was added at the same time. A second operator's cottage and a garage were added later.

Massive turbine engine designed by F.O. Stanley housed in the Fall River Hydroplant in Estes Park, Co.

The Fall River Hydroelectric Plant played a vital role in the development of Estes Park as a summer resort. The plant not only powered the electric lights at the Stanley Hotel, but also illuminated the imagination of Estes Park's promoters. In 1912 Enos Mills could boast that "with the finest of water piped from near snow line, with good sewerage and electric lights, with stores, shops and markets, livery stables and garages, with a bank and two hotels... there is probably no other unincorporated village in the United States so well equipped to supply all the wants of residents and visitors as is Estes Park." With these amenities, plus improved roads to the area and the establishment of Rocky Mountain National Park in 1915, Estes Park stood on the brink of success.

The Fall River Hydroelectric Plant operated continually until the 1982 Lawn Lake Flood damaged its equipment. During the next several years the Town of Estes Park, the National Park Service, environmentalists, and other interested parties debated the plant's future. Ultimately, the groups reached a compromise that allowed restoration of the plant for interpretive uses only.

The State Historical Fund awarded over $400,000 in three separate grants to the Town of Estes Park for restoration of the hydroelectric plant's buildings and original equipment and the development of educational and interpretive exhibits and programming. By preserving the plant and adaptively re-using it as a museum, the Town, its partners, and the Fund have saved a significant historical resource. More importantly, because insufficient attention has been paid to the development of hydropower in Colorado, their research, exhibits, and educational programs will fill a gap in our understanding the state's past. And that's something that people like Brent Wright-who helped restore some of the plant's plumbing after he finished his job at the Stanley Hotel-can be proud of.

By Ben Fogelberg, Editor, Colorado History NOW

**The Historic Fall River Hydroplant** is located at 1754 Fish Hatchery Road. Built by F. O. Stanley to power his famous Stanley Hotel in 1909, it is open to the public as an interpretive center. **Open Memorial Day – Labor Day, 1 – 4pm Closed Mondays**

## The Stanley Museum in Kingsfield, Maine

Founded in 1981, the Stanley Museum is headquartered in Kingfield, Maine, the birthplace of the Stanley's. The Museum is a private 501I(3) non-profit organization, funded by donations through annual fundraising, memberships, income from special programs, gift shop sales and through some grant writing—in that approximate order. The museum owns two Stanley Steamers, a 1910 and a 1916, which it maintains and operates in Maine. There is also a 1909 model used for riding tours. In addition to the important Stanley Archives, the Museum also owns the world's largest collection of photographic prints produced by the twins' now-famous sister Chansonetta Stanley Emmons. (Susan S. Davis, founding director of the Stanley Museum)

## Stanley Museum Kingfield, Maine

P.O. Box 77  Kingfield, Maine  04947

207-265-2729

www.stanleymuseum.org

Chapter Seventeen

# Those Talented Stanley's

*"The most unusual thing I can think of would be a peaceful night.
But if anything is going to occur, don't dare to let me miss it!"* Mary
Roberts Rhinehart, in *The Circular Staircase*

I think it can truly be sad that the Stanley twins, along with their
gifted sister Chansonetta, rarely "missed" out on anything! They ran
after life, as a child would chase an elusive rainbow, confident in the
knowledge they would capture it. From a young age they were
entrepreneurs with dreams of projects and inventions that lay ahead.
Though interested in money, it was a means to an end, and that end
was the thrill of creation, of besting the competition and of creating
things of beauty and longevity. If it fascinated their mind, it ended up
on a drawing board in one way or another. It would not surprise me
to see the names of F.O. and F.E. Stanley listed next to the phrase
"Yankee Ingenuity" in any textbook!

Thanks to Freelan's (F.O.'s) writings, we get an insight of just how
enterprising these two young men were. At the age of 9 they used a
lathe at their father's mill to create wooden tops. These were sold to
playmates until the demographics for that market ran dry. They next
turned their attention to the needs of local women by making
replacements for an important section of a wooden loom that broke
frequently.

A year later the twins were scratching their entrepreneurial itch by entering the maple sugar business and creating their first "toy-sized" violins. At ten years of age, their accomplishments were already amazing. They also kept track of any debts accrued as witnessed by F.O.'s letter to a friend years later on Stanley Dry Plate Company letterhead; the date is Dec. 1894:

"You will find enclosed our check for $20.00. Now will you please cash the same and take the cash to Wm Lane as a present from the two boys that have stolen more apples from his back orchard than any other two boys in existence!" (Stanley Museum Archives)

F.O. Stanley holding one of his violin creations.

At the young age of 10, the twins "whittling" took an artistic turn when they carved their first violin. At the age of 16, F.O. made his first full-sized violin, alluding that the earlier ones were more of a toy-sized instrument. The new violin is signed "F.O. Stanley 1865" directly on the wood interior in ink. He and Francis (F.E.) produced a select number of concert-quality instruments after careful study of the classic violins created by the Italian Masters. It should be noted that the twins were descendants from several American violinmakers including Liberty Stanley, born in 1776, and their Uncle Carlton Stanley.

F.O. traveled to Cremona to purchase Spruce for his violin tops and to Germany to purchase Bosnian Maple for his violin back, sides and necks.

A recent listing online from Fein Violins listed one of F.O.'s violins as follows:

"This violin was originally purchased directly from the maker and played by a professional violinist in musical theaters. It is near mint condition. There are no cracks. The seams have never come open. Even the pegs are original. This violin is truly one of the finest made and finest sounding instruments to ever be in our collection. It possesses the warmth, richness and power of tone of the finest Italian violins."

List Price: ~~$18,000~~
Our Price: $13,500

After F.O. retired from the Stanley Motor Carriage Company, he set up a home-based violin-making shop with his nephew, Carlton Fairfield Stanley (1871-1956), in Newton, Massachusetts. It is believed F.O. produced over 200 instruments in his lifetime, all concert-quality and still sought after to this day.

F.O. began a career as a schoolteacher in rural Maine and was eventually named Principal of Mechanic Falls High School in that same state. He designed a drawing set at the age of 31. The handy case contained a ruler, compasses, a triangle, and a protractor. It sold for one dollar and was highly successful. Unfortunately a fire in 1882 destroyed his small factory, leaving him almost penniless. Although the building was insured, none of the contents were.

Both F.O. and F.E. fell in love with, and married schoolteachers. F. E. married Augusta May Walker, "Gusti", (1848-1927) on Jan. 1, 1870. F.O. married Flora Jane Record Tileston (1847-1939) on April 15, 1876.

F.O. Stanley frequently gave credit to his twin brother for F.E.'s mechanical genius and creative mind. In 1875, F.E. began a new career in Auburn, Maine as a portrait artist. With his usual restless nature, F.E. began looking for a faster way to create high-quality portraits. He began experimenting with atomizers and nozzles in various sizes. The black liquid medium or "crayon" was then sprayed onto the canvas in varying degrees of viscosity. Fine detail or mass areas could be achieved by selecting different nozzle openings. His airbrush was born and patented on September 17, 1876. F.E's following grew with each first prize ribbon he garnered in "crayon portraiture."

The creative itch returned. His popularity as a portrait artist propelled him to a larger studio in nearby Lewiston. The area's leading families came to sit for him. Impatient with the time a person had to maintain a pose while he painted, F.E.'s ever-wandering mind hit upon a new and improved method: photography! Isaiah Woodman, a relative of F.E.'s wife, loaned him $300 for a camera and the driven entrepreneur began yet another career, one that would cement the fortunes of himself and his twin brother, F.O.

## The Stanley Dry Plate Company

In the late 1800's, the accepted way of taking photographs was to use the messy and time consuming method called "wet plate", the collodion photography of the day. The process involved freshly coating a glass plate with a highly unstable, toxic emulsion and then bathing it in a solution of silver nitrate just prior to exposure. In order to achieve a printable negative image, reducing and fixing agents had to also be added.

Unhappy with the complicated process, F. E. began experimenting with emulsions that would dry on the plate without compromising their photosensitivity. Using the knowledge of the few emulsion recipes out there, F.E. headed to his basement laboratory to create his own. For two months in 1880 he experimented on a series of formulas until he came up with a workable gelatin plate. The Stanley Dry Plate took its place in the arena of the American Photographic industry and made it possible for amateur photographers to take quality photographs. Now plates could be ready ahead of time, were non-perishable and available in mass quantities. So, in 1881, F. E. Stanley once again stepped into the spotlight reserved for the intrepid few who went through Life asking "Why? Why not?" and "Why let someone else do it when you can do it yourself?" He began a small dry plate production company and three years later, asked his twin, F.O. to join him. On Oct. 27, 1884, F.O. accepted his brother's offer.

By May of 1885, the Stanley Dry Plate Company was in full swing. F.O. was thrilled to see his financial footing change from depleted to consistently growing. His letters home to his wife Flora, who had remained in Boston while their new house on Pine Street in Lewiston was being readied, were full of enthusiasm.

"We are turning out lots of plates, and no losses!" F.O. wrote home. "We have enough to pay all our debts and leave us more than before the fire. We can count ourselves lucky to get over the fire so soon." Earlier he had written, "Our monthly statements show a profit of $2400 apiece for April." (Stanley Museum Archives. F.O. Stanley letters to Flora Stanley, April and May, 1885)

As the coffers filled, so did the list of hobbies and interests the twins indulged in. They went into the horse breeding business and built a large stable on Canal Street. F.O. was said to own some of the best trotting stock in Maine.

F.O.'s observations of papermaking while at Mechanic Falls played an important role in propelling the Stanley Dry Plate business into further prominence. He designed a dry plate coating machine that reduced the time needed to coat an 8x10-inch plate by hand. Now they could coat 60 plates a minute by machine, where the old method only produced 60 plates an hour by hand! Industry competitors were now taking notice. One of the giants in that industry came knocking, after the twins had built a new factory, extending their business into Canada and across the United States, and built two impressive homes for their wives in Newton, Massachusetts.

George Eastman, of Kodak acclaim, noticed that those Stanley boys were racking in almost $100,000 a month in plates. He offered to buy them out, (highly pragmatic as they were becoming a serious competitor) for the tune of $540,000. They shook hands on the deal in 1905.

It came at an appropriate time as F.O.'s doctors had only recently told him to head west as a last-ditch effort to ease the symptoms of his tuberculosis and possibly save his life. F.E.'s ever-wandering eye for adventure had settled on the new invention of the "horseless carriage," an arena he and his twin had been dabbling in for several years, as F.O. headed to Colorado. Both brothers had just crossed over the threshold of history!

## The Stanley Steamer Motor Car

F.O.'s and F.E.'s best-know partnership was the Stanley Steamer, which they manufactured in Watertown, Massachusetts. F.E. Built the first steamer in 1897, then made another one for F.O., delivered to him July 1898. In November 1898, the Stanley's demonstrated one of their cars at Charles River Park in Cambridge, part of the first car show ever held in Massachusetts.

F.O. and F.E. Stanley in their first Steamer Car.

Within weeks, the Stanley's had orders to build some 100 steamers—while still doing business as the Stanley Dry Plate Co. By May of 1899, however, they had sold the start-up automobile enterprise for $250,000 to Cosmopolitan Magazine's John Briben Walker (Walkers's wealth derived partly from alfalfa farming and real estate in Colorado) and Amzi Lorenzo Barber, the "asphalt king" of the day, who renamed the steamer "Locomobile."

F.E. and F.O. signed a contract with a one-year non-compete clause and were also contracted to promote and advise. When Walker and Barber could not get along, splitting up within a month, Walker, who called his car Mobile, moved his operation to Tarrytown, New York, too far away for the Stanley's to be active. Barber kept the name Locomobile, stayed in Watertown that first year, and made use of the Stanley's.

During the Locomobile association, F.O. Stanley drove a 4 & ½ hp. Locomobile steam car to the top of the northeast's highest and most difficult mountain, Mt. Washington in the White Mountains of New

Hampshire, August 31, 1899. An automobile milestone, this feat was a promotion for the viability of the automobile, for the Locomobile in particular, and was a strategy to promote better roads—Barber's main business, after all, was asphalt.

F.O. and Flora traveling up Mt. Washington in 1899.
Photo courtesy of the Stanley Museum.

By 1901, F.E. and F.O. bought back the original patents from Barber for $25,000 and were building steamers again. Between 1901 and 1924, they manufactured just under 11,000 Stanley Steamers.

During the time F.O. was in Colorado, F.E. expanded the business with a new, pre-stressed concrete manufacturing plant for the cars, took production as high as 700 cars a year, and made auto racing history—with F.O.'s complete support and praise, albeit from a distance.

The Stanley Steamer made racing history at Ormond Beach, Florida, in 1906, with a specially designed Stanley racer with a canoe-shaped body weighing less than 2,000 pounds. On the morning of Friday, January 26, it broke the two-miles-in-one-minute speed barrier, achieving 121.573 mph. That afternoon, the same car set a world land speed record of 127.659 mph that remained unbroken by any car for another four years.

F.O. Stanley in the Rocket in 1906.

Back at the races in 1907, in an attempt to break its own record, the Stanley racer achieved an estimated 150 mph speed—but crashed. The driver, Fred Marriott, survived with a few broken ribs and assorted other injuries and was back to work within a month. Even today, however, no steam car of similar weight and horsepower has surpassed the 1906 speed record!

Though still in Colorado, F.O. is likely to have agreed when his brother and sister-in-law decided to get out of racing after the Ormond Beach crash, choosing not to endanger the lives of their employees. This may well have been the last nail in the coffin for the steam car, since it effectively killed research and development for the Stanley Steamers.

In 1915, the Stanley twins began experimentation with a unit rail car, a self-contained, passenger rail car with its own power plant, to answer the need for dependable interurban railway transportation. That survived until 1919. F.E.'s untimely death on July 31, 1918, signaled the end of family interest in the project when Mr. Stanley's car overturned into a woodpile while trying to avoid two wagon carts that were driving side by side in the middle of the road. He died from the injuries he sustained in the crash. His twin brother, F.O. never fully recovered from his grief.

F.O. and F.E. Stanley riding down Main Street in Estes Park. It was the only time F.E. every visited his brother there. He died shortly after. F.E. is on left with the longer beard, center of photo. Stanley Museum.

## How a Stanley Steamer Works

Stanley Steamer in Estes Park Museum
It takes 20 minutes or more to fire up a Stanley, not much longer

than harnessing a horse to a buggy or saddling up. Until the electric starter was introduced in 1912-1913, the advantage of starting a Stanley with a match rather than having to crank it—necessary with internal combustion gas cars of the year—was a strong selling point, especially to women.

Think of a gas stove in which the pilot lights the burner and the burner heats the water: the Stanley has a pilot that lights the burner to make steam in the boiler. Additionally, Stanley Steamer fuel is under pressure and must be vaporized to burn. To understand this aspect, think of a Coleman stove or lantern: first, the fuel is pressurized by a little thumb pump, then the fuel is turned on and lit with a match, causing a sputtering of the stove flame or lamp mantel. This sputtering indicates raw, un-vaporized fuel. As soon as the flame heats the liquid to vaporization in the Coleman, the flame becomes a low, hot, blue flame on the burner, or a bright white light in the lamp mantel.

After the Stanly pilot is lit, it burns five-to-ten minutes to heat the steel kerosene vaporizer. Then the burner fuel is turned on, vaporizes, ignites, and the lit burner heats the water in the boiler, usually taking about 15 minutes from that point. The boiler is a fire-tube boiler, providing additional heating surface in the tubes which increases the one-to-two square feet of the burner plate to as much as 100 square feet of heating surface.

Once the steam pressure gets high enough—200-500 psi, the throttle lets the steam out of the top of the boiler, back through a super heater that sits above the flame of the burner, then back out of the burner through a steam line into the cylinder block of the engine at the rear of the car.

The engine—called a double-acting (power on both strokes), simple (vs. compound) two-cylinder steam engine—lets steam into the cylinders through D-valves in the steam chest; the steam pushes the pistons back and forth; piston rods connect with the crank of the engine, translating horizontal action to rotary action which turns the drive gear on the crank. The drive gear is married to a pinion or driven/differential gear on the rear axle, turning the axle and wheels, thus moving the car. (Susan S. Davis, *A History and Tour of the Stanley Hotel*)

Rick Mumford, a well-informed volunteer at the Stanley Museum in Estes Park told this author that out of 10,000 Stanley Steamers in the world, there are only 400 left in existence. "The Stanley's were known for more than just a superior automobile. If anything went wrong with one of their cars after it was purchased, they sent a mechanic out to fix it for free! They had a reputation that would make today's customer service look medieval."

## F.O. Stanley's Gifts to Estes Park

Besides building the area's most elite hotel which brought major business to the fledgling town of Estes Park, Mr. Stanley did more to build the tourist town into what it is today than anyone else, with the possible exception of Enis Mills who was responsible for building Rocky Mountain National Park only a few minutes away.

Some of F.O.'s major contributions to Estes Park and to Colorado as a whole are as follows:

1) President of the **Estes Park Protective and Improvement Association (EPPIA)**, which had been founded in 1895 "to prevent the destruction of the fish in the rivers of the Park, the illegal killing of game, and the destruction of the timber by camp fires." The elk population at that time was depleted and the deer and Rocky Mountain sheep populations were dangerously low, along with a declining fish count. By 1907, EPPIA had built a **Fish Hatchery** that soon became one of the best in the state. F.O. contributed one of its three ponds and personally sent his Stanley Steamer Wagons to Yellowstone Park in Wyoming to cart back elk! He reintroduced the elk to Estes Park, and as many residents today will tell you, "there is NO shortage of elk roaming the streets

of Estes Park, oftentimes more plentiful than the enormous tourist trade the town attracts!"

2)     Side by side with Enos Mills, Stanley helped lobby for the opening of a National Park at the outskirts of Estes Park.  Mills petitioned for the park for six years, which resulted in the **Rocky Mountain National Park**'s official opening on September 4, 1915.

3)     In the Spring of 1904, Stanley raised funds from hotel keepers in Estes Park, businessmen in Lyons and Denver, and officials of the Burlington Railroad to have new bridges installed and generally to improve the old wagon road up the South St. Vrain from Lyons to Estes Park.  In March 1907, Stanley kicked off a public-private road partnership with the state of Colorado, Estes Park and other subscribers with $5,000 of his own money. (The state put in $3, 250 and others another, $15,000.)  Work began in mid-April 1907.  The finished road was 18 feet wide, with "plenty of room to pass anywhere."  **The road is now called Colorado State Route 36.** "This road was built by Mr. Stanley, who deserves a great deal more credit for the enterprise than he will get," wrote the local Longmont Ledger on August 23, 1907.

4)     F.O. Stanley was President of the **Estes Park Bank,** purchasing five $100 shares, which helped incorporate the business. He held that position for 11 years.  Today the bank is called United Valley Bank and sits at the intersection of Routes 34 and 36.

5)     Realizing the need or a better water supply, F.O. Stanley, with four other prominent Estes Park leaders, helped organize the **Estes Park Water Company** on September 17, 1908.  Incorporated under Colorado Law October 7, it drew its water from Black Canyon Creek on the MacGregor ranch.  F.O. stayed involved as the company's major and controlling shareholder until the company was sold in 1929 to the Town of Estes Park.

6)     **The Stanley Hotel** was the first all-electric hotel, including an all-electric kitchen, in the world! Because coal—most especially due to its transport into Estes Park—was too expensive in 1908, F .O. decided to use electricity for his new hotel, scheduled to be opened the

following year. Stanley broke ground for the town's first hydroelectric plant on Fall River west of town October 9, 1908. Official incorporation papers were signed October 30, 1908, establishing the **Estes Park Light & Power Company**. Other hotels and lodges signed on, as did eventually the entire population of the town. Because electricity was in its infancy, light bulb sockets were the means of measuring use. Light bulbs bought from the company served as the rate-setting mechanisms.

7)     In September 1909, F.O. provided land in Stanley Meadows— where Lake Estes sits now—for a sewer line. Later, Stanley helped construct a second filter basin and install a septic tank. He later helped with further expansion in 1917 creating the **Estes Park Sewerage Association.**

8)     Along with two other wealthy summer residents, F.O. formed a syndicate and purchased 120 acres of land above Fish Creek on the southeast side of town and built an 18-hole **golf course** that is still enjoyed today.

9)     In 1921, F.O. donated property to the town to be used as the **Estes Park Garbage Dump**, as long as it was properly maintained, "hidden from public view and yet accessible."

10)     In 1936 the town of Estes Park accepted a generous donation of 54 acres of land from Mr. Stanley to be used as a recreation park. Stanley Park today consists of three large sections of land which include the rodeo grounds, a senior center, the Estes Park Area Historical Museum, a school complex (including 4 schools), a swimming pool, county and school offices, and a school athletic field. A gun club, teen center and various athletic fields and courts comprise the northeast section. **The Stanley Memorial Park** was dedicated on September 23, 1941, a year after Mr. Stanley's death at the age of 91.

Estes Park Valley. EstesParkCentral.com

F.O. Stanley brought tourism, city infrastructure, electricity, quality roads, banking, wildlife protection, recreation and the arts to the small town of Estes Park. He was a beacon to those who were fortunate enough to have known him or share in his generosity and achievements. He truly earned the title, "The Grand Old Man of Estes Park."

Freelan Oscar Stanley in Estes Park, Colorado.
Photo courtesy of the Stanley Museum

# THE
# HAUNTING

Chapter Eighteen

# WHAT IS A HAUNTING?

*"There is more between Heaven and Earth, my dear Horatio, than is dreamt of in thine experience."* Hamlet, Shakespeare

The worlds of science and religion are now shaking hands under the evolving umbrella of Quantum Physics. Test tubes are slowly giving way to imagination and a newfound interest in just what part our consciousness plays in creating the things around us. Man has always been fascinated by unsolved mysteries. We follow the clues, unravel the puzzles, and peer through telescopes in search of lost

251

galaxies, hidden meanings and keys. Perhaps we need complete resolution to feel secure in our part of this experience we call Life. I prefer to believe in the insatiability of our minds and the romance of looking for "more" than just what we perceive in our everyday lives.

## Troubleshooting Ghosts: What they are...and are not.

Since the inception of the first edition of *The History and Haunting of the Stanley Hotel,* I've been to many purported haunted houses, interviewed experts in the field of the paranormal, researched historic archives, and written books on some of the most-haunted venues in America. I spoke with George Noory during an interview on his popular radio show *Coast to Coast Am*, about what he thought ghosts were. We agreed, they are energy. Some of his 3 million listeners who called in that evening to ask us questions also felt ghosts "imprinted" the information upon our minds. While they could "see" the ghost sitting there on their couch, or entering a room, others in the same area saw nothing.

While staying at some famous haunted venues on overnight investigations, I've come to one solid conclusion: ghosts do exist, paranormal activity happens to thousands on a daily basis, and we have some very convoluted ideas of how ghosts behave.

Ghosts are energy. Pure and simple. Our bodies are made of energy: we are 99.99% energy and light. There is more space between our atoms that comprise our make-up, than not. That space is vibrating, pulsating energy. When we die, that energy has to go somewhere. You cannot destroy energy—it simply changes form. Picture boiling a pot of water. You can see and feel the water, but after a while, the water disappears and becomes steam. You haven't destroyed the water; it has merely changed into something else.

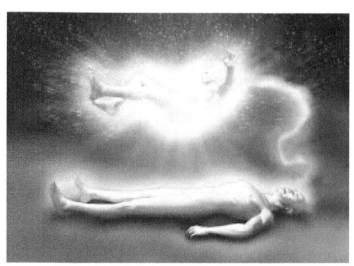

The same is true for human beings. You can call it spirit, or the soul, or any other name, but when this mortal vessel we carry around with us dies, all that energy that comprised us is left behind.

Many people experience that energy in different ways. Some "see it" in a full form, as in a full body apparition, or ghost. Others sense a change in the energy field around them as "something" enters into "their space." The paranormal can be witnessed through the five senses of smell, sight, hearing, touch and even taste. And then, there are those who are more highly tuned, and can experience phenomenon through a sixth sense.

The odd thing is, many stories have come forth where a group of people have been in a paranormal happening, and each witnessed something different. One may have seen a ghost-like shape at the end of the hallway, while the others saw nothing. However, another member of the group may have felt a decided drop in temperature, or smelled perfume, or heard music, while the others did not. How does that happen?

For the simple reason we cannot use the laws that govern our mortal beings with that of the paranormal. We are using a different measuring gauge, if you will. If ghosts are energy, no longer able to use the faculties they did when they were alive, then it makes sense they have no vocal chords. It is why ghost investigators use such paraphernalia as ghost boxes, tape recorders, and such. We do not hear the voice audibly with our ears, but the recorder can pick up interference of electromagnetic fields. Most people do not see ghosts, but they find them later appearing on their camera film or digital pictures. The reason electrical equipment malfunctions so often in the presence of the paranormal is that the energy field has changed. Lights flicker, TV screens go haywire, batteries drain, cameras show strange images, etc.

# How does it work?

I interviewed Loyd Auerbach about his thoughts on ghosts and paranormal experiences. When it comes to the subject of ghosts, few people have more experience or have conducted more research on the subject than Loyd Auerbach. Loyd is the Director of the Office of Paranormal Investigations, a consulting editor for *FATE* Magazine, President of the California Society of Psychic Study, and a professor at JFK University. He is also author of several books on ghosts, ESP and other psychic phenomena. His first book, *"ESP, Hauntings and Poltergeists"* was named the "sacred text" on ghosts by *Newsweek* in August, 1996. Please see more about Loyd in the Bibliography section at the back

When asked, what ghosts are, Mr. Auerbach replied:

"Most of us in parapsychology have used the term **"apparitions"** to refer to that which most people call ghosts. An apparition is what is seen, heard, felt or smelled, and is related to some part of the human personality/mind/soul that can somehow exist in our physical universe after the death of its body. The basic idea of an apparition is twofold: the consciousness must survive and it must be able to communicate or interact somehow with living people.

"When I say that the apparition is "seen" or "heard," I don't mean that this is happening through the eyes or ears. First of all, remember that our actual perception of the world around us involves a process whereby data is received by the senses, then screened and enhanced by the brain or mind. Perception resides not in the senses, but in the brain. Hallucinations, for example, are essentially superimposed images, sounds, smells, etc. that are added to (or in other instances blocked or erased from) the information to our sensory input that is then processed with our sensory data and integrated in what we perceive. In other words, the mind of the ghost is providing our own minds with extra information necessary to perceive him or her. This is an excellent example of telepathy at work."

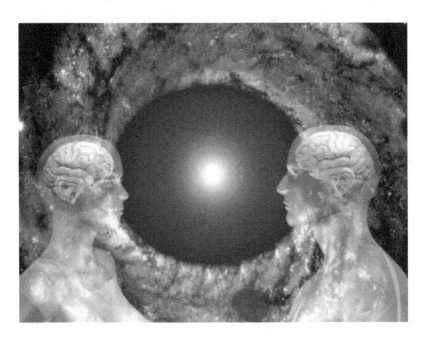

Loyd Auerbach, Paranormal Expert, Professor and Author.

He went on to site the evidence to this theory:

"Besides the fact that when an apparition is present, not everyone experiences the entity, there can be a variety of experiences that indicates subjectivity on the part of the witnesses. Some might "see" the ghost, some "hear" his/her voice (some both), some "feel" a presence or that they're being touched, and some "smell" his/her cologne or perfume.

As not everyone is seeing the apparition, the very idea that one could photograph him/her becomes complicated. If the ghost was reflecting light, people's eyes would see him/her and a photo would be no problem."

I interrupted to postulate that the energy or thought waves from a ghost is what actually imprints onto film and explains why we don't see the apparition as we are photographing an area, but it turns up on the photograph. There are rare cases where people have seen the shape or form and captured it on film while experiencing it in "real time."

Loyd agreed and went on to say, "I should also mention that I have received an interesting wording of apparitions from an *actual ghost*, a deceased woman who was in constant communication with a young boy (and seen by others, as it happens). She said that as far as she knew, she was a ball of energy, of consciousness, though she also said she really didn't know that "ball" was the right word, since she felt kind of formless. How she pictured herself was how others perceived her—she noted that she was more or less connecting mind to mind to the boy (and others), and projecting the idea of her form, clothing and her voice to him."

Physicists are touting the String Theory and other definitions, to tell us there is the possibility of multiple and parallel universes. Einstein believed that the space/time continuum was a fabric that folded over on itself and if a tear appeared in that fabric, we could step into another dimension, another time. Are ghosts simply time traveling? Are they closer than we think, existing just out of reach of this realm? Or are they energy that can make themselves known through the senses?

"Apparitions are often confused with **hauntings**," Mr. Auerbach continued. "The difference is that apparitions are "live" (intelligent consciousness) and hauntings are recordings.

"A haunting relies on the living, not the dead (although in a sense, all of history is "dead"). A haunting is information received by the witness who has the experience. Hauntings actually show that we are all psychic receivers (clairvoyant) to some degree.

"One ability proffered by my psychics over the ages is **psychometry**: the ability to "read" the history of an object by holding or touching it," Mr. Auerbach continued. "Objects, we're told, "record" their entire history, and some can decipher that with **psi** (popular term used to mean any psychic phenomena, psychic abilities, and sometimes inclusive of paranormal disturbances as well). And what is a house (or hotel?) if not a big object?

"…a haunting appears to be stuck in some kind of environmental recording of events and people. Like the small object "read' in psychometry, the house or building or land somehow records its history, with the more emotion-laden events and experiences coming through "louder" and "stronger." That people mostly report negative events and an emotion (around suicide, murder or other violent crimes, or emotional fights) is likely due to a reporting artifact than any unbalanced ration of negative to positive events."

"You might think of a haunting as a loop of video or audio tape playing itself over and over for you to watch. Trying to interact with it would be akin to trying to interact with a show on your TV: sure you can turn it off or change the channel, but I wouldn't expect the actors to suddenly stop and talk to you directly." (Loyd Auerbach Interview on Ghosts)

## The Stone Tape Theory

There is a popular theory as to why some places are "gathering places" for ghosts, or shall we say, have certain properties that make it easier for hauntings to take place. It is called the **Stone Tape Theory.**

The term 'Stone Tape Theory' came from a 1970's British TV play called *The Stone Tape*. Paranormal investigators began to use the term to describe a theory that the materials found in stone or brick may contain properties suitable for recording images and/or sound. It is believed that certain rock formations, stone etc., are able to retain or "tape" energy from living beings. Under certain conditions this energy can be replayed, just like a video recording. Interestingly, some scientists believe these 'tapes' can become worn out, just as with video or tape recordings, when played over and over. Could this explain why some people see ghosts in solid form, looking just like you and I, and at other times we see them as faded or transparent? Would it explain why we don't see other, more ancient ghosts that go farther back than the usual medieval haunts of England? Perhaps these recordings become 'tired' and gradually fade away.

When you add the properties of crystals found in the ground beneath us, you have a very accessible set-up for recording, as found in radio receivers and transmitters. Scientists are now looking closely at the flagstone used in the building of ancient castles as the reason ghosts perform in a continuous and unwavering way; the crystal and quartz found in the stone act as a recorder and transmitter of energy impact from dramatic events, such as a tragic death.

# Poltergeists

Our final member in our haunted cast of characters is a **poltergeist**. Poltergeist is a German word meaning "playful ghost." Some people fear poltergeists as they are the most physically active. They are known to throw things, pinch, rattle, rap, open doors, turn lights on and off and cause items to disappear, only to reappear in some other location. They have been known to pull hair, tug on clothing and are responsible for most of the unexplained noises one hears in a haunting.

A number of investigators, however, believe that poltergeist activity is not caused by ghosts but by certain living people under stress. The agent, in an attempt to relieve emotional stress, subconsciously causes the physical disturbances using mental forces. This is, again, energy at work. Most agents are not aware they are even causing the problem. The mental mechanism that allows the poltergeist agent to unconsciously cause these physical disturbances is called **psychokinesis**. Very often it is attributed to teenagers reaching puberty, who are under a lot of stress, though this has not been proven. Watching to whom the events are targeted, and what type of activity is happening is sometimes a clue as to which agent is seeking a subconscious release of frustration.

Hauntings can involve some or all of the different attributes described above. You can have smells, moving objects, noises, apparitions and recordings all going on at once.

I'd like to relate a personal experience here, if I may. I had a first-hand understanding of our bodies acting as conductors when I witnessed how wrist watches reacted when placed upon my mother' wrist. As children, my sister and I would beg her to take our ticking watches and place them on her wrist. She would sigh and accommodate us and within seconds the sweep hand came to an abrupt halt. She also had a sixth sense about things.

Once, while she, my sister and I were driving to my Uncle's house in California, she suddenly pulled over, with my sister and me in the back seat, and burst into tears. She said her mother had just died. I was 8-years-old at the time and couldn't understand how someone would know this, as my grandmother lived several states away and there were no cell phones at that time. Sure enough, when we pulled up to my Uncle's door (my mother's brother) he came out to meet us with tears in his eyes and said, "Sis, Mom just died." I never forgot that.

My mother also sensed an elderly gentleman who had passed away in the home we bought and she would get black-outs in one small bathroom, following an overwhelming smell of cigar smoke. She was also our favorite party guest. She could look at any person in the group, without ever having met them, and tell them what their bedroom looked like, which parent they were closer to, and other personal things. She even took one of my friends aside during my 20's and told her that her husband was having an affair. My mother had never met this woman before. Sure enough, she found out that he was. It was hard to get away with anything growing up around my Mom! She always seemed to know.

## "Things That Go Bump"

We have come a long way in learning more about the paranormal world. Most experts in the field now agree that you cannot use blanket phrases to describe the events that make up a supernatural happening. There is not just one kind of ghost or just one kind of haunting. Circumstances, environments and the observer vary. Ghosts can fall into different categories such as apparitions, 'recording' ghosts, anniversary ghosts, sentient ghosts, messengers, etc. There may even be sub-types in these categories.

Most ghostly activity tends to fall into two groups, however. "Residual energy" or a "residual haunting" is used to define a haunting that tends to happen over and over again without interacting with people around it. Many ghost stories from old castles in Europe report the reoccurring visages on the battlements, moving along, with hooded head bent down and then disappearing into a wall. The same thing is repeated without variance. It is like a loop playing over and over again. Most ghost hunters and recently, scientists believe the energy exerted when someone dies suddenly or tragically is recorded, leaving an imprint or energy residue on the physical objects nearby that then play that imprint back under the right circumstances. We will discuss this more when we talk about the Stone Tape theory.

The other type of ghostly phenomenon is called "sentient", or an "active haunting". These are the ghosts who are aware of their surroundings and the people therein and actually interact with them. Many cases reported at the Stanley Hotel involve "something" pinching, touching, shaking a bed, tossing something across the room or in some way being mindful it is being watched. Take for example the unaccompanied music coming from the piano in the Music Room of the hotel. If it were just a loop being played back, why would the music stop when someone crosses into the room or opens the door, only to resume when the door is shut again? Why would the ghost of F.O. Stanley elude people chasing after him, only to finally vanish into a wall in the bar area or Billiard Room?

Some ghosts are called "messengers". These are usually loved ones who have come here on a mission, whether to forewarn someone of an impending danger or to sooth a grieving relative and assure them they are happy in a new life. These are usually one-time occurrences and once their mission is served, the ghost is not heard from again. The Bible is replete with messengers in the guise of angels appearing to men to give them direction or warn them of things to come. Many recent movies have dealt with man's desire to hang onto parting loved ones and bring them back or at least feel their presence again.

"Anniversary ghosts" are just what their name implies. They are typically "seen" on an anniversary commemorating something important to them. Often they return to the scene of their death. President Lincoln's ghost has been reportedly seen at the White House enough times to make it seem beyond contention. He has also been seen at the Ford Theatre in Washington, DC where he was shot in the head while viewing a play there.

## An Example of a Haunting

I have a friend who bought an old farmhouse in Denver dating back to the late 1800's. We will call her Debra. The first week Debra moved in she became aware of unexplained noises and pungent smells that would appear and disappear like turning a faucet on and off. She attributed it to the age of the house and went about her business.

The poltergeist activity began shortly after. The house didn't have a modern clothes dryer hook-up, so she would walk out the screen door and into the back yard to hang her wet wash from a sagging clothesline. Upon returning to the house, she would find "someone" had placed the rusted hook into the metal eye on the inside of the door, effectively locking her out. She would then trudge to the front of the house for entry. After this happened several times, she finally banged on the locked screen door and yelled, "Ok you guys. It was funny the first ten times...now will you please leave the door alone?" It was never locked against her again.

A few weeks later, however, things became a little more harmful. There was a bathroom across the hall from her bedroom on the second landing that she used as her own. It had an antique claw foot tub she loved to soak in. Suddenly, from nowhere, a heavy, antique silver hairbrush would materialize out of thin air and go sailing toward her head!

This happened several times. She finally told her father, who did not believe her. He came to stay the evening, to check it out. She waited anxiously as he she heard him run his bath. She next heard the splash of water as he entered the tub. Several anxious moments later, she heard the violent splashing as he hurriedly exited the tub and appeared in the hallway a few minutes later, towel wrapped around his wet body, and sporting a new red welt in the center of his chest. Without a word, he grabbed his clothes, his duffel bag and headed for the car...driving home in a damp towel.

To my astonishment, she stayed on, reluctant to give up on her farmhouse.

The final breaking point came when she was seated on the landing of the stairwell between the first and second floors, talking with a friend on the phone. Her mother had come to visit and was in the kitchen cooking. Debra leaned against the wall, deep in conversation when she happened to look up through the spindles of the stairwell railing on the second floor. An elderly woman in a worn house dress with white hair was walking from her bedroom toward the bathroom where all the occurrences had taken place. She blinked and then called to the woman, "Mom?" Her mother stepped out of the kitchen on the first floor only a few feet below her. "Yes, dear?" Debra went pale and looked up to the second floor in panic. Who was the woman who had just entered her bathroom? She and her mother nervously went to check and found no one in the bathroom, or anywhere on the second floor. Days later, Debra moved out.

This story shows that a haunting can have many elements of paranormal activity. Trying to plot it on a graph is just not going to happen.

The list we've just covered is by no means comprehensive. We are in uncharted territory. I do wonder if with all our scientific equipment...our EMF readers, tape recorders and fancy camera set-ups...we are suggesting that we can capture, chart, bottle and tag the world of the paranormal. It seems most seasoned investigators are declaring that ghosts are reaching out to our minds rather than our

Kodaks. Does that mean you will find me wondering the grounds of haunted houses and hotels without a camera? *Are you nuts?*

Chapter Nineteen

# HAUNTED PLACES

*"I have heard, but not believed, the spirits o' the dead may walk again."*
*William Shakespeare, in The Winter's Tale*

The Stanley Hotel has a preponderance of unexplained things going on. Even the skeptics will give her that. The purest scientific communities have tried to explain it away to noises in the pipes, ancient floorboards, and electromagnetic fields quivering just beneath the hotel in the mineral-laden earth. As Eleanor Lance said in Shirley Jackson's novel, *The Haunting of Hill House*, "Let's just blame it on sunspots."

While researching the hotel in 2009 and 2010 in preparation for the writing of the first edition of this book, I went on Scary Mary's tour and it was amazing! At one point she paused on the landing going up to the second floor and said she wanted to introduce us to two of the spirit children that frequent the hotel. Though we could not see them, she asked them to touch her skirt. To the astonishment of the twelve or so people in the group, the hem of her skirt moved away from her body as though being tugged by someone knee-height. It also vibrated slightly. Then, two pairs of tiny handprints appeared to be pressing into the shiny fabric of Mary's polyester skirt!

A few weeks later, I again attended one of Mary's tours. She was wearing another black skirt, this one a form-fitting pencil style. The guides all wear the same colors of clothing while conducting the tours. We were now standing just outside Room 217 on the second floor, the room made famous by Stephen King staying there, and by the continual paranormal activity that occurs in the room. Here, Mary stopped and spoke again of her "spirit children". She lifted her arms away from her body and all of us leaned forward, expectantly. The hem of her tight skirt began to quiver and move, and then...there they were. Two pairs of distinct imprints, small in size, like that of a child pressing against the fabric of the skirt. You could actually count each finger's outline. I touched the hem and squeezed it a little, looking for some device imbedded in the fabric; I could find nothing abnormal. There was also a faint coldness emanating from the area where the handprints were.

Next, Mary stepped back a few spaces to where you can look up and up through the twisting staircase to the balconies of the upper floors. She called it the vortex of the hotel, the area where energy is generated. A vortex is the funnel-shape created by a whirling fluid or by the motion of spiraling energy. Familiar examples of vortex shapes are whirlwinds, tornadoes, and water going down a drain. A vortex can be made up of anything that flows, such as wind, water or electricity. They can be swirling centers of subtle energy coming out from the surface of the earth. A vortex indicates the rotation of cosmic energy around a central point or axis. Beginning in the mid-19th Century, the word "vortex" has meant any whirling movement of energy or particles. Most haunted venues attribute a vortex being found somewhere on the property and consider it the epi-center of activity and energy. Sedona, Arizona has become world-renowned for its vortices and people come from all over to feel of its energy.

Mary said if you stood in the vortex at the hotel and tipped your head back and stood still and waited a few moments, you would sense a swirling energy that might leave you light-headed. I stood there a moment, but was too aware of the others in the group staring at me to really get into it. Experiencing the "vortex moment" is something best done alone.

Location of vortex at base of 2nd floor staircase.
Photo by Rebecca F. Pittman.

We next ascended the stairs toward the 3rd floor balcony. Mary told us that the ghost of a 14-year-old-nanny named Sarah, was often felt on the landing between the 2nd and 3rd floor and that we might feel a slight coldness when we passed that area. The members of the group dutifully stopped at the spot and then moved on up to the balcony overlooking "Sarah's landing." Mary and I were the last ones to go up. I stopped on the landing and I turned to ask her something I needed for this book. She was standing on the step below me. It was a hot June day and I had a sleeveless top on. In mid-sentence, I stopped speaking and jumped. Something painful was pressing into my right shoulder, the shoulder turned to the corner of the landing. At first I thought I had been burned, and then I realized it was freezing, as those two sensations are closely aligned when first felt. It felt as if a giant 4" ice cube was being pressed into my bare arm!

The group overhead heard me gasp and they turned to look down on us. Several shot pictures with their digital cameras. As they did so, I heard startled exclamations from the people looking down into their camera viewfinders. I hurried up the stairs, my hand pressed to the place on my arm that was still cold. As I looked at the cameras they were offering me, I felt a second chill. On five of the eight cameras that took pictures, were images of me with a giant green orb the size of a baseball floating over my right shoulder. Depending on where the person was standing along the balcony and shooting, the orb was different in each shot; one showed it moving across my throat leaving a wavy tendril-like tail behind it.

After 30 years of wanting some kind of validation that there was something outside the norm at the Stanley Hotel, I was finally, and without equivocation, able to testify that something had definitely happened to me. The cold, burning sensation on my arm stayed with me for hours.

As a side note, Mary told me something interesting as we finally moved along to the 4th floor on her tour. She pulled me aside and said Sarah, during her life, was a very tall girl, something uncommon in the early 1900s. I am 6'2" tall and Mary wondered if Sarah reached out to me for that reason…a common bond, if you will.

During my research into other haunted venues across America I've received some interesting comments from the owners of these places. Most are B&B's, others are hotels, such as the Stanley, and many are former locations of murders, battlefields, and historic landmarks.

The common agreement of these venue owners is that guests coming to stay in their establishments are expecting a guaranteed

Fright Night. Mark Ball, General Manager at the haunted Lemp Mansion in St. Louis, told me he is often amused by the questions of guests checking in.

"I am frequently asked if they can expect something spooky to happen to them during their stay," he says, smiling. "We are talking about paranormal experiences here and they act as though it is Ghost on Demand. It doesn't work that way. The high percentage of activity we do get here validates the world's focus on Lemp Mansion as a very haunted house, but you can't expect something to happen every night."

Other owners of these haunted places have voiced the same concern. One woman at the Whaley House in San Diego, California nicknamed it the "The Dial-A-Ghost" mentality. She said people seem disappointed if the price of admission doesn't come with a guaranteed ghostly experience.

Whaley House in San Diego, California. Photo by Ron Bueker.
WhaleyHouse.org

Frankly, I have learned that most paranormal activity happens when you are focused on something else and not trying to force it. Almost all of my experiences have occurred when I was going about my daily business.

Lemp Mansion in St. Louis, Missouri. Photo Rebecca F. Pittman.

At Lemp Mansion, I was getting ready to pack for a trip to Louisiana when I heard gunshots and a dog bark outside my room on the second floor. The fact that 3 members of the Lemp family shot themselves in that home, one shooting his dog first and then himself, was not lost on me. While sleeping in the attic room of that mansion something kicked the bed and sat on my feet. Flickering lights, running water, voices, all happened while I was thinking of other things.

Many of the staff at Lemp Mansion said they were usually hurrying about their chores when they would notice someone sitting in a chair who would vanish when they looked back, or see a candle light itself, or see a shadow person coming toward them. The people I interviewed at the Stanley Hotel sighted the same thing. It was typically while they were attending to guests, tallying up the receipts, or cleaning that something walked past them, moved their items, or whispered their name.

Myrtles Plantation, St. Francisville, Louisiana.
Photo Rebecca F. Pittman

While writing about the Myrtles Plantation in St. Francisville, Louisiana, my earrings moved out from under my car keys on the fireplace mantle in the Woodruff Room and traveled the length of the board. Something pulled the blanket off my bed in the Confederate Soldiers' Room while I was sleeping. I awakened to see it jerking toward the right corner of the four-poster bed.

For me, running around with EMF readers and fancy equipment can be fulfilling, but I have more luck by simply being still, being in tune, and understanding the story behind the people who lived—and died—there.

In **Appendix I** at the back of this book, you will find a complete guide to Ghost Hunting. Knowing how to take good pictures, and what rules to follow when negotiating a property, are important elements of any investigation. Do your homework. There are a lot of aps, websites and elaborate equipment out there coaxing the amateur ghost hunter to buy their books and wares. Sometimes a hand-held tape recorder and a good camera are all you need. Today's smart phones have some amazing cameras with editing features.

That said, let's take a look at the Stanley Hotel complex and peek through the keyholes at her most famous ghost stories. You will also find submissions from guests who have stayed there, gone on the Ghost Tours, or simply walked her grounds.

Photo courtesy of Big Fish Games.

Chapter Twenty

# THE HAUNTING OF the STANLEY HOTEL:
## The First Floor

Why are scary
movies always in
creepy places like
jails and hospitals?
I want a scary movie
in Walmart .
"Clean up on aisle 13"
"But sir... There is no
aisle 13.."
*dramatic music*

# The Lobby

Stanley Hotel Lobby. Photo by Ron Bueker.

The following paranormal reportings have been accumulated for your consideration. Most names of the contributors reflect only their first name and last initial, unless specific acquiescence was given. I have tried to verify as many of these stories as possible. The abundance of repetitive occurrences adds validity to each area we are investigating. You will find this graphic at the beginning of each

reporting .

We'll begin with the Stanley Hotel **Lobby.**

The Lobby of the Stanley Hotel has seen more activity than any other area of the complex—both human and other. From the time the doors were flung wide for its soft opening in June of 1909 the polished floors have seen an endless parade of guests, celebrities, dignitaries, film crews, and staff. Is it any wonder that the hotel becomes confused as to which era it is?

*Marjorie S., Boston, MA. Nov. 2011.* "My husband and I were staying at the Stanley Hotel for a 5th wedding anniversary. We had always wanted to see it and my husband loves the ghost reality shows that featured it so many times. We had planned on eating dinner in the hotel dining room and were walking across the lobby toward it when I realized I left my purse in my room. I told my husband to go ahead and get seated for dinner and I would be right back.

"I went up to our room, grabbed my purse and walked down to the first landing of the big staircase. As I turned the corner to go down to the lobby, I froze. There was this lady coming up the stairs toward me dressed in a long Victorian gown with a large hat and plume. Her left hand was holding up one corner of her gown to keep from tripping on it. I could clearly see her high top shoes. While my first thought was that the hotel had some of the staff dressed up in period clothes, it was quickly replaced by the startling fear I could see through her to the spindles on the other side of the stairs.

"She passed me without acknowledging I was there. I pressed myself against the railing as she went by and felt my flesh pebble all over. I watched her go up to the second floor and turn the corner.

"My heart was pounding and it took a few minutes to catch my breath. I looked down toward the lobby and realized it had gotten very quiet. When my husband and I had walked through only minutes before it was bustling with activity. Again I felt an icy panic go through me. I took two steps down and peered around. There was absolutely no one in the lobby. Not one soul. Not only that but the furnishings were different...lots of ferns and wicker chairs.

"I finally got the nerve to go down and I literally ran toward the direction of the dining room, even though everything looked different. I remember thinking "What if the dining room is gone? What if my husband is gone?" Just as I got to the fireplace closest to the west end of the lobby there was a popping sound. I felt like an electric current went through me. Suddenly the lobby came to life, people were laughing and rushing around. The furniture was back to normal and the rooms in front of me changed. The noise seemed suddenly deafening. I walked weak-kneed to my husband who was seated studying a menu and told him my story. To my relief he believed me. I have never encountered anything like that before."

*Daniel Ortega, Colorado Springs, Co. June, 2014.* "I was with a group of friends hitting the ghost tours in June. We were waiting on my friend Rick who was in the gift shop looking for some Shining stuff. So we're standing there talking and my friend Jose looks down at the floor, then over to the front window and his face starts frowning. He says...you see that? Look at that shadow on the floor! We look down and it looks like a tall guy's shadow right between our feet on the floor. Only there was no one attached to it! No guy was standing there. We looked toward the window to see if maybe it was from somebody on the front porch but there was no one in front of the window either. Jose put his foot on it and the shadow went right across his shoe. Then just like that it's gone. We told the tour guide and he asked us to show him where it was. We did. He said it was probably old man Stanley cuz he hangs around the lobby a lot. I mean his ghost does."

*Jenn M., New York City, NY. January, 2012.* "There were four of us waiting to check into our room. My daughter was getting married and we were running around doing last minute things at the Stanley Hotel. I wanted to ride the elevator up to our room as I have trouble with my right knee. We were standing in front of the hotel elevator next to the Gift Shop and waiting our turn. My friend suddenly grabs my elbow and says there is a strange shadow going up the back of my white dress. I tried to look over my shoulder but couldn't see my back. The other people in the party gasped and said it was moving. It was the shadow of a tall skinny man. As they watched, it moved from my back and onto the floor where I could distinctly see a long shadow of a tall man with what looked like a fuzzy chin. There was no person nearby who could be casting the shadow. It was blank floor behind it. As we stared at it, it faded away. I had heard the hotel was haunted but this was my first, and only, experience with something paranormal. Thank goodness I had witnesses."

*Mike McGregor, Kansas City, Kansas. May, 2010.* "I went to the Stanley Hotel for a business lunch that a bunch of us were putting on for a new venture we were putting together in Loveland, Colorado. A lot of the guys wanted to see the hotel so we thought it would be fun to eat there.

"We were standing in the Lobby and looking at the Stanley Steamer Car when one of the guys bent his head into the car to look closer at the seat beneath the steering wheel. We asked him what he was doing and he said, "That seat just went down like someone is sitting on it!" We pushed him aside and looked. It looked fine to me. As we were about to tease him about ghosts, one of the other guys shouts, "Look...it's sinking down!" I turned and looked at it. There was a clear indentation on the cushion that wasn't there before. As we watched, it "adjusted" a couple of times, like someone shifting weight, and then lifted back to its normal position. One of the guys...the techie one, laughed and said the hotel probably had some kind of hydraulic device under the seat to freak people out. This was clearly not the case. We took a couple of pictures of the seat but it was too hard to see the differences in the shadowed interior of the car. That was one freaky deal!"

Interior of Stanley Steamer at Stanley Hotel. Ron Bueker.

🔑 *Debbie W., Provo, Utah. August, 2014.* "My sis and I took a tour at the Stanley in 2014. It was my first time doing anything with ghost stuff. I was nervous and she was teasing me about it. I typically don't go to scary movies so this was a big step for me. We got our stickers for the tour and had a few minutes to kill so we went up to the Lobby and looked around.

"I had read from Ms. Pittman's first book that the Lobby walls had been painted by Hollywood to look like real wood when they were originally white. I stepped over to feel the painted wall when I feel something cold on my forearm, like an icy hand closing around my wrist. It startled me and I jumped back. After a few moments I put my hand out again to touch the wall and the same sensation came over my wrist. I hurried over to my sister who was looking at a shirt hanging on the gift shop door and told her what happened. She told me to take her over to where I felt the icy feeling. I did. She reached out her hand to touch the wall and the same thing happened to her. If you want to try it, stand just around the corner from the elevator, where the bathrooms are, and put your hand on the wall there. It is not air-conditioning, or a draft. You feel like a cold, icy hand just wrapped around your wrist...like someone telling you not to touch the walls."

🔑 *Roger Orwell, Atlanta, Georgia. March, 2013.* "I was on vacation in Estes Park, Colorado and my wife wanted to see the Stanley Hotel. Big fan of The Shining. So we go. She's looking at the old piano sitting there by the gift place and asks if I think they will get mad if she plays it. I says Heck Yeah they will. Leave it alone. It's old. Just as I says that, it plays two notes. She jumps. I laugh. But then it does it again. Two high notes. By itself. This hotel lady comes over and asks us not to play the piano. My wife looks at her and says It's playin' itself. Just then it lets out two more notes. The hotel lady's face looks like she thinks we are doing something funny with it. She just says Please don't touch it, and walks away. My wife went out and sat in the car. I thought it was danged funny."

🔑 *Michellie M., Portland, Oregon. March, 2013.* "My

friend Dana and I were at the Stanley Hotel in Colorado. We were looking it over for a friend's wedding reception, along with some other places in Colorado. We were walking toward the Music Room at the end of the lobby when this man comes walking out of that room. He is dressed in black clothes and has a white old-time beard and hair. He smiles at us and keeps going. I turned to look at him to see if he went behind the registration desk, figuring he was dressed like for the hotel guest's amusement, but he didn't get that far. He suddenly disappeared near the base of the big staircase. Disappeared is the wrong word. He more like faded until there was nothing left. Dana saw him too. She wanted to leave, so we did."

Ron W., Denver, Colorado. July, 2014. "I have lived in Colorado for 25 years. I like going to the old historic places like the Molly Brown House and the Broadmoor Hotel in Colorado Springs. I finally got a chance to visit the Stanley Hotel and was very excited to see something built in 1909. I went by myself and was taking photos in the lobby when suddenly my camera wouldn't work. The shutter speed slowed down so much that it wouldn't click right. All my pictures were either coming out black, washed out, or really blurred. The ones I had taken out front and on the porch looked great, so I was puzzled. I was about to abandon the picture taking, thinking the camera had broken when I heard a lady not far me complaining to her husband that her camera wouldn't work. She said the pictures were all blurry.

"I stepped back out onto the porch and aimed it at the mountains. The shutter clicked and the photo was perfect. When I tried again inside, the camera did the same thing. It was all blurred. The picture of the staircase looked really weird, like it was curved sideways."

*Dan Mitchell, Ft. Collins, Colorado. October, 2013.*
"The Stanley Hotel is pretty cool. I've been up there a few times for different reasons. I've had two paranormal things happen to me there. Both in the lobby area. One was in the elevator. I got in and there was a little girl standing there in ringlets and an old-looking long dress. She was looking straight ahead. It spooked me so badly that I got back off and took the stairs. The other one was the flowers on a table in the middle of the lobby started bending over like

someone was pulling them toward them to smell them. There was no wind or anything. I just watched them bend over, hang for a minute, and then straighten back up. Creepy stuff."

Stanley Hotel Elevator. Photo Rebecca F. Pittman

Many stories of time warps happening in the Lobby area have been reported over the years, including this one by Susan S. Davis, former head of the Estes Park Stanley Museum.

In 1995 during the filming of *The Shining*, Paula. P., Head of Sales for the Stanley, was helping prepare for a group coming for dinner in the Music Room. The ABC crew was running late filming a segment in the Pinon Room, and agreed to help when they were done so that preparation time for the hotel staff was cut down and they could finish filming. Something was missing for the buffet tables, so Paula offered to go to the kitchen at the other end of the Lobby to get it.

She took off across the Lobby, and heard her name called behind her. She turned back, and no one was there. In fact, absolutely no one was there. The Lobby, bustling with film crew and hotel staff barely seconds before, was completely empty. She shook her head in bewilderment, but being efficient and unflappable Paula, she turned back to her task and retrieved the missing items from the kitchen. When she returned to the Lobby, it was back to normal, bustling with people and activity. As she got back to her friend at the table, Paula asked her what had happened, why had everyone disappeared. Her friend assured her nothing had happened, they had all been there the whole time. (Susan S. Davis, *Stanley Ghost Stories*)

Another story Susan shares in her popular book Stanley Ghost Stories is the following:

In February of 1984, at 10:30 at night in the small alcove behind the front desk, bellman Mark L. heard seven steps come from the Dunraven Bar, (now the Cascades) and stop. He stepped forward to the front desk, and in the window glass of the front porch, he saw the reflection of a woman with an off-the-shoulder gown, hair piled high, with ringlets. The outfit was a cream-colored southern belle style gown. Mark moved quickly out the door into the Lobby and in several broad strides, he was in the entryway to the Dunraven. No one was there. He checked the MacGregor Room, the front porch, and when he opened the door to the Dunraven Bar, everyone there turned to look at him. Being winter, many were wearing ski clothes with big fuzzy boots (strange what you notice!). He went to the other exit of the bar, looked at the top of the basement stairs and saw and heard nothing. (Susan S. Davis, *Stanley Ghost Stories*)

Reports of F.O. and Flora Stanley ascending, or descending, the grand staircase in the Lobby are numerous. Many have seen them as if they were solid, flesh and blood personages, while others have seen a more transparent shape of the pair. Flora's ghost is often preceded by the strong smell of roses—her favorite flower.

The grand staircase gets its share of paranormal activity as well. While writing the first edition on the Stanley Hotel I was able to interview most of the staff at the hotel. There stories are varied, and poignant.

One such occurrence was given to me by Rob A., a 23-year-old male from Golden, Colorado who was one of the Ghost Tour guides at the hotel. Rob is a gregarious, warm person who loves what he does. When I asked about some of the paranormal activity that he had witnessed lately or had heard reports of from the guests who attend his tours, he said that there had been some strange things happening on the grand staircase lately.

"I have had three people on three different occasions on completely different tours report to me as we climbed the main staircase that someone or "something" had just kicked them in the shin! This was a new one to me, but all three reports came within a 36-hour period. One woman claimed to be 'sensitive' to environments and said she thought a small boy was following them around and might be responsible for playfully kicking a few people as they climbed the steps. One woman even showed me her newly red ankle."

Stanley Lobby with Grand Staircase. Photo by Ron Bueker.

When Stephen King decided to shoot a TV mini-series based on his book *The Shining*, he knew exactly where he wanted it to be filmed-- the hotel that started it all, The Stanley Hotel in Estes Park, Colorado. The series, starring Stephen Webber and Rebecca DeMornay was filmed throughout the hotel and grounds, but there were several poignant scenes shot in the Lobby. Hollywood resorted to fake blood for one of the scenes filmed in front of the registration desk at the hotel. Unfortunately, it left a stain on the rug that was in front of the check-in counter. One evening, after the shooting was completed (film shooting that is), a photograph of Mrs. Stanley that usually resides calmly on the wall behind the registration desk suddenly flew off and over the front desk, (a good 5 feet of distance) to land soundly on the offensive red stain. It was her way of showing her displeasure at having her beautiful hotel defaced. The stain was immediately removed and the picture placed back in its place on the wall.

Flora and F.O.'s portraits above the registration desk cubbyholes.
Photo by Ron Bueker.

While Flora's spirit has made itself known throughout the Lobby area, she favorited the Music Room where she can still be heard playing her beloved Steinway piano. We will learn more about her when we hear the ghost stories reported from that room.

Another frequent report of paranormal activity circulated throughout the Lobby is that of seeing the wicker rocker chairs on the front verandah move of their own volition. Without a breeze to be felt the chairs have rocked rhythmically back and forth as though someone is seated there, idly enjoying the spectacular views of the Rockies.

There are many photographs of floating orbs throughout the Lobby. Some undoubtedly are dust/light reflections caught when a flash goes off. Others seem more ominous and tend to defy the usual explanations. It usually requires a sequence of rapid fire camera shots to show if an orb is acting in a manner unnatural to, say, a dust particle. A video that can follow the movement of orbs is a better indicator of paranormal activity as reflections from the many windows throughout the Lobby, brass fixtures and other hindrances can impact a camera shot and lead the happy photographer to think they have captured a ghostly phenomenon. That is not to say the Lobby isn't replete with authentic photographs of paranormal activity. The same can be said for the rest of our tour of the Stanley Hotel.

Stanley Hotel looking down from first landing. Photo Ron Bueker.

# The Music Room

Music Room entrance from Lobby.
Photo by Rebecca F. Pittman.

The Stanley Hotel Music Room is a hot bed of activity. Reports of the piano playing when no one is seated there are constantly being relayed to the hotel staff.

Many people have heard the piano music and glimpsed inside the Music Room to try and catch the phantom pianist. The music stops as soon as the pocket doors slide open or someone crosses the threshold. There have been an audacious few who have seated themselves at the piano (something the hotel prohibits) and felt unseen hands pushing them away.

Chris Bechard with Alpenglow Media took one of the most compelling photographs I've seen of an ectoplasm form. The picture was taken January 18, 2004, using a Nikon D100 camera on a tripod with 10-second exposures @ f/5.6 with an 80 mm (28-80mm zoom) Nikon-G lens and circular polarizer filter and a film speed setting at ISO/200. The photograph was taken following staff reports of a period of out-of-the-ordinary activity.

Chris Bechard told me the following story that precipitated his being at the hotel with his camera:

"A paranormal research team had been doing some snooping around at the hotel. The front desk clerk that I was good friends with back then had called me in the early evening, stating that she had experienced a Bible flying off the bookcase at the front desk and chairs in the Music Room being strewn about after just being set up for a banquet only moments before. She called me and told me to get my camera and get over there, so I did.

"The heck of the matter was, I went around and photographed all over the hotel, with my camera on a tripod. I was nervous with anticipation that I might see something—I did not. I took a couple hundred images on my camera to show her. It was she that caught something unusual on a few of the frames, so I went home and scrutinized each one. Some of the photos showed images I had not seen while taking the photos. They showed up on the film. There were things I could not explain...I still can't." (Chris Bechard/Alpenglow Media)

One of the photos from the Music Room shows a woman seated at the piano wearing a long gown, high collar and up-swept hair-do. Her hands are on the keyboard. Standing next to her is what appears to be a small girl, wearing a long pinafore dress, with long curled hair held in place with a bow. You can see an ectoplasm-type material swirling through the forms and a bright orb rests each transparent shape.

Chris Bechard's photo of Flora Stanley's ghost in the Music Room.

Jerry B., former General Manager of the Stanley Hotel told this author that he has himself noticed the pungent smell of roses suddenly appear from nowhere when he has been in the Music Room. He told me that there is no build-up to it; it's just suddenly there, then gone just as fast. He said he has smelled it before in the Lobby as well.

The interesting thing is that there are no roses in the Lobby or Music Room unless a wedding reception is in progress or a special centerpiece is added. The times these fragrances have been sensed was when the Music Room was empty, with only Flora's beloved Steinway adorning the alcove. Likewise, the Lobby was void of flower arrangements.

Becky R., Naples, Florida. December, 2014. "We were enjoying Estes Park's winter beauty. It was one of those gorgeous Colorado days when it was 70 degrees and the sun sparkled on the snow-capped Rockies. My husband and I stopped at the Stanley Hotel just to look around. The hotel is amazing. The views are breathtaking. We stopped to grab a snack and took it out on the verandah to stare at the sun on the snow. I happened to glance to my left where there were some doors at the end of the verandah. A woman was standing there, peering at me through the glass. It wasn't her appearance that startled me at first, it was the eerie feeling that came over me as she seemed to be looking right through me. In fact, I had the feeling I was invisible to her. Then I noticed her hair piled up in an old-fashioned bun and her high lace collar. It was then I realized I couldn't make out the rest of her from the waist down.

"I turned quickly to my husband and grabbed him. "Look over there!" I whispered frantically. "Do you see that woman in the doorway?" He looked surprised at my frightened face and looked past me toward where I was pointing. I looked as well. The woman was gone. He asked what was wrong. What had I seen? When I told him, his eyebrows went up in the way it does when he thinks I'm nuts. His mouth curled into a twisted grin and I wanted to punch him. I know what I saw. When I asked inside which room the door leads to, they said the Music Room. It was then I saw the woman's portrait over the registration desk and felt like throwing up. It was the woman I'd seen in the doorway glass."

Flora Stanley.

*Gianni Markus, Newark, New Jersey. June, 2012.* "I was visiting the Stanley Hotel in June of 2012. I was with three of my girlfriends. We were just there to have lunch, grab a souvenir from the gift shop and go through Rocky Mountain National Park on the way to Granby. Melissa was showing me her scarf she bought as we were all standing in the lobby. Just then we heard the sweetest piano music coming from a room at the end of the lobby. It said Music Room over the door so we thought maybe a recital was going on. We walked over to the closed door and listened. It had this lilting, sadness to it. The music ended, but there were no applause like I suspected there would be. We waited a minute and Melissa cracked the door open. The room was completely empty except for a few tables with tablecloths folded on them, and a few scattered chairs.

"Maybe whoever was playing went out that door over there," Melissa said, pointing to a door across the room that looked like it leads out onto a balcony. We shrugged and closed the door. Just as we were about to walk away, it started playing again. Surprised, we turned and before I could stop her, Melissa whips open the door. The music stopped in mid-key. No one was sitting at the piano. It's the first time I have ever had what they call goose bumps, but right then, they were running all over my body."

Some people have reported seeing Flora Stanley's image in the large glass windows of the Music Room, staring at them with her drooping mouth and sad eyes. Often the smell of roses would waft through the room at those times. One report was that she was seen floating outside the glass going from window to window. People tend to feel a sudden melancholy come over them when they see her visage and smell the floral scent. It may be due to her possible dealings with manic-depression, or the blindness that robbed her of the views of the Rockies from her beloved Music Room.

# The Pinon Room

Entrance to the Pinon and Billiard Rooms at the east end of the Lobby.
Photo by Rebecca F. Pittman.

The Pinon Room at the Stanley was originally the men's Smoking Room when the hotel first opened, as mentioned earlier. It has a decidedly masculine feeling to it, in part owing to the massive keystone fireplace dominating the south wall. Years of tobacco smoke and conversation have been absorbed into these Colorado stones.

Reports of paranormal activity from this room, and the Billiard Room which is through the adjoining doors to the north, are quite frequent. While they tend to revolve around appearances put in by Mr. Stanley and he strolls his favorite area at the hotel, the reports are by no means restricted to the proprietor's spectral form.

Giant keystone fireplace in the Pinon Room. It remains the largest of its kind in Colorado.

Mark Williams, Los Angeles, California. May, 2011. "My girlfriend and I were walking through the Pinon Room at the Stanley Hotel. It was a pretty quiet day...not a lot of people around. I liked this room a lot. It was a little dark and the fireplace is super huge. So we're standing there talking about what the room was like in the 1900s when the hotel opened and all of sudden a really strong smell of pipe tobacco started filling the air. It actually made my girlfriend nauseous to the point she went out into the lobby. I looked into the billiard room next door since the door was open to it, thinking it was coming from there but no one was in there. I mean this was really strong, like 50 guys all blowing smoke at the same time.

"Just as I was about to leave, because to be honest, it was making me a little queasy, it just stops. It was gone just as fast as it came. That's really strange because a smell like that doesn't just cut off. When my girlfriend came back into the room she was really surprised and asked if I opened the door to the balcony to air it out. Pretty weird."

Pinon Room. Photo courtesy of Rebecca F. Pittman.

Monica Roberts, St. Paul, Minnesota. February, 2009. "I wanted to submit a story from a time I was at the Stanley Hotel in 2009. I was with my parents on a vacation to Estes Park. I'm 19. We were getting ready to eat lunch at the hotel and were just walking around and looking at the rooms on the main floor. It wasn't super busy at that time of the year. When we walked into the room called the Pinon Room I remember not wanting to be there. I couldn't explain it, and my Dad was teasing me about it. I had liked all the other rooms but this one made me feel funny. My heart started beating a little faster and I just felt like I wanted to get out.

"I told my family I would meet them in the restaurant and started for the doors. One of them had been propped open. They are swinging doors. Just as I got to it, it swung shut in my face. It was like someone grabbed it and shoved it really hard. It almost hit me. My Mom came running over to see if I was okay. She opened it back up and I bolted out of there. I had barely made it to the lobby when it suddenly swung shut really hard behind me. I had the feeling I wasn't welcome in that room."

The mirror cabinet in the Pinon Room has a fascinating history of its own. It was once part of the original bar housed in what was then called the Dunraven Grille at the hotel. F.O. was not a big fan of alcohol and it wasn't until 1946 that an actual bar was installed at the Stanley. When the hotel later fell onto hard times, it was looted and the original bar, along with its brass railing, disappeared. This cabinet is all that is left.

The TV version of *The Shining* was shot at the Stanley Hotel. The mirrored cabinet is featured in some of the scenes with Jack Torrance.

Steven Weber as Jack Torrance in the TV mini-series version of Stephen King's *The Shining*, shot at the Stanley Hotel.

Orbs near the mirror cabinet in the Pinon Room. These were shot in several successive photos. They moved erratically around the mirror and out as dust particles.
Photo courtesy of Marilyn Rudgers.

Pinon Room. Mirror cabinet on the left, fireplace on the right. At the back are doors leading out to balcony. Photo Rebecca F. Pittman.

The mirror of the bar cabinet has been the reported sightings of several specters. Flora Stanley, F.O. Stanley and various unknown entities have peered out at the passing guests from this antique glass.

In the previous photo and the one below you can see a ghost image of what looks like an old Calvary soldier in the mirror of the original bar cabinet in the Pinon Room.

Close-up of ghost photo.

298

Kris Tennant is part of the investigative team of the Rocky Mountain Ghost Explorers. During a recent investigation at the Stanley Hotel she filmed some footage in the Pinon Room. When she looked back over her results she was surprised to see a spectral image forming outside the Pinon Room doors that lead out to the west balcony. It began as a mist-like ectoplasm and slowly evolves into a more solid mass on the video. The form is seen peering into the room and bears a resemblance to Flora Stanley's features. These black-and-white photos do not do the video justice. You can view it on Kristen's website at www.rockymountainghostexplorers.com.

Photo on left shows the mist at the window beginning to take shape. The photo on the right shows it solidifying.
Video stills courtesy of Kris Tennant with Rocky Mountain Ghost Explorers.

Kris's comparison of the ectoplasm to Flora Stanley.
Photo courtesy of Kris Tennant.

# The Billiard Room

The original billiard ball rack and balls made in the J.C. Cane Company
in Boston.
Photo by Ron Bueker

Stories emanating from the Billiard Room at the Stanley Hotel
of the other-worldly type are varied and interesting. The expected
reports of hearing the familiar sounds of a pool game underway
(when the room is completely void of tables and people), are sent to
me and told to the hotel regularly. Yet, there are a few that have
surfaced since the publication of the first edition of this book that are

out of the ordinary.

Rick Haverson, Dayton, Ohio. September, 2014. "My family was staying with some friends at their cabin in Estes Park in 2014. We're from Ohio and it was a treat to be in the mountains in the fall. There were a lot of elk running around Estes Park, which delighted my 10-year-old son to no end. My two little daughters, who are 7 and 9 were not as thrilled.

"Our friends took us to the Stanley Hotel for dinner one night during our stay. After dinner, we looked around. I wanted to see Room 217 because I'm a huge King buff but we were told it was booked and the hotel had to respect the guest's privacy. All very understandable. My wife and daughters were looking at the Music Room with the piano. My son Jeff and I went into the rooms next door. They were both set up with tables and chairs for a conference or something. When we walked into the room where the billiard tables used to be my son stops and points at a big mirror on the far side of the room by some steps going up to some hotel rooms. I looked and didn't see what he was pointing at.

"What?" I asked.

"There's an old guy playing pool in the mirror," he announced.

I looked again and saw only our reflections and that of the room's tables and chairs.

"Too much sun, Jeff," I said playfully and messed up his hair.

"Dad!" he said in a way only a 10-year-old can when they are looking at you as an idiot, "he's right there! There are two other old guys standing around a table holding sticks and watching him. He just hit the ball with the stick! Now he's walking around the table and they are all patting him on the back. I don't hear anything though."

My son has never played pool. I have no knowledge of him being around a pool table yet he described the scene to me in great detail. He became upset when he looked around him and did not see a pool table or the people he was describing. He looked at me as if to see if I thought he was nuts, and then ran out of the room to find my wife."

Shamir O., Salem Massachusetts. May, 2010. "I come from Witch Country. I get spooky stuff. After seeing three bare-chested Indians walk through the room at the hotel called the Billiard Room, and then disappear through the wall on the west side of the room, I gotta give you guys credit. That is one whacked-out place!"

Harve Richards, Denver, Colorado. (No date given.) "I have been to the Stanley Hotel several times. I am a Stanley Steam Car aficionado. After ah tour completed I had taken, I walked around the hotel. There was some of the staff clearing away tables in the Billiard Room from what looked like a wedding. I apologized for interrupting them and they were really nice and said I was free to look around.

"I was studying the padded bench along the wall at one side of the room and could hear one of the men right behind me. Without turning around, I asked, "Is this the original cushion for the bench or is this new?"

I felt this weird chill go through me. All the sounds of clinking glasses and voices that had been going on behind me just shut off. It was the deepest quiet I've ever experienced. My ears felt like someone had stuffed cotton in them. I remember the hair on my arms stand up and feelings of electricity go through me. I had this weird thought that if I turned around I would see something I didn't want to see. I finally turned my head and the minute I did, all the noise came flooding back and people were bustling around the room like before. The hairs were still standing upright on my arms and my scalp was tingling. I don't know what happened. I just know it was a very strange occurrence."

Taylor R., Ogden, Utah. January, 2009. "Just wondering if anyone else sees Native Americans in the Billiard Room at the hotel? I saw their reflection in the glass windows in that room one night when my husband and I stayed overnight. A friend of mine said her cousin saw these men that were wearing animal hides walk in front of her and go through a wall. The ones I saw were two men and a woman. My friend's cousin said they didn't look at her. They just walked across the room. She couldn't see through them but they were also not really clear. Like an old faded movie. Is the hotel built on old Indian grounds maybe?"

Stories of F.O. Stanley are the most-frequently reported paranormal sightings in the Billiard Room, but stories such as those of seeing Native Americans and even an occasional mountain man have been turned in. It seems to be a very active room at the hotel.

# The MacGregor Room

The entrance to the Macgregor Room entrance flanked by F.O. Stanley portrait (left) and Dunraven's (right). Ron Bueker

Perhaps the area at the west end of the Stanley Hotel Lobby most conveys the hotel's history in one anecdotal grouping. The MacGregor Room's double doors lead into the Stanley's largest gathering place. Named for Alexander Q. MacGregor, its position between the two portraits of the hotel's creator, F.O. Stanley, and his nemesis, Lord Dunraven, is poetic and accurate. MacGregor was an early settler in Estes Park, who, along with a handful of other hearty souls, went to battle to stop Lord Dunraven of Ireland from unlawfully scooping up most of Estes Valley for his own personal use. Due to MacGregor's efforts, Dunraven finally gave up on the location and moved on. Enter F.O. Stanley who bought up Dunraven's parcel of land and built his famous hotel. So there hang the two portraits of the two men who owned this parcel of prime mountain property, with the name of the man in the middle, who helped facilitate the final outcome.

An empty MacGregor Room. This area is used for weddings, conferences, the Stanley Sunday Brunch and other special events. Ron Bueker.

As mentioned in the former chapter on the hotel's early history, the MacGregor Room was the original Dining Room when the venue opened in 1909. It remained such for quite some time before a formal dining area was added at the rear of the hotel. It is this room that housekeeper Elizabeth Wilson landed when she was blown through the ceiling from Room 217 above. We will go into detail about this famous occurrence at the hotel when we talk about Room 217's ghost stories, but for now, suffice it to say that Mrs.

Wilson landed on a dining room table in this room, breaking both her ankles after a gas explosion from 217 blew her through the floor and into the Dining Room (MacGregor Room) below.

Here also is the setting that most Stephen King's fans associate with his cameo appearance in his T.V. mini-series of *The Shining*, shot at the Stanley Hotel. King appeared as the band leader, frenetically conducting from the apron of the large stage that dominates this room.

Stephen King in his cameo appearance for the TV mini-series of *The Shining* shot on stage at the Stanley Hotel MacGregor Room.

306

The views from the large windows of the MacGregor Room are beautiful: some facing the mountains, other looking out over a reflecting pond or manicured walkways and historic out buildings. Some, who have stood at these windows looking out at the moonlight drenched mountains, have seen other things as well.

Bethany W. New York City, New York. July 20, 2013. "Here is a story I thought you might find interesting. I was at the Stanley Hotel in July last year. We were staying the Manor House but wanted to look around the main hotel after dinner. I followed my husband into the MacGregor Room. There were other people there milling around. I noticed a group of them were gathered around one of the windows facing the front of the hotel and making a lot of excited gestures. I figured it was an elk or bear on the grounds. I went over to the window next to them so as not to butt in on their group and looked out. I was looking for a large animal. One of the people next to me said, "There is goes again!" I looked to where she was pointing and saw this band of blue light streaking through the pine trees just outside the window. One of the men standing with her said, "It's just some car headlights coming up the road." The other people, including some guys, disagreed with him, saying car lights aren't blue, and they wouldn't be coming at the angle all of them were looking at.

"Just as my husband came over to me to see what all the fuss was about, the blue lights streaked across the front yard area again, only this time they climbed a tree vertically! They actually went up the trunk and disappeared into the branches. By now one woman is screaming, and other people are coming over. All in all we saw the light four times before it stopped appearing. It was three stands of light, all the same color of blue, laid on top of each other like guitar strings. It was not headlights. Even the guy claiming that changed his mind. There were no cars visible."

Rodriguez Mathis. Rapid City, South Dakota. "We had my sister's wedding in the MacGregor Room. There were 75 people there. During my brother's wedding toast to her and her husband, all the lights went out. It was night time, so it was kinda scary. A few people were making jokes about ghosts. There was this sound of glass clanking overhead. Like little bells almost. I thought it was chandelier glass tinkling. My mom got nervous and said she was afraid the lights were going to fall on us because they all heard these glass prisms clinking real hard against each other.

"Just then the lights come on and we all look up. There aren't no [ms] chandeliers up there. Its [ms] these big white glass balls handing down. Even they managed to swing and hit each other they wouldn't make that little tinkling sound we heard. It was really freaky."

Light fixtures in MacGregor Room.

Stories of the lighting fixtures in the MacGregor Room have been long standing. Many have seen them swinging on their own accord. These are heavy globes that no amount of vibration from overhead could have set them moving at the pace this author and others have seen.

Staff members at the hotel have reported seeing the lights turn off and on of their own volition.

Most of the stories coming from this area are those of music playing when no one is in the room, and that of small children laughing and running across the floor when no one is there.

Selma Ortiz. Stanley Hotel staff Oct. 2001-May 2004. "I was a dining room supervisor/waitress at the Cascades Restaurant at the Stanley Hotel. One day I was in the kitchen and I heard lots of small kids running and playing and having fun in the MacGregor dining room, so I peeked in to see what fun they were having. There was no one there, so I closed the door and a few minutes later you could hear them again running and playing just like in a school yard. So again I looked in and no one was there. I went to the front desk to ask if there were kids there and they said "No." No kids checked in at that time or seen on the first floor."

Deb Winters. Loveland, Colorado. (No date given) "I've been to two events in the MacGregor Room. One for a wedding, and one for the *Shining* Halloween Ball they have every Halloween. At the wedding a tablecloth went flying off a table by the stage…glasses, dishes and everything. Everybody was seated there so there was no explanation for it suddenly swooping off like someone grabbed it. At the *Shining* Ball my friend Orie was dressed as a vampire. Two people came up to him and asked how he got his fake blood to stay looking fresh all night. He looked down to his sleeve they were looking at and said, "I didn't put any blood on my clothes. Just my neck." It was pretty scary. He put his finger in this blob on his sleeve and it was wet and looked like real blood. He went into the bathroom and washed it off but he kept looking back at his sleeve the rest of the night like he expected it to come back."

George Onafrey. Lakeland, Florida. October, 2010. "My wife and I were at the Shining Halloween party. There were a lot of creative costumes, some pretty expensive. I asked a guy while I was in the Men's room at the hotel how he got his face to glow like that. He smiled, went into one of the stalls and never came out. In fact, when I peeked beneath the door, there was no one there."

A couple from the *Shining* Halloween Ball. Photo courtesy of
Estes Park Trail Gazette.

On March 23, 2008, Nancy and Mike C. from Tampa,
Florida were visiting with friends at their cabin in Estes Park. The
men had been fishing all day and the women had talked them into
getting cleaned up and taking them out for a nice dinner. They
decided on the Stanley Hotel.

The foursome entered the hotel Lobby, commenting on its beauty
and warmth and headed toward the Cascades Restaurant. The double
pocket doors to the MacGregor Room were open and it appeared to
be empty.

"Let's peek inside," Nancy whispered to the others, who followed
her into the large room. "That's where Stephen King was standing
when he played the bandleader in the TV series," she whispered
excitedly, pointing to a spot on the apron of the stage.

The others walked over to the stage and sat down on its edge,
discussing the movie and how it differed from the original with Jack
Nicholson.

"The two guys were debating who made the best Jack Torrance,
Jack Nicholson or Steven Webber who played him in the mini-series.
They were talking a little too loudly and I was about to tell them to

quiet down, as I wasn't sure we were supposed to be in the room, when all of a sudden the gold drapes that are hanging at the back of the stage started to billow out. My first thought was that some staff member was coming from someplace behind the curtain to tell us to please leave. The curtains settled down...no one came out from between them, and then....they did it again. This time they blew out so far onto the stage that you could see beneath them. There was no one there. I got nervous and my husband turned around to see the curtains, about 7' away from him heaving in and out as though they were breathing. He got up and walked over to them, saying there was probably a door opening and closing behind them or a window. He pulled the still heaving curtain aside and looked behind it. There was nothing there but a small alcove stuffed with extra tables and chairs. It wasn't very big. As he stood there, watching the curtains go in and out, the hair on the top of his head started to stand straight up...like he was standing in electricity. He jumped back and almost fell down. Then just as suddenly as they had started, the curtains became still and his hair settled back down onto his head. My husband's hair is rather long-- it touches his shoulders. It was the strangest thing I have ever seen. Then the knucklehead goes back over and pulls on the curtains again to see if it would happen again! Nothing happened. By now, I just want to get out of there. So, he jumps down from the stage and starts making a joke about old hotels being drafty. The minute he said that, the curtains started billowing out again. I grabbed his arm to pull him toward the open doors. My friends were already hightailing it out to the Lobby. When we got to the door and looked back, the curtains were still. My girlfriend told him she thought whatever was in the room didn't like how loud and disrespectful he was and the moving curtains and electrical shock were to get him to leave. "It's almost as if the curtains were trying to sweep you off the stage," she laughed.

Stage in MacGregor Room. Photo by Rebecca F. Pittman

"After dinner, we peeked back into the room, but the curtains weren't moving. My husband asked the bartender if anyone had reported the curtains moving by themselves on the stage—were there any vents or breezes back there? The bartender looked at him like he had three heads, chuckled and said, "No... that's a new one!"

I would love to learn what that was someday."

Mary Ann M.is a sweet, warm woman who is part of the wait staff at the Cascades Restaurant in the Stanley Hotel. She has been with the hotel for over 18 years. When I asked her if she had had any paranormal experiences at the hotel, one in particular came to mind.

"I was working the night shift and as it turned out, I was the last one to clean up that night. There is something a little spooky about being the last one in the MacGregor Room and in charge of turning off all the lights. The switch for them is inside the swinging door to the kitchen and I stepped inside the doorway and turned them off, one by one until the room was completely dark.

"I went down to the parking lot and got into my car and began driving off when I happened to look up at the giant windows of the MacGregor Room and saw the light closest to the southwest window shining brightly. I was surprised to see it on as I had just made sure they were all off and actually walked through the dark room on my way out.

"The next night, I was again in charge of turning off the lights. This time I double-checked to make sure they were all off, especially the one I had seen lit the night before. It's the light right beneath Room 217 and I remember thinking that it was at that exact spot that poor Mrs. Wilson had landed when she was blown through the floor from a gas explosion.

"Well, I am in my car and driving away from the hotel when I look up at the window and the hanging light was on again! Same one! None of the others were on. I remembered thinking that maybe Mrs. Wilson was trying to let me know she was still around."

December 30, 1970, housekeeper Arty R. was to clean the dance floor in the MacGregor Room for the special New Year's dance for which the Stanley opened every winter. She entered the MacGregor Room, and it felt like she was entering another time. People were dressed in period dress: long skirts, high collars, and tuxedos. Concerned, she turned around and walked back to the night clerk at the front desk to ask her what was going on. The clerk was eating her dinner and appeared not only not to notice Arty, but apparently not to notice any of the noise emanating from the MacGregor. Arty returned to the room, where she went about her business. She did not feel threatened by the room full of spirits, and they appeared oblivious to her scrubbing. (Susan S. Davis, Stanley Museum, Kingsfield, Maine)

Ghost dancer's illustration.

There have been many stories of phantom parties heard and seen in the MacGregor Room. Some have reported hearing music, the sound of voices and laughter, the clatter of tableware and crystal, but seeing nothing. However while walking through the large ballroom they are aware of bumping into unseen things, having to dodge to the right or left as they encounter invisible dancers and tables.

Others have reported seeing the scene play out before them as if it was happening in real time; dancers from another era waltzing about the room in styles and fashions of another era. They are oblivious to the spectator standing there, mouth agape and shivers running up their arms. The thing I find interesting is that the period pieces reported reflect not one, but several eras from the past.

Madame Vera, the wonderful psychic at the Stanley Hotel told me she "sees" images from the 20's, 30's, 40's, etc. She calls them "smoke in the walls," a term I particularly like. There have been enough reportings coming from this 100-year-old ballroom to make it compelling, to say the least. The fact that it resides one floor beneath Room 217 makes it all the more delicious.

# The Whiskey Bar and Cascades Restaurant

The Cascades Restaurant. Photo courtesy of *EPTrailGazette.*

The Cascades Restaurant and Whiskey Bar location were once the area of the hotel which housed the Children's Dining Room, Barber Shop, back porch and a section of the courtyard.

Once accessed from the Dining Room (today's MacGregor Room), due to a coat check and cigar desk blocking the way to the where the door is today, patrons of the hotel were not originally offered a bar in the traditional sense. F.O. was not a proponent of heavy liquor.

In the 21$^{st}$ Century bars offering beer and hard liquors are moving over to accommodate the trendier martini and whiskey bars. Appealing to a more sophisticated and knowledgeable palette, these toney new venues offer up hundreds of variations on their chosen libation.

While the Whiskey Bar and Cascades Restaurant pander to the discerning traveling public, the rooms' histories are no so fast to join the modern day confluence.

The Whiskey Bar at the Stanley Hotel. Photo courtesy of the *Estes Park Trail Gazette.*

Matt R. Aubrey. Tallahassee, Florida. June, 2014. "Hanging out with friends in Estes. Went to the hotel for a few brews. We were sitting at the bar watching some sports when—not lying—my buddy's glass slides past his plate a few inches. We're all cracking up cuz he's gone white as a sheet. We told him it probably had a wet bottom and just slid on the slick counter. He puts it back and about ten minutes later it slides again, only the other way. Now he's freaking out. We checked and the bar wasn't wet and his glass wasn't either on the bottom. I guess Dunraven was thirsty."

Alicia V. Bangor, Maine. (No date given) "I'm from Bangor so of course I'm going to check out a Stephen King locale. I was on vacay with a few girlfriends. We stayed in Room 418 at the Stanley. 217 was booked. So we're eating in the bar area of the hotel, having appetizers and stuff. The empty chair across from us at a table where a couple was sitting slides away from their table like someone kicked it. The lady jumps so hard her glass turns over. A waitress comes over to see what the fuss is and starts mopping the wine out of this woman's plate. I hear her husband tell the waitress that the chair just slid away from the table on its own. She didn't look convinced but smiled, slid it back and said she would get the lady another glass of wine and some more food.

"The woman is clearly freaked out. She's looking under the table at the chair legs and begging her husband to tell her if he is doing it as a prank. Which is pretty much what we're all thinking when just then it slams away again. I was looking at his feet when it happened. He wasn't near it. My friend jumped and we all laughed, but the woman who spilled her drink got up and left. The guy hung around to pay the bill and I heard him tell the waitress that he thought the place was haunted. Some guy seated next to them said, "Duh!"

Rod Burgess. Longmont, Colorado. July, 2010. "I've had dinner at the Stanley a few times. Their chef is pretty good and the service always nice. My wife and I had just finished eating and I was getting my wallet out of my back pocket. Just as I reached around my back for it I felt this cold spot on my wrist. It felt like an ice cube. I jerked my hand away and looked down and behind me to see if maybe I bumped a serving cart with cold drinks or something. Nothing is there. My wife is looking at me with this amused face. I put my hand around again to get the wallet and it happens again. A cold spot about 2 inches wide on my wrist. Now I'm worried. What the heck is it? I tell my wife. She slides into the chair next to me and puts her hand down there. Nothing happens. She makes a quip about me trying to get out of paying. I reach again and it happens again. Same place. This time I leave it there while I look around my arm. Nothing. I go ahead and get the wallet out but my hand is shaking a little. When the waiter came to pick up the tab my wife jokingly tells him that a ghost is trying to get at my husband's wallet. He laughs, picks up a couple of plates and says, "You should have let him pay. He hangs around her a lot. A woman last week sitting where you are said something icy kept touching her neck." I may try sitting somewhere else next time."

Reports of napkins moving and lights sporadically flickering have all been reported in these two rooms that share a large, welcoming alcove of the hotel. Their doors lead out to the back courtyard where a waterfall, rock groupings and up-lighting invite guests to sit in this mountain retreat's open air vignette.

It is also from this courtyard that a few people have seen faces peering down on them from guest room windows overhead; Lord Dunraven's visage being the most-oft reported.

Back courtyard of the Stanley Hotel viewed from upstairs' guest room. Photo courtesy of Trip Advisor.

# The Kitchen

A report of the Stanley Hotel's first floor would not be complete without the stories coming from the kitchen. This area is accessed through a small doorway behind the Whiskey Bar. Staff working in the kitchen turn in reports on a fairly regular basis concerning the sounds of clinking glasses, the ice machine, and black shadow people on the back stairs.

J.T. Thompson, Chief Engineer at the Stanley Hotel is a wonderfully efficient man who helped me tremendously when I was researching the book and doing some faux bois painting on the main floor. He told me he has had strange happenings in the hotel kitchen, just inside the door to the beverage area. He heard noises near an area where stacks of glasses are typically kept. He went to investigate it and found no one in the area. As he turned to leave, they began clinking again as though someone was stacking them against each other. He turned to look at the rows of glistening glassware. Nothing was moving. It happened again, the sound of clinking glass. He was unable to explain it, but "it gave me the creeps," J.T. told me.

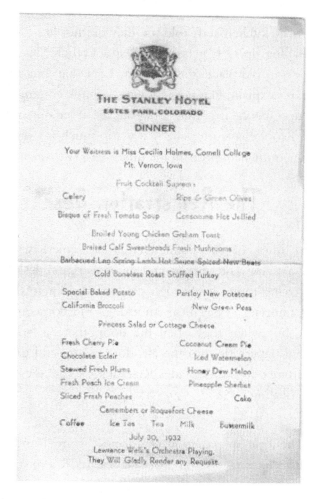

Menu from July 30, 1932. Lawrence Welk's Orchestra is playing.
Photo courtesy of Linda Elmarr with the Stanley Museum, Estes Park.

Selma Ortiz. Stanley Hotel staff. Oct. 2001-May 2004. "I was a dining room supervisor/waitress at the Cascades Restaurant at the Stanley Hotel. On the top of the stair case by the kitchen where we would deliver room service we would catch a glimpse of Dunraven's ghost watching us. We would go back to see and he'd be gone. We also saw him by the elevator."

Some of the kitchen staff told me they did not like being there late at night cleaning up. "It gets kind of spooky here," one young man told me. "It's an old place, things creak, I get that, but sometimes it's stuff you can't explain, like pots moving, sounds coming from the ice machine like someone is getting a big bucket of ice out and there is no one there. People have quit cuz it was too much for them. One girl had someone untie her apron all the time when she was doing dishes."

# The Registration Desk

The first floor of the Stanley Hotel is replete with stories of paranormal activity. The staff behind the registration desk has reported something trying to get in through the locked door to the hallway by the grand staircase. They hear knocking, and someone rattling the door knob, but when they open the door, there is no one around. Some of said papers fly into the air, doors slam, and the office door near the entrance to the Cascades Restaurant sometimes shudders like someone is beating on it.

There is a plethora of stories from front desk clerks reporting hearing music from the MacGregor Room and the Music Room. Others have heard the elevator operating when no one was aboard. There are two entrances to this area, one directly into the front desk and the other into the office that adjoins it. In the past the staff has stated the old brass doorknobs have jiggled late at night as though someone wanted entry. When they have checked the hallways on the other side of the doors, no one was there.

Several desk clerks have reported looking up from their duties to see F.O. Stanley standing there, looking down on them as though inspecting their work.

Sometime during 2003, Clarissa D., night clerk at the front desk, felt someone looking at her or over her shoulder as she was working. She looked up, but saw no one. It happened again; again, she looked up and saw no one. Soon again, she felt the presence, but this time she raised her eyes only, rather than her head, and there was F.O. Stanley standing at the counter watching her. When she raised her head to look in his eyes, F.O. faded away. *(Susan S. Davis, Stanley Ghost Stories)*

Dave M. walked into the massive hotel lobby in the spring of 2005 and stood staring at the magnificent staircase before him. Light was pouring in from the large Palladian windows that crowned the landing leading to the second floor. As he stood admiring it, he noticed someone smiling at him from the front desk in the form of a greeting. He smiled back, and walked over to the large front desk counter.

The woman behind the counter wore a long dress with a high lace collar. Her hair was piled into an old-fashioned bun. He particularly remembered her elaborate butterfly pin that was holding her hair in place; it dominated the left side of her head.

Just as Dave was about to speak to her, requesting room prices for an upcoming anniversary he was planning for he and his wife, a young man came through a door to the left of the reception area, behind the counter. He was smiling brightly, saying, "Good morning and welcome to the Stanley Hotel!" As he did so, the lady in the long gown, smiled once more at Dave and faded from view!

"What may I help you with today?" the cheerful clerk asked him, placing his hands on the counter top in efficient readiness.

All Dave could do was stutter, try to speak, and stutter again. Not being able to wrap his mind around what had just happened, he merely grabbed a brochure from the desk counter and sputtered, "I'll get back to you," as which point he departed the Lobby.

"I couldn't bring myself to tell this guy that a lady just faded into the cubbyholes," he laughed later. "I took my wife elsewhere for our anniversary but I am determined to go back there and check this whole thing out. I mean...that is just *WHACK!* I thought the old car in the Lobby was cool, but dang!"

There are several stories, as I've reported, of desk clerks seeing the rattan rocking chair on the front veranda move when no wind or people are around. These clerks stand behind the reception desk and gaze out the window at the increasingly common occurrence. Paranormal research teams have set up cameras on the porch to try and catch its movement, even taping toilet paper streamers to the other chairs to measure wind or movement. It seems to begin rocking on its own accord, as the reception desk clerks look on with fascination.

# The Gift Shop

I was unable to unearth many stories concerning the Gift Shop. With the daily activity that goes on in there, it is probably difficult to witness anything through the entire bustle. There is a decided feeling of someone watching you if you are in the back office area. Its fan-shaped windows overlook the Billiard Room on the other side. The times I was there interviewing its owner, I would get the sense that if I looked up, there would be a face at the window watching. This area was once part of the back verandah.

It is hard to feel "haunted" when you're surrounded by a plethora of enticements in the form of jewelry, clothing, toys, books, mugs, photography and whimsical home décor. However, one glance at the section of the gift shop dedicated to The Shining with its host of movie memorabilia, and the shivers return.

Chrysalis Gift Shop tribute to The Shining.
Photo by Denise Brandy.

Chapter Twenty-One

# THE HAUNTING OF THE STANLEY HOTEL:
## The Second Floor

"Ghosts make the papers along with celebrities every day of the week." (Dr. John Markway, The Haunting, a movie based on Shirley Jackson's book, The Haunting of Hill House)

## Room 217

Without doubt, the most talked about guest room at the Stanley Hotel is the notorious Room 217. While Stephen King's fortuitous stay in this room during his virgin visit to the hotel in 1975, and the hotel's subsequent inspiration for his blockbuster book The Shining, may have put the second floor room on the map, it was reported to be haunted long before he arrived.

So what does some remnants of carpet, scraps of antique wallpapered drywall and shrapnel have to do with a ghost story in this room. Plenty!

Room 217. Photo by Ricky Ranvich.

"It was a dark and stormy night..." This is how our story begins. It was the evening of June 25, 1911. A rocky mountain thunderstorm was shuddering the rafters of the two-year-old hotel. Suddenly the power went out. The hotel staff hurried the worried guest to the lobby and asked them wait there while the back-up acetylene gas lamps were lit in each guest room.

A small gas leak was emanating from the dual light fixture in Room 217, slowly building up an invisible vapor wafting out into the room that was at that time called the Presidential Suite. It was an L-shaped room that took up the space that now houses two rooms: 217 and 215.

Housekeeper Elizabeth Wilson from Lancaster, Pennsylvania went through the rooms on the 2nd floor with her lit candle, turning on each back-up gas switch and lighting the fixture. Meanwhile, in Room 217, the odorless gas was expanding. Ms. Wilson came to the door of the Presidential Suite and turned the doorknob. The moment she passed into the room with the lit candle, and explosion blew off the northwest face of the hotel. She was blown through the floor of the room, landing in the MacGregor Room below. It is here that the story takes several detours, depending on which newspaper article you read from the time.

Some of the area papers report that the explosion destroyed 10% of the 70,000 square foot building. It was essentially the entire west wing. Dubbed a compression fire by some articles, it was said the fire was extinguished on its own, saving the massive wood hotel.

*The Denver Post*, however, ran its own story stating a fire did break and "added to the damage." According to this article there two other maids involved in the explosion. One was Eva Colbern who was supposedly blown through the wall onto a hotel porch but was merely stunned. A third maid, Mary Donaldson, was also caught in the explosion. She and Ms. Colbern each grabbed fire extinguishers and attacked the blaze, putting it out. The Rocky Mountain News reported there were actually two explosions, about an hour apart. The only thing the newspapers agree on is that it happened around 8 p.m.

An example of housekeeping maids during the early 1900s.

The explosion details were not the only disparities in the reports. Ms. Wilson's name appears in various accounts as Elizabeth Wilson, Lizzie Leitenbergher, and Elizabeth Lambert. Lambert may have come from the name of the General Manager of the hotel at the time whose name was Alfred Lamborn. *The Rocky Mountain News* reported that Mr. Lamborn, his wife and daughter were having dinner in the hotel Dining Room, which is today called the MacGregor Room. Suddenly, an explosion rocked the hotel, the ceiling above them caved in. "A large steel girder from the second floor crashed down, landing between the three, smashing the table," stated the News. "The party escaped with bruises."

Other reports state the explosion and subsequent expulsion of Ms. Wilson through the floor happened "just as a fashionable throng of guests was finishing dinner."

It seems the 5 area newspapers differed as well on the extent of Ms. Wilson's injuries. Two have her mortally wounded, while two submit she sustained two broken ankles. The accepted version is that she did indeed break both ankles and Mr. Stanley paid all her medical bills from the Longmont hospital. After she recuperated she was made head chambermaid and worked at the hotel until her death in the 1950s.

But our story does not end here. It is merely the beginning. Elizabeth Wilson's ghost, and housekeeping habits, continues to haunt the room to this day. She reportedly folds guests' clothes occupying Room 217, and puts them away for them. She has been known to turn on the bathroom light for them in the wee hours of the morning, just in case they need the area illuminated for a midnight bathroom run. People have felt themselves tucked in, their pillows plumped up, and small items arranged neatly on a formerly cluttered desk. And perhaps most ominous of all, a black stain continues to appear just outside the bathroom door where the gas light had been, indicating the spot Ms. Wilson was blown through the floor.

Michele Bartlett. Richmond, Virginia. August, 2011.
"My boyfriend and I were staying in Room 217 at the Stanley. He

had his video recorder set up on a tri-pod pointed at the floor of the room in front of the bathroom. He heard a black stain sometimes appears there to show where a maid got blown through the floor shortly after the hotel opened.

"We went to bed and he left it running all night. I teased him it better be pointed only at the floor. The next morning he eagerly checked the feed. He yelled at me to come and look. I was really surprised to see a black spot in the video tape start out as a small dot and then grow to about the size of a small rug. It spread out like a water mark. It was pretty scary, but he was all excited. He marked the time the stain began to appear on the tape.

"We had to check out soon so we were cleaning up the room and packing. He went back to look at it again on the tape. I heard him swear and asked what was wrong. He told me to come over and look. He rewound it twice to the time stamp he wrote down but there was no dark spot. I told him he probably wrote down the wrong time. Bad idea! Now he starts watching it from the beginning...over 8 hours of tape! I told him he would have to do it at home...we had to check out. He was in a black mood all the way back to Denver.

"For three days he went over that tape and could not find the black stain again. I saw it as well. It was very obvious on the tape and we watched it grow. It took probably 3 minutes from the start of a small hole to a big one. I don't know what happened to it."

Daniel P. (No other info given) "Before calling it a night, I had opened a single window and set up a fan to blow the cool mountain breeze toward my bed. If you listened very carefully, you could just make out the sound of the wind blowing through the trees outside.

"While I lay sleeping (and probably snoring) under a mound of blankets, I felt my wife crawl out of bed. She padded across the carpet, either tiptoeing or taking tiny, quiet steps. I opened one sleepy eye, looked at the bedside clock, and then saw my wife standing at the open window, her face pressed against the screen.

"'You have to see this,' "she said and turned to me. She beamed, and her dimples deepened the way I'd always loved. She said, 'There's a family of elk just outside,' and the fan blew her long hair about her head so she looked like she was either floating or under water.

"I stared at her for a long time.

"My wife had been dead for five years."

Staff members of the hotel have reported seeing a woman dressed as a chambermaid wearing old-fashioned clothing in the area. Museum site manager Ellie DeLeone took a group to see the room one day and was so alarmed by the door first opening, then closing, that she refused to take tours to the room after that. (Susan S. Davis, *Stanley Ghost Stories*)

Daniel S. Parsons of Las Vegas, Nevada was on a Ghost Tour in 2007. He was enjoying the stories of the hotel's past and present. He had mainly signed up in order to learn more about the Stanley Steamer car he had seen in the Lobby. He was a professed car nut.

When the tour climbed to the second floor and was taken into Room 217, he was impressed with how nice the room was. Many people were taking pictures, hoping to capture an orb or an impression of Mrs. Wilson, the maid said to haunt the room. Others just wanted to a picture with the caption "Stephen King slept here."

As he watched in amusement, a motion from the corner of his eye caught his attention. He turned and looked to his left where he saw the bedspread's hem quivering lightly. As he watched, it lifted out slightly and "tugged" at the coverlet until an indentation made by an overzealous woman wanting her photo taken while sitting on the bed, was pulled straight, returning the spread to its pristine condition.

"I looked around to see if others had noticed, but no one seemed to, which I found amusing as I was one of the few on the tour who wasn't going "ga-ga" over the ghost stories and history of the room.

As the tour guide continued talking about a Mrs. Wilson and how she was known to keep the room tidy, I watched as the delicate leaves on a tall Boston fern to my left fluttered as though someone were brushing against them. I was the closest to the plant, with no else between the window where it stood. It was also only a foot or two away from the bed in the same area in which I had just seen the bedspread's movement. I will admit, I got a little chilled and chided myself for being so susceptible to the atmosphere and ghost stories. But, just at that moment, the door to the bathroom slammed shut, causing everyone to jump, then laugh nervously.

"Say what you want, I don't tell stories like this without substantiation. That is what happened and I can't explain it."

Arnie M. Branson, Missouri. February, 2015. "We were visiting friends of ours at the Stanley Hotel. They had booked Room 217. I was looking out the window of that room at the view of the mountains and listening to them talk about Stephen King and a maid that was blown up in the room. Those kinds of stories don't mean much to me. My parents had a haunted B&B when I was growing up and I got used to all the stories and strange stuff happening.

"I went into the bathroom and shut the door. While I was "sitting there," looking over the claw foot tub, the faucet in the sink suddenly shoots on. This blast of water hit the basin. I jumped a little because it was so sudden. Then it just shut off. I put it down to an old hotel with some typical maintenance issues. Then a wet towel draped over the shower curtain railing suddenly falls on the floor. I'm not sure how that can happen as I had just noticed it hanging there and it was halfway over the railing. You would have to yank it down. Just as I'm reaching for the toilet paper, the entire roll starts spinning, throwing paper onto the floor in a big ribbon. That was it. I finished up and ran back into the room. I told everyone it was time for lunch and headed out the door into the hallway."

⚿ Missy Calhoun. (No other info given.) "My friend Denise was at the Stanley Hotel for her friend's wedding. She had Room 217. She told me later when she got back home that her hairbrush kept moving no matter where she put it. She said her bobby pins always ended up in a trash can. It bothered so bad she threw the hairbrush away before she came home cuz she was afraid whatever had been moving it around might attach to it and follow her home."

⚿ Marshall R. Colorado Springs, Co. December, 2014. "I was in Estes Park for a Christmas party at my friend's condo not far from the Stanley Hotel. We went over to the hotel for a drink in the bar after the party. There were some guys at the bar talking about their shoes missing. I didn't pay much attention until the one guy said he was thinking of suing the hotel for his shoes.

"Turns out, he was staying in 217 and when he came back to his room after going around Estes his brand new expensive athletic shoes were missing. He was whining he spent $200 for them. Just then some guy comes in and puts a hand on this guy's shoulder and says your shoes are in the bathroom in the room "Dude." The guy gets really mad and says he looked there twice and besides, they were packed in a suitcase when he left. He hadn't unpacked yet."

Photos taken in Room 217 show a preponderance of digital abnormalities. Some show the room distorted as if going through a time warp, others show gigantic orbs usually appearing before the bathroom door where Ms. Wilson met her fate. A vertical purple bar appears frequently in the viewfinder and in the photo when pictures are shot at the end of the bed. Some people have seen strange shadows on the ceiling and walls that show up as well. While shadows are not unexpected, especially with moonlight and dancing pine boughs outside the window, when they take the form of a person and move in an unexplained manner, it can give one pause.

Renee S. Asheville, North Carolina. October, 2013. "I took this photo in my boyfriend's room at the Stanley Hotel. It's Room 217. Tell me what you think. To us it looks like a woman in an apron like a chambermaid might have worn. She looks like a light purple image and you can see through her."

Room 217 photo of what looks to be a chambermaid standing at the end of the bed.
Photo courtesy of Renee S. of Asheville, No. Carolina.

Back to the beginning of our story about Room 217: what does scraps of antique-papered drywall, some carpet and shrapnel have to do with the stories of Room 217? It turns out that while the hotel engineer was checking the air handlers in the tunnel beneath the hotel in February of 2015, he came across some large chunks of drywall with antique wallpaper adhered, scraps of pale green carpet and other fragments. These long-lost articles from 103 years ago matched the photos of the décor in Room 217 from the hotel's early days. Here was proof in Flora Stanley's distinct floral patterns of red, pinks and greens on the wallpaper, and a green carpet with her red and blue detailing. Over the years staff has still found old pieces of the exterior molding and even an antique doorknob on the less-used portions of the front property. Sometimes old hotels do give up their secrets.

The area to the north of Room 217 is where the hotel vortex is found. It is the corner by the staircase where the linen closet is. Guests have reported feeling light-headed here and even nauseous. I myself, did not experience anything, but others in my group did. The doorknob on the linen closet at this location has been known to light up with a cluster of small colored pin points that travel up the door. The only light in this area is from white bulbs so the colored lights are unexplained.

# Room 202

Some years ago, while taking one of the Ghost Tours at the hotel, the guide informed us that Room 202 was where items tended to turn up that had been reported missing from other guest rooms. He called it the "sticky-fingered ghost room." Supposedly, whenever a guest reported a piece of jewelry, a book, comb or other small object missing overnight, it tended to "materialize" in Room 202. Just a warning, there may be a ghost roaming the premises who was a kleptomaniac in a former life!

# Room 206

Room 206 seems to have a phantom lamp that resides closest to the window. Several guests over the years have reported it going on and off, at times even hearing the filament burn out, only to have it pop back on. Faulty wiring is one thing, but a burned-out bulb becoming "enlightened" is another!

# Room 234

Elizabeth B. Longmont, Colorado. October, 2008. It would seem that Room 234 could rival the stories of other more notorious rooms. This guest room has been the scene of many bizarre happenings, some unparalleled by the rumored history of others such as 401 and 418.

In October of 2008, a Ms. Elizabeth B. of Longmont, Colorado, revealed the following story:

"I brought my family to the Stanley because I had very much enjoyed coming here as a child. My 16-year-old son, Zach was in Room 234 (adjoining at the time to my room, Room 236.) My mother and 12-year-old son stayed in Room 238.

"We returned from dinner around 8:30 and Zach popped his head into my room and said, "What was THAT?" I told him I didn't know what he was talking about and he swore he heard children laughing. We went to sleep around 10:00 and I was awakened at 12:30 when he crawled into my bed (he hadn't done that in 14 years!). He was shivering violently and was very cold when I touched him. He finally went back to sleep in my room and we slept soundly until a knock on my door woke me up at 7:00 a.m. My 12-year-old son (Jacob) was anxious to go to breakfast and I was surprised Zach wasn't still in my bed because as I hadn't heard him leave. Jacob and I went through the adjoining door and sat on Zach's bed to wake him up. He talked to us for a couple of minutes and moved to try and sit up. This is when we discovered he was tucked into bed all the way up the side with his arms stuck in the bed. I do not sleep walk and did not hear him get up or go into his room before 7:00 a.m. We still laugh that someone knew he was cold and tucked him in to help get warm.

Martha Westport. Miami, Florida. June, 2010. "My sister and I stayed in Room 234 at the Stanley Hotel. She was reading in bed when I came out of the bathroom and stopped short. Her long brown hair was standing straight up on her head and moving like it was in a breeze. She glanced at me over the top of her book and said what? Your hair is standing up I said. She frowned like she thought I was pulling a prank on her and raised her hand up to her hair. When she felt it standing up she bolted out of bed and turned to look at her pillow as if she thought the problem was her place in the bed. Her hair was still standing up. She went into the bathroom and started putting water in her hands to mash it down. By the time she came back to the room her head was wet. She refused to get back into the bed so she slept in the chair."

Winston B. Baton Rouge, Louisiana. January, 2011. "I was on a ghost tour at the hotel. The guide was talking about the ghosts and said most of the rooms were haunted. I thought was a tad far-fetched. Then some of the people on the tour started sharing their ghost stories of staying at the hotel. One woman's was pretty amazing. She said she was staying in room 234 and the pillow kept moving out from under her head and onto the floor. She bent over and picked it up several times and put it back. I'm thinkin'...lady...I would have been out the door! But this woman says she was just annoyed and wanted some sleep. When it did it again, she threw it across the room where it landed on a chair. She bunched a different pillow under her head and turned on her side to get some sleep. According to her, a few minutes later the pillow she had thrown across the room sailed over and hit her in the back of the head. She swears she reported it to the hotel desk."

# The Housekeeper's Stairs

There has been emphasis placed on the back stairs at the rear of the West Wing of the 2nd Floor. This is a small staircase primarily used by the hotel staff. Just to the north of it is a door that leads outside to pristine white wooden steps leading down to the back courtyard or up to the other two floors.

It is here at this hallway staircase that Mary Orton (Scary Mary) summons her spirit children to come down and play.

Mary points out that she doesn't have anything special about her going on. She has had clairvoyants and psychics who come to the hotel from year to year tell her that they see certain spirits around her. She has been given the little children's names and a description of what they look like. There is K.T., Emily, Mathew, Elizabeth (who is usually found in the Music Room...she likes to be called Beth, she is always saying, "Call me Beth, call me Beth, call me Beth"), Clara, and Sarah, the Nanny who Mary sees most frequently on the landing between the 2nd and 3rd floors in the vortex.

Scary Mary Orton at the Stanley Hotel.
Photo courtesy of Patrick Andrade, *New York Times*.

It is here at this hallway staircase that Mary Orton (Scary Mary) summons her spirit children to come down and play.

K.T. Is about ten-years-old, and is a tomboy. Her mother made her wear a bow in her hair, which she doesn't like and is always tugging at it. Her real name is Katherine Trumont and she is Canadian. We think she may have died on the 4th Floor from tuberculosis, which was a very prevalent killer in those days. Mr. Stanley himself almost succumbed from it, until he came to Colorado and the fresh mountain air. Many people were sent out West in those days to regain their health.

Emily never came to the Stanley, or to Estes Park for that matter, Mary told me. She is from England and somehow is attached to K.T.'s spirit...they are bff's (best friends forever) in the spirit world.

Mathew is a fun-loving little boy who likes to play games and is very mischievous. He teases Mary Orton and sometimes pinches her leg. He allows her to call him Matt but prefers to be called Mathew when she is talking about him to others.

Clara reminds Mary of Nellie from the TV show *Little House on the Prairie*. She has long ringlets and is very careful of her appearance.

Sara is the 14-year-old nanny who used to watch over the children on the 4th floor, Mary continues. She thinks Mary looks like her younger sister because of her hair and eye color. She followed Mary around the first week she was tour guide, because Sara knew Mary was nervous.

While researching the first edition of this book, Mary was kind enough to show myself and a couple staying there from Texas this back housekeepers' stairway. Mary called up the staircase to the "children" and then instructed Susan, Bruce Brown and myself to watch her skirt. She was kind enough to give us a private tour after Susan and Bruce, who were visiting from Texas took us into their guest room they had rented for the evening, the infamous Room 217. Bruce had an EMF reader with him and he, Susan and I watched Mary's black pleated skirt closely.

At first, we noticed some light tremors around the hemline, but didn't feel it was conclusive. Mary moved down the hallway to where a small hallway branches off and strong light from a window plays across the carpeted floor. There she stopped and had us watch. A few minutes went by and then we saw the middle pleat push in several inches as though a small child had leaned into her. She laughed and said it was Mathew.

Bruce Brown had placed an EMF reader on the floor. He was not touching it. It remained at a steady setting, without variance. Then Mary asked Mathew if he was here, and if so, to make Bruce's toy move. (She was talking about the EMF reader.) Nothing happened. She then asked K.T. to make the needle move, if she was present. Just then the reader did a *major* jump, the needle went clear to the far edge of the scale. All of us jumped. No one had touched it, and it was sitting solidly on the floor where it had been for almost 30 minutes with no reaction, until she asked if K.T. would interact with it. I was very impressed.

Madame Vera has stated that there is a huge energy around this back staircase and the children love to play here. There will be more about them when we talk about the 4th Floor.

Chapter Twenty-Two

# 3rd and 4th Floors

*"There are nights when the wolves are silent and only the moon howls."*
*George Carlin*

The 3rd and 4th floors of the Stanley Hotel have their own oft-reported paranormal activity. The 4th floor in particular has some of the most-haunted guest rooms in the establishment. What is interesting about the stories coming from these rooms is that they are so similar in their theme, yet at times, there is just enough diversity to let you know these were intimate experiences. In other words, thousands have witnessed similar occurrences, yet some have added small details that happen to ring true with the facts known about the area of activity.

## The 3rd Floor

Several guest rooms on the 3rd floor have recurring reports of something strange happening within their walls. Many have been verified by the hotel staff. But the rooms are not the only places where paranormal activity is captured on film and recorders. The long hallway connecting these rooms seems to be a popular hangout for ghosts as well.

The 3<sup>rd</sup> floor hallway showing an entity at the far end morphing into shape. Photo by Chris Bechard with *AlpenGlowmedia.com*.

Dubbed the Pillsbury Doughboy of the 3<sup>rd</sup> floor by some guests who have seen the image pictured above in their own camera lens, this ghost seems to be a residual haunting, as he is always at the east end of the hallway doing pretty much the same thing. A white shape begins to shimmer, it fills out into a somewhat copious form, stays there for a moment, and then fades away. Several people have captured him on both traditional cameras and smart phones. He (or she) is one of the few entities at the hotel that is seen by the naked eye, while also appearing in photographs. No one is quite sure who it is. The ghosts of people most reported at the hotel are F.O., Flora, and Lord Dunraven—all very svelte. The large form may represent a former guest at the hotel, or a member of the staff, or even someone who lived in Estes Park long ago and has decided he likes the digs at this posh hotel. To date, it remains a mystery.

Another area of the 3rd floor with some interesting activity is the old Otis elevator.

Stanley Hotel elevator in hallway.
Photo courtesy of Ron Bueker.

341

"We were in the elevator on the 4th Floor and pushed the button for the basement," writes Pastor Winford S. C. He was visiting the hotel with his daughter, Victoria. "For some reason the 3rd Floor door opened instead. A maid was standing there in a long gray skirt. We pushed the button and nothing happened except the door trying to shut, but not shutting. "Okay, let's Go," I said to my daughter and we took the stairs to the basement.

Pastor C. enclosed a drawing of the maid. It is a Victorian-style dress with high lace collar, long mutton-sleeves, and an apron. No one wears that style of dress at the hotel today.

Black and white sketch by Pastor C.
of maid he saw standing on 3rd floor hallway.

*Pastor C's story was reported in the First Edition of this book. At that time he had misplaced the drawing he made. To my delight he contacted me last year saying he found it in one of his "sketching pads." His granddaughter had drawn on it. My deepest appreciation.

Some of the most reported occurrences on the 3rd Floor are doors operating under their own volition. The hotel night watchmen have encountered several rooms where the doors refused to behave in an acceptable manner.

One of the watchmen was doing his rounds on the 3rd Floor. He checked each room for closed and locked windows, lights off, and to be sure everything else was in order. He completed his check of one particular room, and as he walked away from the locked room, the door opened. "Maybe it's one of those fussy doors," he thought to himself. He went back, looked in the room to verify the windows were indeed shut, closed and locked the door again. As he walked away, the door opened again. By this time he was getting annoyed, so he went back, checked again, and this time as he turned to leave and lock the door, a rush of cold air caught him. Enough of this, he thought to himself, shut the door and left, the hair standing up on the back of his neck.

Another night watchman doing his rounds tried in vain to close and lock the fire escape door at the end of the west wing corridor. Each time it opened, he returned, locked it, only to have it open as soon as he turned away. Finally, he gave up, and as he walked down the hall, the door closed with a bang, and locked on its own. (Susan S. Davis, *Stanley Ghost Stories*)

# Room 317

George O. from Des Moines, Iowa was a guest at the hotel and staying in Room 317. It had been a long day with a tedious drive from DIA airport in Denver through snow flurries and car accidents. He sank into the soft bed with a grateful groan, plumped up two pillows, picked up his well-thumbed paperback and settled back with a sigh. He reached for the drinking glass he had filled on the nightstand next to him, took a sip and set it back down.

He was well into the chapter of his book, when he heard something fall and shatter in the bathroom just to the left of his bed. Surprised, and a little shocked, he sat for a moment and listened, then swung his long legs out of bed and walked timidly toward the open bathroom door. After fumbling for the light switch, he poked his head into the room. At first he saw nothing out of place. Then he looked into the bathtub. Lying inside the tub was a drinking glass, shattered to bits. He stood there blinking. How in the world did a drinking glass end up broken in the tub? He had only used the room once since he arrived and he had not noticed a drinking glass in there.

He turned back toward the bedroom and stood there scanning his memory to remember if he had at any time set a glass on the tub's ledge. Just then his gaze fell upon the nightstand by his bed. The drinking glass he had been using while reading his book was gone. The hairs on his arm were standing up as he walked gingerly toward the table and looked at the floor beneath it to see if the glass had fallen off. It was nowhere to be seen.

With trembling fingers he dialed the front desk and asked that housekeeping be sent up, that he had accidentally broken a drinking glass. He came close to asking for another room but couldn't bare the embarrassment or the thought of repacking everything after the long day.

The remainder of the night went by without incident. The housekeeper dutifully cleaned the glass, though she did look surprised to see the broken glass in a bathtub. He tipped her, locked the door, twice, shut the bathroom door soundly and slept with the lamp light on for the rest of the night.

Bartender Jason Kurtis was called to deliver ice to Room 317. When he got to the door and knocked, a man answered the door and responded in a surly voice, "What do you want?" "Here's the ice you ordered, Sir," Jason responded politely. "I didn't order any ice," the man snapped, and slammed the door shut. Jason returned to the bar, scratching his head about this one.

When he got back to the bar, the call came in again, "Where's my ice?!" Jason figured he must have gone to the wrong floor. So he took the ice to Room 417, one floor *above* the other room he had visited and was greeted by the *same* man with the same surly response. At this point, Jason's skin got cold and clammy. (Susan S. Davis, *Stanley Ghost Stories*)

# Room 318

Wesley Morris, Loveland, Co. October, 2010. "My friends were staying in Room 318 at the Stanley. We had dinner downstairs and then came back to the room. We sat on the bed and started playing poker. We had played about three rounds. My friend starts scooping up the cards to shuffle for a new game. Before he got them all over to him, a bunch of them flew into the air. Two of us jumped up and ran out into the hallway. I told him I wouldn't spend the night in that room for anything."

Sometime in November 2003, while Dawn, the housekeeper, was cleaning Room 318, she felt like she was being watched. She looked but no one was around. She went back to her cleaning and again felt like she was being watched, and this time looked toward the closet. She tried to ignore it and continued cleaning the room. She looked again and saw a see-through image of a woman standing just inside the closet. The spirit appeared to be wearing a long striped dress (either gray and white or blue and white) with a white high neck and long sleeved shirt, and a white apron. Her hair was piled up into a bun.

Dawn thought her mind just imagined this until a week later when two women asked her about ghosts. One of the women did not believe, but the other swore she had seen a ghost in Room 318 in the closet doorway. When she described the ghost, Dawn simply smiled and replied, "Yes, I saw her last week."

# Room 325

On Monday, August 24 of 2009, Stacie H. and her mother were staying in Room 325. "I was awakened at 1:51 a.m. when I felt someone holding my hand. It startled me quite a bit. We also had something or someone that kept covering us up with the comforter and bedspread all night."

# Room 332

Mike D. and his wife stayed in Room 332 on July 11, 2009. "My wife and I went picture taking upon the 4th and 2nd Floors. We had been gone about three hours, returning around midnight. When we walked into our room, it was filled with the smell of roses! Lasted at least an hour...it was awesome!"

Wendi Heights, Denver, Colorado. November, 2014. "A friend of mine was a maid at the Stanley Hotel for about a year. She said the 3rd floor bothered her more than the others. She always felt a kinda dread going along to the rooms down the long hallway. She said she always felt someone was following her. Room 332 was the one she disliked the most. She told me a few times that the bathroom door would shut behind her when she went in there to clean, she would hear noises in the closet and be too afraid to look. She finally quit and is now working at the Brown Palace in Denver. Funny thing is the Brown Palace is supposed to be haunted too."

# Room 340

Two young girls staying in Room 340 were watching TV. Although sure they were alone, the bathroom door suddenly slammed shut, and they heard the door bolt.

I have received emails from other guests of this room claiming weird things going on. People knocking on their door at all hours of the night. The problem is the knocking is coming from inside the closet. Two accounts were concerning the bathroom faucets. The TV will suddenly turn on, tuned to *The Shining*. Pictures rattling, whispering... It seems each floor at the Stanley Hotel has some *long-term* guests hanging around.

The following photo was taken by Kris Tennant with the Rocky Mountain Ghost Explorers. I had been staying overnight at the hotel and was taking photos all over the premises. She said when she began shooting the 3rd floor hallway at the top of the stairs from the 2nd floor her camera started acting erratically.

"All the photos were turning out fine. But as soon as I got to that spot the camera shutter speed went way down. It took forever for it to click. When I looked at the picture the stairway is all blurry. But it was the thing standing just down the hall that freaked me out. I call him the Shadow Boy and I'm pretty sure he's why the camera went haywire. The other pictures where he is not there turned out fine.

Kris Tennant's photo of Shadow Boy at the top of the staircase on 3$^{rd}$ Floor. Rockymountinghostexplorers.com.

3$^{rd}$ floor hallway with orbs. Photo by Spiritbearparanormal.com.

# The 4ᵗʰ Floor

The Stanley Hotel 4ᵗʰ Floor Hallway with abundance of orbs.
Photo courtesy of Chris Bechard with Alpenglow Media.

The fourth floor of the Stanley Hotel reports more haunted activity than any other area of the complex. While Room 217 may be the most infamous, the sheer number of reports coming from the hotel's attic floor is hard to ignore. They typically center on the sound of children running and playing, erratic television behavior, missing toys, a haunted couch, and of course, the antics of Lord Dunraven.

## Room 401

Photo by Linda Grouper.

Room 401 was originally the Nanny's Lounge when the hotel was first built. You can see where the small balcony off the room used to be. It is now enclosed and offers a table and two chairs for the guests of the room to relax and enjoy the view of Lumpy Ridge. Today it is frequently booked as a Bridal Suite. In the fall of 2009, it underwent a complete renovation. Many wondered if that would increase the ghostly activity in the room, even though heaven knows it receives enough as it is!

Kevin L. sent a letter to the Stanley Hotel on August 19, 2009 to describe the paranormal occurrences that happened to himself and a friend who were staying in Room 401.

"After arriving and checking in, only about a half hour later I walked into the bathroom and very quickly heard my name being called. I opened the door immediately and asked my friend Jon what he wanted only to find out he'd said nothing and most definitely did not call my name!

"We also had a flashlight pushed off a table. During an EMF (Electromagnetic Field) session, the K-2 meter pegged out as far as it would go and the room electrified to the point all the hair on both of our arms and legs stood up. My skin also had a tingly feeling that lasted for about 20 seconds, and then went completely away.

"We caught more than a dozen EVP's (Electronic Voice Phenomenon) of everything from children laughing and women having conversations to a couple tapping responses to direct questions. As far as video, we captured a few orbs, but nothing special."

Room 401 is known for its spooky closet. Lord Dunraven is said to haunt this room and many have seen him standing near the closet. During several tours, guests have stepped into the closet, closed the door and reported feeling a light touch, as well as having their jewelry played with. One woman actually filed a report with the hotel that her ring was removed from her finger while she was in the closet. As of this writing, it has not surfaced.

As the room is used as a Bridal Suite, it has given rise to a plethora of stories involving the hapless grooms as Lord Dunraven has fun with the men's possessions.

The week of June 16, 1996, Rev. Kimberly Henry and her husband came to spend the week of the summer solstice at the Stanley. It turned out that Rev. Henry knew the Head of Reservations, Karen

Lynch. Since they were staying for a week, Rev. Henry thought a room on the 4<sup>th</sup> Floor would be best, so Karen arranged for the couple to stay in Room 401. After the first couple of days, Rev. Henry reported to Karen that she kept smelling cherry-flavored pipe tobacco. Karen was mystified, explaining that Room 401, also one of the hotel's choice honeymoon suites, was a non-smoking room.

The third night, Rev. Henry reported to Karen that they had both seen a ghost standing in the corner of the room next to the closet, watching them. She described the spirit as a man who was bald on the top of his head with a distinct ring of hair around the bold spot.

She also reported that at one point, her husband had been next to the sink, put his wedding band down on the sink, and it mysteriously swept into the sink and down the drain. The couple called the front desk that called Engineering who rescued the ring. Another time, the husband had put his glasses down on the table, and they suddenly flew onto the floor, as if someone had swept them off the table. During the course of the week, it was clear to both of them that the spirit did not like the man, because it didn't do anything to annoy the woman during the time, beyond his appearance.

The two friends had talked of getting together for lunch, so on the fourth day the couple came downstairs at noon to join Karen, whom they met at the front desk.

The couple walked through the Lobby toward the restaurant corridor, and as Karen came out her office door to meet them, the woman suddenly gasped, pointing to the picture of Lord Dunraven hanging on the wall in the hallway next to the MacGregor Room.

"That's him! That's the man I saw in my room!" (Susan S. Davis, *Stanley Ghost Stories*)

She was pointing at the enigmatic face of the notorious Lord Dunraven, Adare Viscount.

In April of 2003, Donna H. and her two daughters were shopping in Estes Park when they decided to have lunch at the Stanley. After lunch they strolled around and asked permission to go up to the other floors. They were told they could do so quickly, if they did not disturb the guests.

Donna led the way up the various staircases, stopping to comment on this décor and that. As they were finished touring the 4th Floor, they decided to take the elevator down to save steps. While waiting for the car to arrive, they heard a squeaking sound and looked to their left. The door to the room nearest the elevator was slowly opening. Donna watched to see who emerged, but no one did. It was the way it opened that caught her curiosity; not swung open with purpose as most people do when exiting, but very slowly. The room number was 401.

One of her daughters, a vivacious 18-year-old stepped softly over to peer into the room, curious to see what the guest rooms looked like. Donna chided her and told her to come back.

"There's no one in there," the girl whispered. "I just want to peek."

Before Donna could call her back, the girl had stepped quietly into the room. As she did so, the door swung to with a loud bang. The girl's startled cry could be heard from inside. Donna ran to the door and tried turning the handle but nothing happened. The room door automatically locked when closed and required a room key.

"Open the door," she shouted to her daughter.

The handle rattled back and forth as the girl tried to get it to open.

"I can't!" she cried, her voice becoming distressed. "It won't open! Mom...get me out of here!"

Just then, the girl emitted a loud scream and Donna heard her fall against the door on the other side.

"What's wrong? Are you hurt?" Donna cried, looking around frantically for someone to help them. She instructed her other daughter to run down to the front desk and get help.

Just as she did so, the door handle turned and opened with a soft clicking sound.

Donna bolted into the room to see her daughter on the other side of the room, huddled in a chair with her face in her hands, shivering. She had been nowhere near the door to open it just now.

"What happened?" Donna cried, looking about the room in worry. Had her daughter startled a guest who might have been in the bathroom when she sneaked into the room. The bathroom door was closed.

"I couldn't open the door, then the closet door swung open and something cold whispered into my ear. I couldn't tell what it said. Then the closet door slammed."

Without further explanation, and fearing the front door would close on them again, the girl got up and bolted from the room, her mother close on her heels.

As they left the room, the door once again slammed behind them, causing both to jump out of their skins. Donna's daughter squealed and ran for the stairs on the far end of the hallway. As she was making her way down, her sister was coming up, saying the desk clerk was on her way. The frightened girl told her the clerk could talk to their mother, but that she was getting out of the hotel. She took the stairs two at a time and was found leaning against their locked car when the mother and her sister finally found her.

The clerk had checked the room thoroughly and assured Donna that no one was checked into 401 at that time as check-in was at 3 o'clock. Donna informed the confused clerk that no one in their right mind would stay in that room and departed the hotel.

Many people equate Room 401 with the Ghost Hunters from the Sci-Fi Channel. It was this room that Jason was investigating overnight and caught the closet door opening on film, as well as a drinking glass next to him on the nightstand exploding from the inside out.

Raneen H. New York, New York. May, 2012. "My son Ben was playing on the floor of Room 401. I noticed he kept looking over at the closed closet door and watch it for a moment before he would return to pushing his cars around the carpet. When he paused and stared over at it again, I asked him what he kept looking at. He looked up at me and said something in the closet wanted out. Well I can tell you a statement like that from a 4-year-old will cause the hairs on your arm to stand up.

"I walked over to it, opened it and peered inside. It's a small area with a slanting room, an ironing board, iron, clothes railing and some hangars. I stepped aside for him to see that there was nothing there. He shrunk back and told me to shut the door.

"I picked up my magazine and he returned to his cars when he stopped again, scooped them up, and backed away from the closet. He began to cry and say he wanted to go home. He refused to sleep in the room. My sister, who lives in Estes, came and got him and my husband and I spent the night. When he began asking if I heard a noise in the closet I was ready to check out early."

Room 401. The closet door is straight ahead to the left of the wall clock. Photo courtesy of Mike Arnett.

There are indeed a number of stories about the room, but it is not the only room to be reckoned with on the most-haunted floor in the hotel.

# Room 405

Room 405 seems to delight in its own private parties. Blaring music is oftentimes heard coming from the room when no one is checked into it. The music often continues for days. Perhaps the ghost of John Phillip Sousa stays in this room, as he was once a revered guest at the hotel.

# Room 406

Wendi Watson. October 2014. "I was visiting my friend who was staying in 406. She was telling me how it used to the nannies area back when the hotel opened. She was telling me that she would never be a nanny and watch after someone else's "brats." Just as she said that the bathroom door slammed really hard. It shook the room. We both jumped. I told her it was probably wind coming in through a window. She was too scared to look, so I finally opened the door and wasn't happy to see the little window shut tight. Just as I was coming back into the room, the door slammed again so hard I jumped a foot in the air. She didn't want to stay alone that night so other friends came and stayed with her."

# Room 407

"My name is Madison M. and I have stayed in Room 407. I was taking a picture of the floor to test out my camera and the picture was perfectly normal. The next picture turned green and was kinda blurry.

When we went on the Ghost Tour, our guide was talking about the nannies who had stayed there. At that moment the closet door in the hallway slowly opened but no one came out. The weird thing was the door was locked the whole time.

Back in our room, we heard someone talking about our room on someone else's Ghost Tour, so we opened our door a crack so we could hear what they were saying. The door suddenly shut by itself. We were kinda freaked out, but were excited so we opened it a crack again, and said, "If anyone is here with us, please shut the door." We waited and nothing happened. A few minutes later, it shut by itself. I was very excited and convinced something was there. It was a ghostly experience that was very cool. Maybe you should consider this room as one of your haunted rooms. I am convinced it is!"

A strange form of what looks like a tall man with slicked back hair have been seen in the window of Room 407 from people in the courtyard below. An image that resembles Lord Dunraven has been seen looking down from that very window. Though he haunts Room 401 and much of the hallways of the 4th Floor, Room 407 has been accredited as "his" room.

# Room 418

Room 418 has been called the most-haunted room at the Stanley Hotel. While 217 carries the most publicity and tends to house more celebrities, 418 seems to attract a lot of paranormal activity.

This author sat in this room for a few hours in 2010, wanting to get a sense of it. It is not an overly large room, as most of the rooms on the 4th Floor were reserved for the "help" and vacationing children. It is warm and cozy and once-again, done in Flora's Stanley's signature colors of burgundy and gold. I was comfortably ensconced in an over-stuffed chair, eying the closet door I had heard so much about in terms of EVP readings when the sash on the wooden window to my right began to rattle. I will admit that when one is seated in a reportedly haunted room the atmosphere lends itself to an over-reaction to common things. So, I chided myself and told my imagination that it was the wind sighing through the gigantic pines outside the window and rattling the sash of a hundred-year-old window.

The noise would stop, then come again a few minutes later. Curious, I got up and went over to the window and pushed on it. Sure enough, it rattled. I smiled and was about to return to my seat when I glanced out that same window to discover there was no wind. Not a single branch was quivering outside. I frowned and stood there for a moment. As I did so, staring at the motionless landscape beyond, the window shook, the rattling startling me out of my shoes. I was only an inch from it as I watched it vibrating, clacking like old bones. I could feel no vibration under my feet or around me that would account for it. I even placed my hand on the window next to it to feel for anything that would cause the window sash to bang against itself. Nothing! After a few moments it stopped, leaving me the one who was rattled! (The Author)

There are stories galore of guests staying in this room and hearing the sounds of children running up and down the hallway outside their door. Reports of balls bouncing, nursery rhymes being sung in sweet, high voices, laughter, jacks being tossed onto a wood floor, even though the hallway has been carpeted for years, and running feet are all reported.

Many EVP's have been captured in this room, including a very clear one of a small child, female in tone, saying "Mommy?" Other voices have been those of older people having conversations and even one report of two men arguing. They seem to center around the open closet door of this room.

Room 418 is also a room many of the cleaning staff is not happy to go into. Impressions of a full reclining body suddenly appearing on the smooth coverlet of a freshly made bed have often been seen here. The television turns on and off and when it comes on of its own volition, it is always tuned to Channel 44, the station that carries *The Shining* on a continual loop. Even when the channel is placed on another channel, if the television turns on by itself, it is always back to Channel 44.

Jesse D., a hotel clerk who once worked at the front registration desk and is now head manager at Mary Lake Lodge, has had a few stories of his own to report about the going's-on at the hotel. His story about his overnight stay in Room 418 was especially compelling.

"I got off work and went out to the car to get some things for the ghost children in Room 418, as I was going to spend the night there. My mother, knowing of my plans to stay overnight in the room, to me to bring along this special light I have. It is flat with one-inch squares that light up.

"As I entered the room, I said, 'Kids, I brought you something!'. I immediately felt the energy in the room pick up. I was going to make a run to McDonald's and I felt a pressure to get the toy out, so I got the light out showed "them" how to use it and I set it up for them.

"I got my food and returned to the room. I was watching TV and the commercial came out really loud. I turned the TV off...this was about midnight. The window started tapping, about every 30 seconds--one tap. Then I felt this squeezing pressure on my arm and my one side and on my stomach. I was *on* my stomach!

"The tapping continued, two taps in a row. I sat up in bed. The thought occurred to me that maybe they wanted the light toy turned back on. It is on a 90-second timer and turns off after that. I got up and turned it on and said, 'There you go...now let me go to sleep!' There were no more taps or feelings of pressure."

## Room 432

"My wife and I stayed at the Stanley Hotel on the night of Wednesday, October 14, 2009. We took the Ghost Tour at 5:00 pm given by Kevin. I have always been a skeptic, and never have experienced any ghost experiences while staying at many "ghost" plantations or hotels.

We went to bed about 10:00 pm. I woke up around 4:00 am and was wide-awake. I tossed and turned for several minutes trying to decide if I should get up, because I am often an early riser. I got up to go to the restroom. I had the feeling that my wife followed me into the bathroom and she stopped in the doorway, and then she said, "Hurry, get back to bed." I turned to my left and said, "Huh?" Nobody was in the doorway or the bathroom except for me. I assumed my wife had returned to bed. I returned to bed and found my wife asleep.

Around 7:00 am I asked my wife if she spoke to me during the night, and she advised me that she hadn't. I am 100% positive that I heard a woman's voice speak to me while she was standing in the doorway of the bathroom. This event occurred in Room 432."
Fred V., Topeka, Kansas.

# The Haunted Hallways of the 4th Floor

The 4th Floor hallways have two specific areas that report strange happenings. Some of these are not just reports turned in by guests on tours or staying the night, some of the paranormal happenings are witnessed in real time.

If one goes to the east hallway where Room 418 is housed, you will see an interesting conflux in the carpeting. A large burgundy-red square of carpet can be seen interrupting the continual flow of hallway fabric. At the back of this square, against the west wall you will find an ordinary looking couch. But this couch receives a good deal of paranormal activity. This is the area where children gathered in the early days of the hotel to play games, roll balls, toss down jacks and dance in circles as they chanted nursery rhymes and songs. Their vestiges and faded whispers are still heard on a regular basis, and are in fact, the most reported hauntings turned into the hotel staff. Due to the plethora of stories of children in this area, guests leave small pieces of candy and toys on the couch where most of the activity seems to center. The next day, the treats are reportedly gone. People have set up cameras to make sure it isn't other guests making off with the treats. Nothing shows up, including the removal of the candy. It seems it's just there one minute and gone the next.

4th Floor couch with candies and an orange resting along the back.

Many people have snapped photos of ghosts on this floor that are quite extraordinary. When the floor was being remodeled the activity increased. Giant orbs could be seen down by the doors leading to the stairway out back. Some of these orbs looked lit with a strange glowing light. This area continued to be a hotbed of shapes, orbs and workmen's things moving as they repapered and repaired.

The following photograph was snapped at night after the men had left for the day. Note not only the abundance of orbs, but their strange light. There is also some type of white form rising above the open door on the left.

Photo courtesy of Chris Bechard with Alpenglow Media.

The following photograph by Chris Bechard is one of the best ghost photos I've seen. You can see the white transparent mass hovering over the couch on the 4th Floor. Across from it is a bright orb and dark figure. This is where the activity in this hallway seems to center.

362

4<sup>th</sup> Floor hallway ghost near couch.
Photo courtesy of Chris Bechard, Alpenglow Media.

The reports of children heard running and playing in the hallways when no children were booked into the hotel is prevalent. It is rumored that Stephen King may have either heard the stories or witnessed something himself, inspiring him to put the phantom children in his famous book, *The Shining*. Psychics have mentioned sensing a small girl's death on the 4<sup>th</sup> Floor in the early 1900's from the prevalent killer of that day, tuberculosis. They believe her name to be Katherine Trumont, or K.T. as we discussed earlier.

One of the spirit children we have discussed is Emily, a young girl from England whose spirit is often "seen" and felt here. Emily was from England and many of the nursery rhymes overheard by the unseen children are old songs from Great Britain.

An illustration of how many apparitions are seen with balls of energy somewhere on, or near, their person.

The second most- reported occurrence on this floor is that of people feeling their hair rise into the air. Little children while playing ring-a-around the rosy near the couch have suddenly felt their hair rise up on end as though an electric current has passed through them. It was personally witnessed by myself and five others on a tour as one little girl who had joined in Scary Mary's Ring Around the Rosy dance suddenly felt something begin pulling on her skirt. All of us watched in shock as her skirt was tugged on by unseen hands. At the same time, her long straight hair began to rise from her head until it was standing straight up. She burst out crying and ran for her mother. It slowly let down until it returned to normal.

This has happened to a number of people who circle near the couch and recite nursery rhymes. The children from the past seem to want to continue the games they played over a hundred years ago.

Near the elevator on this floor is the other area where the "hair raising" tends to occur. The following photo was submitted by Kristen Tennant who was on a tour and witnessed a teenage boy, who was on the tour as well, suddenly look up as he felt electricity pouring through his tingling scalp. As you can see, people looked up in shock as his light blond hair began moving up and away from his face. You can see it standing out to the right of his head. We were given permission to use the photo with the tour group in it.

Photo by Kris Tennant of Rocky Mountain Ghost Explorers.

As mentioned before, reports of smelling Lord Dunraven's pipe tobacco have come from the 4th Floor hallway, sounds of men deep in conversation, women feeling their fannies pinched and sensations of being touched.

Lord Dunraven's fondness for pinching the female staff's tushies as they cleaned on the rooms on the 4th Floor became so rampant that for a time the housekeeping was done entirely by males in this area.

While investigating the hotel on Friday the 13th, 2009, this author was walking down the 4th Floor hallway with some friends and my 21-year-old son, Ryan. We were discussing various things, all in animated tones, when suddenly we all gasped in unison and came to an abrupt halt. A huge blast of tobacco smoke hit us smack in the face just as we neared the staircase leading down to the third floor. It was as if someone had taken a great draw on a pipe and leaned forward to blow it directly into our faces. I actually coughed and blinked my eyes. All of us felt and smelled it at the same time.

My son dashed to where the hallway branches off (a mere two feet away), leading to Room 407, Lord Dunraven's purported dwelling, but no one were there. The odd thing was that the smell disappeared as quickly as it had come...not gradually dissipating as it normally would. The rest of us just stood there, shocked but excited. The hotel is a non-smoking facility and there was simply no explanation for it. (The Author)

And finally, a rare capture of what looks like a female in an old-fashioned high neck collar, black satin dress with hair piled in a bun. She appears to be carrying something in both hands. This was snapped on the 4th Floor hallway. The person taking the picture said her camera speed suddenly slowed down resulting in the blurry appearance, just as this image came out of a wall in front of her.

Photo courtesy of Natalie R., former tour guide at
the Stanley Hotel.

We have covered all of the main hotel but the garden/basement
level. Due to the high amount of traffic there for the Ghost Tours, it
would be hard to recognize much paranormal activity, and few is
reported. The only exceptions are the Ladies and Men's Rooms
where people have reported feeling sudden cold spots, hearing doors
open and close when no one is in the room, and feeling someone
enter the stall next to them, shut the door and latch it, only to see no
feet when they peer under the stall wall.

The tunnel which is found through the door next to Madame
Vera's room is very haunted and numerous stories come from here
of voices of small children calling out, and even disembodied voices
calling out the staff's names as they walk past the small cave entrance.

The main hotel is not the only building on the vast Stanley
complex that houses entities who refuse to move on. The other
buildings have their own stories of shadows, voices, and eerie
happenings.

Chapter Twenty-Three

# The Manor House/Lodge

*"A house is never still in darkness to those who listen intently; there is a whispering in distant chambers, an unearthly hand presses the snib of the window, the latch rises. Ghosts were created when the first man awoke in the night." J.M. Barrie, in Little Minister*

The Manor House/Lodge at night. Photo by Rebecca F. Pittman

As mentioned earlier in the book, the Manor House, built in 1910 as a year-round hotel on the Stanley complex, was originally used to house the bachelors staying at the mountain retreat. Since then, its use was expanded to house couples and all who wanted to book a room there. Now, in 2015, it has bowed to the current trend of offering lodging for those travelers who enjoy having their four-footed companions accompany them. The name of the building has hence changed as well to The Lodge.

The Manor House/The Lodge at the Stanley Hotel. Photo by Rebecca F. Pittman.

Many ghost stories come from The Lodge; tales from the staff, overnight guests and people attending events there. The rooms within have their own sense of atmosphere, and, due perhaps to the lesser traffic here, one is often left to experience the main floor rooms without interruption. It may be wise to mention here that The Lodge is off-limits unless you are an overnight guest there, or attending an event. It is not included on the tour.

In the basement level of this building is the Parlor, an upscale Spa catering to the hotel's guests or others by appointment. The back courtyard of the Lodge is an area frequently used for weddings, receptions and banquets.

# The Main Floor of the Lodge

The main floor of the Lodge seems to often echo scenes from another time. Housekeepers have reported people dressed in Victorian-era clothing walking about the floors as if in no hurry to be anywhere. Entire scenes have played out of people sitting amenably in wicker rocking chairs chatting away and laughing. Staff has also seen people drifting up and down the staircase, their shapes transparent and soft. Maids have reported their cleaning items moved around, often times vanishing completely, only to turn up in another room they haven't even been in yet. One reported a strange white powder that kept appearing on the floor near the base of the stairs. She said it wasn't like anything she had ever seen. It sparkled and was "super fine" … "far finer than sifted flour."

Main staircase in the Lodge. Photo by Danielle Moniker.

# The Library

Mark Dewberry. Fort Collins, Colorado. January, 2015.

"I'm a professional photographer. I was asked by a bridal party to take photos of their upcoming nuptials in May. I went to the Stanley complex in January to scout out the area I would be filming. It was to be the back courtyard of the Lodge at the hotel. The staff were kind enough to let me go into the Lodge to look for possible photo ops, as well as look over the back patio.

"While I was in the building I peeked into the public rooms on the main floor. I began taking some test photos, checking for light, etc. The minute I tried to take photos of the room they call the Library my camera refused to work. It was the strangest thing. Here I was, clicking all over the place, but the minute I aimed it into that room it refused to work. Nothing showed up in the viewfinder, only black. The shutter wouldn't click. I walked away, took photos of the Ranch Room—all good. I step back into the Library, same thing. I have no idea what's going on with that room."

The Library Room in The Lodge. Photo by Rebecca F. Pittman

Jose Ladera. Denver, Colorado. August, 2014. "I was taking a few pictures of the inside of the Lodge. While standing just inside the doorway to the Library in that building, a loud bang came from the far right corner of the room. It startled me. It was very loud. The thing was there was nothing in the room to make the sound. It was pretty much empty but for a table with some tablecloths on it. I had just decided it must be coming from outside when it did it again only this time it was in the center of the room. This huge BANG! I jumped because it was only about a foot from me. I actually felt the vibration of it. I was backing up when it suddenly went BANG-BANG-BANG-BANG about an inch from me. I felt the impact of it in my chest. I just turned and ran out into the parking lot."

# The Ranch Room

Ranch Room at the Lodge. Photo by Danielle Moniker.

Susan S. Davis with the Stanley Museum is always kind to share her stories of the hotel. She was the head historian when the Stanley Museum was once housed in the hotel basement. Here is a story she shared concerning the Ranch Room of the Lodge:

Arty R., who has been a housekeeper for years at the Stanley, tells of meeting Mrs. Stanley on the stairs of the Manor House. One of Arty's most repeated spirit sightings was of the Lady in Green, whose identity became known to her in yet another incident in a restroom in the Concert Hall. (see Concert Hall section)

While cleaning the Ranch Room at the Manor House—the equivalent room to the Pinon in the main building—Arty happened to glance up the hallway to see a lady in a green dress standing in the doorway of the last room on the corridor. The dress went to the woman's mid-calf. Short hair and a broad-brimmed green hat framed her pretty, and very white, face. Most remarkable was the smell of her lovely perfume, a smell Arty noticed every time she cleaned in that part of the Manor House. (Susan S. Davis, *Stanley Ghost Stories*)

Roger M. San Diego, Ca. March, 2012. "My buddies were having a bachelor party for one of our friends who were getting married at the Stanley Hotel. We were staying next door in the Manor House. We'd had a few beers when we were headed back to our room from the main hotel. As we came into the lobby of the Manor House and were waiting for the elevator we hear this argument coming from our right down the hall. So, dumb drunk guys decide to see what's up. The voices were coming from a room at the far end of the hall. It sounded like two older guys really going at it. We're tiptoeing down to eavesdrop. When we get the door and look in, the voices just shut off. There is no one in the room! We could hear them shouting right up until we looked in! The only part I caught was "If you think you are going to get the better of an old peg puller like me, you might had better check your senses."

"When we got to our room my friend Googled "peg puller." We couldn't find what it meant other than a tool to pull tent pegs and stuff like that. We never heard the voices again, but that was pretty spooky."

Dave Douglas. Denver, Colorado. June, 2014. "I was in a meeting in the Ranch Room at the Lodge at the Stanley. My chair faced the stairs that go to back rooms, I guess. During the presentation something caught my eye on the hallway at the top of the short flight of stairs. A man was standing there staring at us. For some reason the hair on my arms stood up. He was all in black with a black beard that reached to his chest and he was just standing there with his hands clasped behind his back. He never moved. I couldn't even tell if he was breathing. I poked my friend next to me and nodded to the stairs. He looked and shrugged, like "What?" The guy was still standing there. I leaned over and whispered, "That guy standing there... Doesn't he give you the creeps?" "Dude, I don't see anyone standing there. Are you okay?" Just then, the guy turns slowly and walks off down the hallway, going really slow. He's got a billiard cue stick clasped in his hands."

Stairs in the Ranch Room leading to guest rooms.

# The Dining Room/Ballroom

The Lodge Dining Room. Photo by Danielle Moniker

The most prevalent ghost stories come from the area of the Lodge that was once the Ballroom. From as far back at the 1990s, the staff at the Stanley Hotel complex have reported some strange goings-on in this beautiful room of white whose windows command yet another breathtaking view of the Rockies.

There have been several reports of happenings in the Manor House ballroom. The windows to that room look out over the main parking lot and you can also see them from various places inside the main hotel if you are looking from the east wing.

People have seen the ballroom, lights ablaze, and figures dancing past the windows, music blaring and laughter heard tinkling on the night air. If someone approaches the windows for a closer look, or is bold enough to enter the Lobby of the Manor House and tiptoe toward the ballroom door, the lights are extinguished, the music stops and you are found staring dumb-founded into an empty room, moonlight playing on the dark walls in patches of spectral white.

These stories have ended since the room became the Dining Room for the Lodge. Perhaps the addition of new furnishings and the more-frequent visitors to this room have put a damper on the ghostly activity. There is one amazing story that was shared with this author in 2009.

(This housekeeper preferred to remain anonymous.) "I was cleaning the Manor House one night after a party in the Ballroom. I was almost done and was just sweeping up when the lights go out. I stood there a second. I could see cuz of the moonlight and parking lights and such. A few seconds later they come back on. I went back to sweeping when they go out again. My heart was pumping a little. It was so quiet in there all alone. This chair falls over behind me and I jumped. Then another one falls over right in front of me. I felt something touch the back of my night and I screamed. The scariest part was this shadow that moved around the room really fast. He was like streaking around the room. I dropped the broom and ran out. I was running back to the big hotel when I looked back over my shoulder to the windows of the room I had been cleaning. The lights came back on just at that second. I didn't go back to clean. I asked to not work over there anymore."

# Guest Floors of the Lodge

The Lodge has two floors of guest rooms. These rooms are very spacious with large bathrooms and tubs. They are now pet-friendly. Stories of odd things happening come from these areas.

Amber N., a member of the housekeeping staff at the Stanley Hotel in 1998 was cleaning on the 2nd Floor of the Manor House. She heard a board creak overhead and turned to look up through the spindles of the staircase to the 3rd Floor landing. There was a small boy standing there in bib overalls and a striped T-shirt. She was a little surprised to see him as she was not aware of any children booked into the Manor House and it was the first time she had seen him around anywhere.

"Hi Sweetie," she called up to him. He turned away from her, as if to look over his shoulder to the seating area behind him.

"When he turned, I screamed. I could see right through the back of his head! I just dropped my cleaning stuff and ran out of the building. I quit the next day."

# Room 1214

Room 1214 has the dubious distinction of being called the Chair Room. This title is due to the number of reports of a chair mysteriously appearing in the middle of the room out of nowhere. The room keys also have a habit of bending sideways. More than one group staying in the room has reported these occurrences.

# Room 1217

Oleia D. Longmont, CO. February 14, 2011. "My boyfriend surprised me with a Valentine's present when he took me to the Stanley Hotel. We stayed in the Manor House, room 1217. He likes spooky stuff. I didn't know he had packed a Ouija board in his suitcase and I wasn't very happy about using one in a haunted hotel. After teasing me he sets it up on the bed. Nothing happened for a long time and I was getting bored. I wasn't thinking this is how I want to spend Valentine's. I took my fingers off the thingy that comes with the board and begged him to take me to dinner. He finally stood up and started for the bathroom. The plastic thingy slides across the Ouija board and onto the bedspread all by itself. When he walks over to pick it up it goes flying across the room and hits the wall. I screamed. I'm yelling at him to pack it away. At the same time the temperature in the room drops really fast and I'm freezing! I don't want nothing more to do with the Stanley Hotel."

# Room 1301

Room 1301. Photo by Rebecca F. Pittman

While this author was at the hotel researching the first edition of this book, I stayed in what was then called the Manor House in Room 1301. The hotel had asked that I do some repair work on the faux bois paint finishes in the Lobby area of the main hotel that had been done for the filming of Stephen King's TV mini-series, *The Shining*. I am a professional faux painter and muralist, and spend my time writing books when not covered in paint. I offered the hotel management my services in touching up some wall scratches in return for room and board while I researched this book.

Each day I would walk over from the Manor House to the main hotel and spend the day painting, talking to guests and listening to their stories. I also interviewed the staff on their off hours. I would usually return to my room around 4:30 or 5 pm and take a long soak in the luxurious Jacuzzi tub.

The first evening I was there, it began to snow outside, coming down in large fluffy puffs, turning Estes Park into a winter wonderland. As I peered from the antique lace curtains at the snow piling higher outside, the boughs of the pines soughing softly, I thought of Stephen King and his inspiration to write his book, *The Shining*. It was coming to this very hotel at the end of the summer season, as the roads to Trail Ridge were being closed for the winter, that he got the idea for a caretaker snowed in at a deserted hotel with his family for the winter. There is indeed a profound sense of isolation in the Rockies when the snow encapsulates your small existence. To top it off, I was in the Manor House all alone! Now that is formidable. Here I was, a female, spending the next 5 nights in a haunted hotel complex and there was no one else in the Manor House at that time! No one...nadda! Not a soul in the other 38 suites! The kitchen is not used except for events, and the only staff is next door at the main hotel.

So, I flip on the TV to quiet my nerves and find I am on a channel featuring *Ghost Lab*! Great! And....like an idiot...I keep watching it! Finally, at 10 pm., I put my watch on the nightstand next to my wonderfully soft bed, and drift off to sleep. Ok, I will admit to keeping one eye open for a good two hours! But I eventually fell asleep.

The following morning, I awoke at 7 a.m. was quite proud of myself that I had passed the night without incident. 'Won't my four grown sons be proud of me?' I thought. I dressed in my "paint clothes" and picked up my watch. It had stopped. To be precise it had stopped at 1:17 in the morning! "Oh Poop," I said, as I am known to favor that word under moments of exasperation. I put the watch on anyway, hoping it might start later and headed for the main hotel.

I was painting in the Cascade Restaurant when I happened to look down at my watch. It had not only started, but it was on the correct time! J.T. the lead engineer at the hotel was nearby and I said, "J.T.? What time do you have, please?" "11:20," he said. My watch read 11:20. "Hmmmmm," I thought, and then went back to work, thinking it just a quirk of a simple watch with perhaps a moody battery.

That night, same routine. I had gone out to dinner with friends, come back, crawled into bed, set the watch on the nightstand and eventually (cough) dozed off. The next morning, the watch is stopped at 1:17. Now I'm interested! I put it on, went about painting and around 2:30 in the afternoon I thought to check it. It was on 2:30! I sat there staring at it, perplexed. When it happened again for a third night, I told my friend Sara who owns the Chrysalis Gift Shop at the hotel. She got excited and said, "What do you think it means? Do you think someone died in that room at 1:17?" I said, "Or, it could be a date, January 17." Her eyes grew big and she said, "Let's Google IT!" I laughed and said, "Google WHAT?" She typed in 1:17 and the first 4 links came up with James 1:17 from the Bible. It read, *"Every good gift and every perfect gift is from above, and cometh down from the Father of lights, with whom there is no variableness, or shifting shadows.""*

It wasn't enough that the phrase "shifting shadows" was in the text. The next thing Sara suggested to me gave me bumps. She said, "You said your mother passed away last year. Maybe the watch was her way of saying she is looking down on you and "watching" over you and not to be afraid that you are the only one in the Manor House with ghosts, or 'shifting shadows'!" After I thanked her for reminding me that I was over there alone, I said, "Hey....wait a minute! Why was that the only Bible verse that came up when you typed in 1:17? Do you realize how many books in the Bible have a Chapter One with a verse 17? There has to be tons! Why did just that one show up?" She smiled and said, "Because that is the one you were meant to see!" I thought it over for a while. It gave me a feeling of comfort. The odd ending to this story is that the watch stayed on that time.

For the rest of my time at the hotel, it stayed stuck on 1:17. I figure it is my message from someone...I choose to think it's from my mother.

I didn't look over the photos I took of my room (1301) until I got back home. Since I had been staying next door to the most-haunted room in the Manor House, Room 1302, I was curious to see if my photos showed anything. I was startled to see what looks like a face, fingers and some odd shapes in one of the photos. It is the one posted at the beginning of this story. (The author.)

# Room 1302

Room 1302 gained notoriety when the team from the hit show Ghost Hunters on the Sci-Fi Channel investigated the room in 2006 during a night-long live coverage episode from the Stanley Hotel for their TV show. In the footage they took, Grant Wilson is seated at a small table in a step-up alcove in the room, where there are two chairs. While one of the staff is monkeying with some equipment, you hear Grant yelp and the sound of a table and chair slamming into the wall. Grant explains that the table jumped and it and the chair across from him slammed into the alcove wall.

Since this filming, countless guests have gone to the room and sat in the chair hoping the table will put on a similar performance.

It seems the Manor House mirrors its big brother next door in more ways than one. Guests here, as well as in the main hotel, have reported hearing sounds of people walking about overhead, or furniture crashing, while they were staying on the 3rd Floor. (This would be the equivalent to the 4th Floor at the main hotel.) The problem with this story is that those respective floors are the top floors in the structures! There are no rooms overhead; only a roof.

Room 1302. The sitting area with table and chairs is in the background. Photo by Debbie Overton.

# The Courtyard and Stairs

The outdoor courtyard and the white wooden exterior stairs leading from the guest floors at the Lodge have had a few strange reports.

Several sightings of something white moving across the outdoor courtyard at the Lodge have been turned in. The stories carry a lot of similar detail of the sightings. Although the shape spotted is non-gender in detail, all get "the feeling" it is female.

"It just floats in a feminine manner," one woman emailed. "It moves from the back door of the Lodge, floats across the stone floor, up the steps to the parking lot and fades away. I've seen her twice and she always does the same thing."

"It looks like a woman, though I don't know why. There really is no shape to it. Just a white mass with trailing tails. But when you watch it you just feel it's a woman," reported one man.

If the shape is doing the same thing each time, then it seems to be a residual haunting where the ghost is on a loop. It never deviates from its course.

Rachael M. Bridgeport, CT. June, 2013. "I was getting married in the courtyard at the Manor House at the Stanley Hotel. We were running a rehearsal run with about 30 people in attendance. As we were waiting for the coordinator to tell us where to stand, everyone gasped. This white thing floated out the back door of the Manor House and went right past us! It was the scariest thing I've ever seen. It was broad daylight but you could see it plain as day. Several people snapped pictures with cameras and cell phones but it didn't show up on any of them! We watched it go up the stairs and when it got to the gate there it just dissolved and was gone. I was really shaken and so afraid this thing was going to show up for the wedding. It didn't but everyone kept looking for it."

Chapter Twenty-Four

# The Concert Hall

*"I'm here, because you believe I'm here. Keep on believing and
I'll always be real to you."*
*Capt. Gregg in The Ghost and Mrs. Muir, by Phillip Dunne and
Joseph L. Mankiewicz*

View of the Concert Hall from the west. Photo by Ron Bueker.

During the research for the first edition of this book this author became friends with the head engineer at the Stanley Hotel. J.T. Thompson is a most competent man who handles all the maintenance issues of this giant complex. He was showing me around the basement of the Concert Hall. We were in a carpeted room with a dressing area, complete with make-up mirror and an attached bathroom. There were 3 stacks of event chairs piled high in this room. J.T. stopped, plucked a chair from the pile and set it in the middle of the room. At first I thought he just wanted to sit down for a minute, but then he told me his story.

"I was down here checking on some things for the Engineering Department and I was in this room," J.T. said in his wonderful Mississippi drawl. "I'm in here and all these chairs are stacked up, just like you see them now." He gestures to the towering stacks of chairs, their legs fitting snugly into each other.

"Well, I had just left this room, and I hear a *thud*. So, I come back in here and this here chair is lying out in the middle of the floor, upside down. I stand there a minute, thinking that the law of gravity would not have put it in the middle of the room even if it did fall off the stack. Besides, just try and get one of those chairs off the stack."

I walked over to the first stack of heavy metal chairs and tried as hard as I could to dislodge one. I couldn't even get it to budge. I even committed something like, "How in the world do the event people get these down?"

J.T. nodded sagely and continued. "So, I pick up the chair and rather than mess with putting it back up there, I just set it by itself on the floor back against the stack." He demonstrated by placing the chair he had positioned in the center of the room back over by the stack of chairs.

"So, I am leaving the room again, and what do I hear? *Thud!*" So I come back in and there is the same chair, upside down back clear over here in the middle of the room! Ok, now I'm getting a little buggy about it! That chair does not topple over like that...try it!"

So, I stood it upright and tried shoving it. Nothing. I tried tipping it slightly to see if it would go all the way over. It was bottom heavy and settled back onto its legs. Frowning, I pushed it all the way over, but I literally had to have it almost sideways before it finally tipped to the floor.

"It happened three times that morning and finally I just said, 'Heck with it!' and left it there. I guess somebody else used it when they set up tables for some to-do over here."

As we continued through the basement, we stopped in the other dressing area, which is pretty much like the one we had just been in, only smaller. Here J.T. stopped and said, "Now in this room, one of the workers was in here and he had just opened a bottle of water, took one sip and was called into one of the other rooms for a minute. When he came back and reached for his bottle of water, it was almost empty. I mean, he had only taken one sip of it! He was too weirded-out to drink anymore of it."

Many of the staff at the Stanley Hotel dreads going into the Concert Hall more than any other area in the complex. Stories of things flying across a room, narrowly missing their head, trash strewn across a hallway that had not been there moments before, lights shutting off, suddenly leaving them in darkness, and furniture in the basement level moving about are all reported. There are a few that refuse to go into the building at all.

Long-time housekeeper Arty R. tells of being locked in the Men's Room. More frightening, and this time with a witness, Arty was cleaning the bathrooms in September 1994 when she felt her wrist being grabbed and her hand forced to write, "Mary Donovan, Aug. 18, 1927" on the mirror. Arty had been chasing the identity of the Lady in Green she had seen in the Manor House on another occasion for some time; she was convinced Mary Donovan was the name of the Lady in Green. (Susan S. Davis, *Stanley Ghost Stories*)

One of the more bizarre stories (I realize that is an oxymoron when talking about the Stanley Hotel) is from a woman in the cleaning crew. She was at the Concert Hall and noticed that the roof of the Concert Hall would be black with ravens when she went to clean it, and they would fly off when she left.

# Paul and Tim: Ghosts of the Hall

Candace C., part of the event staff at the hotel, and a person with some intuitive abilities, told me about her experiences at the Concert Hall, especially those concerning three ghosts: Paul, Tim and Lucy.

"There was a Gospel group called Legacy 5 who was finishing up a concert at the Concert Hall," Candace told me. "Those of us on the staff were in the balcony watching the entertainment until it was time to clean up after the performance. When the evening ended and everyone had cleared the building, we organized the basement, including the Green Rooms that the entertainment performers use. We finished up, shut off all the lights, shut the interior doors to the Green Rooms, bar area, backstairs, etc. There is also a closet door with a dead bolt that was securely locked.

"As we are leaving, we heard noises from the basement where we had just been. When we went back down the stairs, all the lights were on, all the doors were open, including the closet door with the dead bolt. We had made sure no one else was in the basement and no one could have opened the closet without a key to the bolt. Besides, during the performance someone was always stationed at the stairs to make sure no one went downstairs who wasn't authorized to do so."

Candace spoke of another time when many of the hotel employees were attending a Movie Night at the Concert Hall. The movie playing was....you guessed it....*The Shining!*

"A lot of us were sitting in the balcony watching the movie. We turned off all the lights to watch the show. The screen drops down from the ceiling above the stage. To the left of the stage is a small alcove, more like a closet. There is an old piano sitting there and some extra tables, stuff like that. To the right of the stage is a door leading to the back stairs that go to the basement. That door was ajar a few inches. As we're watching the movie, the lights to the right of the stage start flickering on and off and suddenly the door to the stairway leading down, *slams*! Then the lights on the left side of the stage start flickering on and off. No one was back there."

Ghost in chair in back row at the back. Photo by Kevin Lynn.

Courtney K., a bartender in the Cascades Restaurant at the hotel said she also would see the lights in the basement turn back on after she had shut them all off, locked the doors and was driving away. "I would look back, and there they were...all of them on after I had just shut them all off. The Men's bathroom light comes on all the time there as well."

I asked Candace C. if she had any guesses as to who was playing around with the lights.

"Paul was a maintenance man who died here in 2005 while trying to leave a snow-packed parking lot. He was having heart problems and was clearing snow near his car as he tried to get to the hospital. He died of a heart attack. He is one of the ghosts at the Concert Hall. He is calm and non-violent. It may be his footsteps we here overhead when we are in the basement. Someone walks from the front door toward the back of the hall all the time when no one is up there.

"The other male ghost is Tim. Tim used to work here long ago as a dance partner for the older ladies. He was suave, charming, and handsome, but he had an angry edge to him. He had dark hair and was in his 30's or 40's. Some people feel him caressing their hair. It has a malicious feeling to it. You can sense a lot of angst. Tim is a pacer and I sense him pacing a lot, especially by the back stairs and stage area."

# Lucy, the Resident Ghost of the Concert Hall

By far the most-reported stories from the Concert Hall revolve around a ghost by the name of Lucy. Lucy has no last name. Lucy was a transient woman who crawled into the basement of the Concert Hall (at the time it was the Casino) one winter to try and stay warm. She managed to pry open a window and sat huddled through the night. She was found dead from cold and exposure, frozen in the tattered clothes that were her only protection for the chilling Rocky Mountain winter nights.

Lucy has been known to shove people who have been in the basement on Ghost Hunts. These groups differ from the Ghost

Tours in that a select number of guests are given ghost hunting equipment, such as EMF's, tape recorders, etc. to try and capture activity in the Concert Hall basement. A woman on that "hunt" in the summer of 2009 was shoved into a wall by unseen hands. Mary Orton, the head tour guide at the hotel, said the woman had a bruise on her wrist where she hit the wall. Reportings of anyone being physically assaulted by the ghosts of the Stanley are very rare, and they seem to center around this particular one.

When J.T. was showing me around the basement, he paused in the open area at the bottom of the stairs leading up to the main foyer of the Hall. There is a small ledge there with a row of small casement windows. The ledge goes back a little ways behind a protruding wall.

"There," he said, pointing back into that corner. "They think that's where she died."

I felt a sadness looking at the lonely little alcove. I could see how easy it would have been to get in if the window was loose from the elements. At that time the main hotel and the Concert Hall were not heated and were abandoned in the winter months.

Area of the Concert Hall basement where Lucy is most active.
Photo by Rick Larsen.

The Ghost Hunters from the Sci-Fi Channel and other paranormal researchers, psychics included, have all reported evidence that someone is indeed haunting the basement. Sounds of footsteps coming down the steps toward you, only to pass right by you with no one there are reported. Hangers moving on the coat rack, as though a breeze has caressed them, doors slamming, furniture moving, etc. have all been reported.

If you are interested in booking one of the Ghost Hunts, please contact the reservation desk in the Ghost Tour Office at the Stanley Hotel.

Candace C. told me that while on a controlled Ghost Hunt in the basement, they had placed a flashlight on the floor and asked Lucy if she would turn it on. It came on. They asked her to turn it off...the light went out. This went back and forth for some time until they asked her to "Stop". The light remained off. Candace also said that if they asked for some kind of audible evidence that someone was with them, they would hear a scraping sound coming from a metal floor strip at the door entrance, as though a foot was dragging across it.

Possible image of Lucy's ghost (left) in Concert Hall basement.
Photo courtesy of Rick Larsen.

There are many more stories about this area of the hotel complex. They pour in daily. Please remember that unauthorized visits to the outbuildings of the Stanley Hotel complex are prohibited. The staff at the hotel is very gracious with their time and is usually willing to answer questions or book you on a very informative tour.

Concert Hall at night. Photo courtesy of Beckyphotography.com

Chapter Twenty-Five

# Carriage House & Out Buildings

"Where there is no imagination there is no Horror." Arthur
Conan Doyle, Sr.

The Carriage House at the Stanley Hotel. Photo by Dwayne
Elmarr.

There aren't many reports of ghostly activity concerning
the old Carriage House. In 2014 *Ghost Adventures* staked out the

inside and gave us a rare glimpse of a building that is strictly off-limits. The structure has been in need of repair for some time.

During the ghost hunt inside the Carriage House, the *Ghost Adventures* crew "hit on" a moving orb, cold spots, and a shape that seemed menacing. They pointed out a few stacked mattresses in the area and said these were called "dead beds." Whenever anyone passed away in a hotel, the mattresses had to be taken away. It was an eerie image to see the mattresses there, few though they were.

The building is being remodeled at this writing in readiness to turn it into the Stanley Motor Car Museum. There are several Stanley Steamers in Estes Park private collections. The Stanley Hotel is one of those collectors.

F.O. Stanley in 1910 giving a ride to a pair of twins. Perhaps they are the older version of the two girls who appear in *The Shining.*
Photo courtesy of the Stanley Museum.

There have been a few reports of blue orbs hovering outside the Carriage House doors, and once or twice people have reported hearing noises that sounded like a TV blaring from inside. Perhaps it's a residual haunting from when the building was a Motor Lodge.

# The Former Gate House/Presidential Suite

Former Gate House/Presidential Suite.
Photo Rebecca F. Pittman.

On December 4, 2003, Mr. And Mrs. Derek K. from Austin, Texas, and Mr. And Mrs. John C., from Buda, Texas, were staying in the Presidential Suite. At 10:30 p.m., the couples bolted the front doors shut and retired to bed. Derek heard footsteps in the kitchen and near the first-floor bedroom. Around 4:30 a.m., Mrs. K. heard a man and woman talking upstairs.

The next morning, the K.'s asked the C.'s about having gone out again after they'd come in together. Mr. C. was surprised. "I thought you guys went out again!"

Neither party had left their rooms after 10:30 p.m. (Susan S. Davis, *Stanley Ghost Stories*)

395

In the summer of 2007, one of the housekeeping staff was in the Presidential Suite doing a routine cleaning. The main door to the outside was closed behind her as there was a fairly strong wind blowing and she didn't want dirt coming into the Suite. As she went about her duties, there came a knock at the door. Assuming it was probably a guest wanting to peek inside, she went to the door and opened it. There was no one there. She looked to the left and right of the door, but there was no one on the path. Frowning slightly, she went back to work, wondering if the wind was playing tricks on her.

About five minutes later, the knock came again, slightly louder. This time she paused, now wondering if it might be children or the teenagers she had seen around the pool area earlier playing a prank. She tiptoed to the small windows flanking the door and peered out. She could see no one, nor did she hear footsteps running away.

Determined not to be made fun of, she posted herself near the large window to the right of the main door, keeping herself hidden from anyone who was looking toward the front of the structure. She waited several minutes, and was about to give up and get back to her work when the pounding at the door came again...four loud deliberate banging sounds. She jumped. She was looking at the small porch in front of the door. There was absolutely *no one* out there and the wind had actually abated only moments before. Her arms covered with goose flesh when suddenly the door shook from the force of three more loud bangs. She squealed, grabbed up her supplies and ran for the door, not caring who or what she ran into as long as she was away from the building. As she threw open the door, she felt a very cold sensation, as though she had passed through an open freezer. The day was hot, at least 88 degrees and the wind was no longer blowing. She shut the door, locked it with trembling fingers and ran for the main hotel.

David Radcliffe. New York, NY. June, 1014. "My story is not about staying in the Presidential Suite building. Some of my friends have and all of them have said you hear strange noises at night and things moving around. I witnessed something outside the Suite. I was having a romantic weekend with my wife at the hotel. After dinner we were out walking around the grounds. As we passed the building called the Presidential Suite I stopped short and pointed at the front door. "Do you see that?" I asked her. "She looked and blinked a few times. It was clear she saw what I was pointing at as she gripped my arm and backed around behind me. There was an old guy in dirty bib overalls sitting by the front door in a high-back rocker, rocking back and forth and grinning at us. He was puffing on one of the pipes with the really long skinny neck. He was looking right at us and grinning. There was no color to him. None at all. He just looked like a dirty grey. Have any of your other readers mentioned seeing something like that at the Presidential Suite?"

# Former Manager's House/Executive Offices

Former Manager's House/Executive Offices.
Photo by Rebecca F. Pittman.

The former Manager's House is today used as the Executive Offices for the Stanley Hotel. Set amid the pines, it is a beautiful setting with views from the General Manager's office window worth salivating over.

The tall, erect form of F.O. Stanley is the most reported sighting in the Executive Offices. He has been seen peering over the Management's shoulders as they go about running his beloved hotel. There are also reports of doors closing on their own and one of a shadow that appears on the wall of the steep staircase as one ascends to the offices above. This shadow appears to be female with long-flowing skirts. Perhaps Flora is also making sure the wheels of her beautiful hotel are well oiled and moving smoothly.

# The North and South Dormitories

North and South Dormitories. Photos by Ron Bueker.

The two buildings serving as living quarters for many of the out-of-state staff at the Stanley Hotel sit at the top of the back driveway at the rear of the complex. Nestled into the jagged rock and towering pines, staff have reported feeling slightly isolated from the hectic activity of the main hotel only a few yards across the paved drive. These employees typically enter the hotel via a side door that leads to the underground tunnel of the hotel. It is also here that the head housekeeper has an office, and the employee dining room is just off to the left of the entrance from outside.

The dorms have quite a few stories that add shivers. Here are a few:

In the summer of 2001, a housekeeper, who worked for the hotel for the three-month season, related that everyday brought a new paranormal experience in the main hotel. But it was what was going on in her dorm room that finally rattled her into leaving.

In the dormitory, she had an upstairs room on the north side. Every night she would lock her door and lay out her shirt, her hairbrush and other items she would need first thing in the morning so that she could get dressed in a hurry. Come morning, her door was still locked, but the items she had set out were all gone. She never "lost" anything. She might find her brush in the kitchen, her shirt in the bathroom, and other items scattered in other public areas of the dormitory. These morning searches were an annoying, not to say disturbing, way to start the day.

Aware that old buildings have door keys that often fit more than one door, she went to Ace Hardware and bought a sliding bolt, which she installed on her door. Even then, her clothes disappeared, clearing her fellow staff of the crime. She finally gave up putting out her clothes because she spent too much time looking for them.

The scariest situations that she encountered would happen if she woke in the middle of the night. She would see shadow-type people walking on the walls of her room. This really scared her. She would roll up in a ball in the middle of the bed and hide under her covers, too scared to open her eyes again until dawn. She said many of the housekeepers had similar experiences. She was thrilled and relieved when her three-month commitment to the hotel was up and she could get away from the Stanley. She refuses to ever set foot on the property again. (Susan S. Davis, *Stanley Ghost Stories*)

Selma Ortiz. Stanley Hotel Housekeeping. "As I was living in the dorms, it was winter of 2003 and all the employees for the summer were gone, and I was alone (I sometimes would bring my 14-yr-young daughter Felicia on the weekends to work there with me as a busser in the restaurant.) I would be in the shower and I could hear someone trying to open the door and I would say wait, then they would just walk up and down the stairs and hallway and keep trying to get in turning the door knob. The bathroom was on the corner of the stairway and my room was down the hall. They just walked constantly, waiting impatiently to get in, so I came out and no one was there. I went back to my room to check on my daughter and tell her she can go to the bathroom now but she was sound asleep. I asked her if she got up she said no!

"Being alone, there were other times I would hear the same things: lots of pacing up and down the hallway and stairway!!!!!! There were 2 buildings for the dorms. In the other one there were about 4 guys living there and one of them would tell me if I ever needed assistance to let him know. I would lock the place up really good and I checked all the doors and windows before going to bed, since I am a female living by myself. So, one night around 2 or 3 am I woke up to hearing footsteps walking around my door. I stayed very quiet. Then they were trying to turn the door knob to get in and all I could think of was who was trying to get in (which I knew they can't get in). I kept quiet. Then they started knocking but with three knuckles. You can tell it was a boney knock...it sounded very eeerrrie!!! Whoever it was they kept it up for a little over an hour. I was so scared. I had my phone under my pillow and I was too scared to move or even open the window to call for help, so I just laid there till they left. I had to be at work 5:30 am. When I got up to get ready I checked everything and all of the doors and windows were still locked up tight! I was very tired and mad when I got to work and asked who dared try to get in the dorm and my room (the guys didn't know which room was mine) no one knew what I was talking about, so that is when I knew it was the ghosts I'd heard about from other women who had stayed in the dorm! Other times I would feel someone getting into bed with me and touching my back. I got used to it; it happened a lot. Also the clock I had in my room; in the mornings I would notice it would always stop working at 2:26 am every night. I would reset it and it would be at 2:26 am when I got up again.

# The Former Laundry/Engineering Building

Former Laundry/Engineering Building. Photo Ron Bueker.

Stories coming from the Engineering Building are

401

mostly those of tools missing, and things being moved around. J.T., head engineer reported that there is an atmosphere in the old Laundry building. The planked walls are reminiscent of a barn. Towering shelves packed with everything from paint to wallpaper, varnish to hardware is everyone one looks. He says there are times he will look over his shoulder sure there is someone watching him. This building, and the Concert Hall basement, is the only two places that give him the shivers.

# The Ice House and Pond

Former Ice House. Photo Ron Bueker.

The only stories emanating from the Old Ice House are ones of an equestrian nature. The small house also served to house a few ponies that were used to give children at the hotel rides. You can see the corral fence. A few people have said they hear a horse whinnying as they go by. There have not been horses housed there in a long time.

The pond near the Ice House is all but dried up unless a Rocky Mountain thunder Storm empties into it. It will be the location of the new Pavilion and Amphitheater going in soon.

Those are the paranormal reports regarding this amazing hotel complex set in the majestic Rockies. Stories continue to fill the FB messenger and email box dedicated to this book. It is one of the spookiest venues in the world for a reason. It's haunted!

Frequent hotel guests courtesy of the Rocky Mountains.

# Appendix I:

# THE COMPLETE GHOST HUNTER'S GUIDE

*"From ghoulies and ghosties, And long-legged beasties, And things that go bump in the night, Good Lord, deliver us!" Scottish Prayer*

David Juliano, from his website *The Shadowlands: Ghosts and Hauntings,* was kind enough to give me permission to reprint his advice and guides to successful ghost hunting. The following excerpt is from his **Ghost Hunting 101**.

Photo courtesy of diy.allwomenstalk.com

## What you may encounter:

There are generally two types of spirits you may encounter. One was a human at one time and it has remained on this level for some reason. It may not know its dead, maybe held by unfinished business, guilt, etc. These spirits are like the person was when they were alive, so they could be good or bad, just like the living, but not normally dangerous. This human spirit is the type you will encounter 95% of the time. You could also witness a residual haunting which is just a playback of a past event. This is just like watching a video from the past playing over and over. The other types of spirits you may encounter were never human and are generally bad news. You must be aware of this type but not obsessed with them. The chances that you will encounter them in a regular ghost hunt are slim. I have experienced both types and I just want to make you aware of their existence. So be aware and protect yourself and you should have no problem.

## General Tips:

- Check out the area in the daylight so you are familiar with the area. Look for    dangerous places and obstacles that you will not be able to see in the dark.

- Make sure you are not trespassing. Ask for permission to access different areas of the property.

- Never go alone. If you get hurt, who will get help?

- The best times are from 9 pm to 6 am, these are the psychic hours, but anytime can produce results. Photos have historically been better in the dark but don't let that discourage you from taking them during the day.

- Find out all you can about the history of the locale.

- Bring your I.D. in the event the police or property owner questions you.

## What to Bring:

## The Basics:

- 35mm Camera—Nothing fancy with at least 400-speed film. 800-speed film is also good at night but you'll have to test your camera flash strength to see which speed works best for you. More experienced photographers may want to try infrared film. If you are having someone develop your film, be sure and tell them you want

ALL of the photos, even the ones they may think are bad. These "bad ones" are normally your best ectoplasm mist photos.

• Digital Camera. Regardless of what you've heard, digital cameras are great tools for ghost researchers. Not only do they allow you to see instantly if you have a positive photo, they can also take photos in limited infrared range of light.

• Flashlight with spare batteries. Due to spirit activity, batteries often run down very fast and you don't want to miss anything. I recommend using a red lens flashlight to help preserve your night vision. (You can find out more about red lens on *The Shadowlands* website.)

• First-Aid Kit, just in case. You can trip in the dark.

• Notebook with pens and pencils. You need to log everything that happens. A high EMF reading along with anomalous image, gives the image more credibility than if mentioned separately. Take careful notes of location, time and readings.

• Jackets or weather appropriate clothes.

• Watch, so you can log in the times of events and their arrival and departure.

**Advanced and Optional:**
• Video Camera and optional tripod. Video cameras are an important instrument for an investigation. Unlike still cameras they provide us with constant visual and audio surveillance for review and observation. The video cameras we use are equipped with infrared capability and this is the mode we use. With video any phenomena occurring can be documented in its entirety. This will show the length of time the phenomena occurs, what is happening, the conditions surrounding the phenomena, and the possibly even the cause of the phenomena. The Sony line of camcorders has an infrared night shot feature that enables you to videotape in complete darkness and see beyond what the human eye can see. You can use these on tripods or walk around with them. You should also invest in an infrared light

extender, which will help your camera see in the darkest places and make the quality of the video better.

• Tape recorder with external microphone and high-grade tapes. Recorders or digital voice recorders are without a doubt one of the most important pieces of equipment that you should have in your investigations. Audio recorders are used for many different purposes throughout an investigation. Recorders are used for interviews, spontaneous thoughts, your notes and electronic voice phenomena (EVP). You have to use an external microphone when recording EVPs (ghost voices). If you rely on internal microphones you will also be recording the internal gears and motors and this will make your tape worthless. The type of tape that is most recommended is high bias tapes or metal tapes.

• Digital Audio Recorders. This recorder is small and easy to carry. You can also use the voice activation feature so there is less audio to review. I use this for my notes as well. Most units record the time of the recording as well which is very useful. When using audio recorders, be sure to state the location, time of investigation, and investigator's names. When recording investigator's names, it would be wise to have each individual present state their own names, which will make it easier for distinction amongst voices heard on the tape during review. Voice activation mode should be deactivated on *tape* recorders during use when EVP is trying to be achieved due to the fact that it usually cuts off beginning of words, sentences and phrases. This is not necessary with *digital* recorders and they actually seem to work better in voice activation mode.

• EMF Detector. The Electromagnetic Field Detector, also known as an EMF, is the modern day ghost researcher's tracking device, a very important piece of equipment. With this instrument it is possible to locate and track energy sources. It will detect fluctuations in electromagnetic fields and low strength moving EMF fields that have no source. It is a common theory that spirits disrupt this field in such a way that you can tell one is present by higher than normal readings with this meter. Before using EMF's as a ghost research tool on an investigation, be sure to walk around the area and take initial readings you receive while scanning the area during the investigation. Most units purchased come with a manual describing most household and major appliances and their corresponding electromagnetic reading. When using the EMF as a tracking device, look for fluctuations of 2.0 to 7.0. This usually indicates spirit presence. Anything higher or lower is normally a natural source.

• Cellular phone for emergencies.

• A Compass. When used on an investigation this will indicate spirit presence when the needle cannot come to a precise heading or spins/moves erratically. This works on the same principle as an EMF meter.

•     Candles and matches as batteries often run low during ghost hunts. Be careful using candles around motion detectors, as they will set them off.

•     Motion Detectors. These can be used to sense movements by often-unseen forces or spirits. You can get battery operated ones for about $20 and they are great for inside but I have seen them used successfully outdoors as well, just watch the placement. You don't want a tree branch setting it off.

•     Thermometer or Thermal Scanner. Thermometers are an instrument that are very useful. There are two types used: regular digital thermometers and infrared non-contact thermometers. When used on an investigation this will aid as a detection system for spirit presence. Rapid temperature drop of 10 degrees or more could indicate spirit presence. I recommend using the infrared non-contact thermometers because they react in less than a second to a temperature drop and you can scan a large area quickly.

•     Hand Held Radios, or Walkie Talkies are very useful in a large outdoor area and a building with groups spread out in various rooms. Be sure to be aware they could interfere with your EVP recording though.

**Taking Pictures:**

**For 35mm cameras**: Open your film and load your camera after walking around the location for about 20 minutes first. Use at least 400-speed 35mm film. 400 and 800 speeds work best. Black and White film also works well. You may want to try infrared film if you are an experienced photographer.

•     Make sure you note other light sources in the area so that you don't think a streetlight is an orb.

•     Make sure you clean your camera lens regularly.

•     No smoking on location. This can appear like mist on the photos so you don't want to contaminate your evidence.

- Watch for dust or dirt being stirred up in the area you are photographing. They can give false positive pictures. (Many "orbs" are really dust reflecting off camera flashes. Author's note)

- All long hair should be tied back, again to eliminate any false positives.

- Remove or tie up camera straps. It can look like a vortex when photographed.

- Don't bother with your camera viewfinder. Hold the camera out in front of you and aim at the area you want to take a picture of. Many newer digital cameras do no not even come with viewfinders. This also helps in cold weather by keeping your camera away from your breath (which can appear as spirits or mist in a photo).

- Watch for reflective surfaces such as windows or shiny tombstones. They can look like an orb or other anomaly.

- Let fellow investigators know when you are taking a photo so that you don't get double flashes and the night scope operators can look away.

- Many people like to ask the spirit if they can take their picture. It can't hurt.

- Take photos whenever you get a positive reading on any piece of equipment. (The naked eye may not see something there, but it may imprint onto the camera film.

- Sometimes you will see an orb, mist or sparkles in your flash or other's flashes, take more pictures right there, you may be near a spirit!

- You may only get about 1-2 pictures for every 50 you take, which is about average.

- Don't pay for fancy developing. Discount photo stores are fine and remember to tell the processor you want every photo, no matter what it may look like.

## Audio and Video Recording:

• You can set up stationary recorders and just let them run or you can walk around with them. During audio recording, ask questions whether general ones or specific ones to a certain spirit.

• Make sure you view or listen to the whole tape. EVP's are usually not heard at the time of recording but are heard only after the tape is reviewed.

## More tips:

• If it is raining, snowing or foggy and you are scheduled to do an outdoor ghost hunt, reschedule it. You cannot conduct a proper investigation in these conditions.

• Keep an open mind. Any negative feelings may drive the spirits away. Be respectful of the location and the dead.

• Be skeptical when it comes to looking for causes for any phenomenon such as natural or man-made.

• No smoking, alcohol or drugs at an investigation for obvious reasons.

• No whispering, it can taint your recording results.

• The Tax Assessors Office can give you historical info on many locations you visit.

• Do not wear perfume, cologne or anything else with a noticeable scent. This is so someone does not mistake the smell for a supernatural occurrence. Spirits often use scents and smells to get our attention.

• Make sure you let someone know where you will be so they will know in case of an emergency.

I want to thank David Juliano with *TheShadowlands.net* for his invaluable information. His website also carries Ghost Hunting equipment and much more information for the paranormal enthusiast.

# Ghost Hunting Equipment That Went Viral

Mike Coletta is part of a team of paranormal investigators who formed the Rocky Mountain Ghost Explorers. He and partner Kris Tennant have a long history of understanding what "goes bump in the night." Mike is a retired Department of Defense Logistics Specialist and has worked on UFO cases. He has been featured on many TV shows and specials, including *My Ghost Story, America's Secret Structures*, and featured in numerous articles on *NPR, CNN, Huff Post*, and more. He and Kris have researched numerous "haunted houses" and hotels. Mike is the originator of Radio *Shack Hack* 12-470 ghost box, also known as the spirit box, as well as the creator of other numerous prototype paranormal devices. He was kind enough to share with me how he came about creating his unique spirit box:

"In 2007 there were very few, if any, devices that could be called high-tech paranormal investigation tools. Of course there were the standard "tools of the trade" that were used by the few that really dabbled a bit deeper than most. Audio recorders, dowsing rods, crystal pendants, flashlights, meters that detected electrical charges and other common household items were in use during investigations.

"Among the more interesting tools of that time was a device called a "Frank's Box", or, telephone to the dead, as some called it. Invented by a man named Frank Sumption (now deceased), this box spit out audio snippets at variable rates; and was used or claimed to be used, to communicate with those in the afterlife. Frank made very few of these, so the demand for them was extreme. At that time there were only approximately ten in the world. They were extremely rare.

"I became very interested in the workings of this Frank's Box, so I studied schematics of the device that I found online. After understanding how the box worked, I formulated a way to alter an ordinary radio to do the same thing a Frank's Box could do. I was able to take a Radio Shack model 12-470 multiband radio, and after altering some of the internal circuitry, make it perform just like a

Frank's Box. Since there were just a few real Frank's Boxes out there, and since so many wanted one, I decided to share with the paranormal world how to make your own Frank's Box using a number of Radio Shack radios. It became very popular.

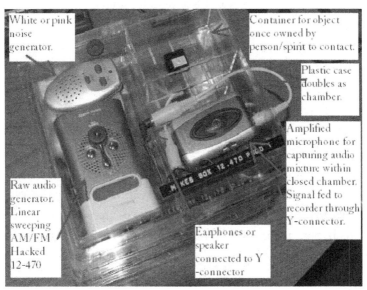

White or pink noise generator.

Container for object once owned by person/spirit to contact.

Plastic case doubles as chamber.

Amplified microphone for capturing audio mixture within closed chamber. Signal fed to recorder through Y-connector.

Raw audio generator. Linear sweeping AM/FM Hacked 12-470

Earphones or speaker connected to Y-connector

Mike Coletta's Shack Hack spirit box. Photo courtesy of Mike Coletta with the Rocky Mountain Ghost Explorers.

"I produced two videos, the first ever produced, that shows this process, on how to "hack" a model 12-469 and 12-470, making it function just like the telephone to the dead. My videos went viral! Over a million hits in all by the time I took them down. Also going viral were the sales of the two Radio Shack model radios shown in my videos. Now thousands of people around the world could make their own Frank's Box-type paranormal tool, just by following the instructions in my video. Real Time Spirit Communication (RTSC) was the name, and the *Shack Hack* was born!

"Between 2007 and 2009 I went on to make a number of other prototype paranormal devices. Probably about 15 in all. These I placed online in a how-to book, so others could make them if they desired.

Some of Mike Coletta's paranormal equipment in Room 401
at the Stanley Hotel in 2009. Photo Mike Coletta.

"Two of these devices, an 8-in-1 micro box and a shadow
detector caught the attention of the TV show, *Ghost Hunters
International.* Their tech guy wrote me numerous times asking if
they could use these devices for their show. I told them NO, because
I had not fully tested them. I was contacted by the Stanley Hotel, I
assume after being contacted by the show. The Stanley kindly offered
to let me stay in room 401 for free so I could test my devices.

"I stayed in room 401, tested the devices, allowed a number of
tour groups at the Stanley to view the devices and tests, and then told

the *Ghost Hunters International* show people I did not feel the equipment was ready to air on TV, at that time.

After perfecting the devices, I eventually got on a number of TV shows, in books, in magazines, on radio, on web articles.... and the rest is Paranormal History! (By the way, some of the devices you see on the market today, I made as prototypes long ago, and they were shown in my free how-to book.)"

Mike Coletta checking out Lord Dunraven's portrait in the Lobby of Stanley Hotel with his Mel meter. Photo Mike Coletta.

416

One of Mike Coletta's paranormal detection devices outside the closet door of Room 401 at the Stanley Hotel. The device is called the Micro Box. Among other things it has a camera, tests temperatures, has a proximity detection alarm, Ion detector and more. It is this closet said to be haunted by Lord Dunraven. Photo courtesy of Mike Coletta.

For information on Mike's devices, or to request a lecture or paranormal investigation from him and Kris Tennant, please reach out to them at contact@rockymountainghostexplorers.com.

# Appendix II:

# THE STANLEY HOTEL FLOOR PLANS

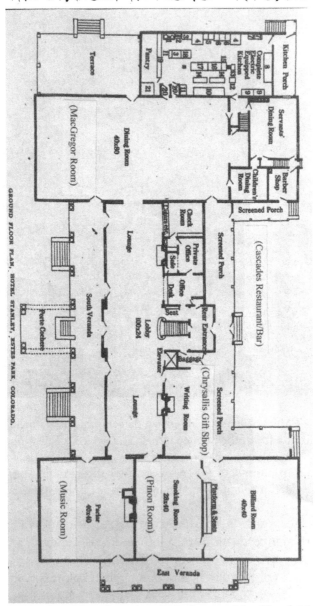

Stanley Hotel Lobby Floor in 1909, featured in *Hotel Monthly*.
*The names of the rooms today have been added in parenthesis.

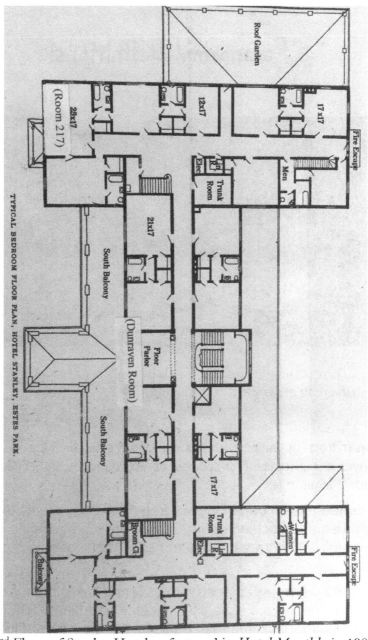

2nd Floor of Stanley Hotel as featured in *Hotel Monthly* in 1909.

# Appendix III:

# Paranormal Definitions

This is just a partial list but one that will aid you in understanding the world of the paranormal.

**Apparition**- an image with distinct features that enables one to recognize it as a person or specific object; typically associated with residual hauntings.

**Banshee**- Death omen spirit of Ireland that manifests to herald an approaching death.  Heard wailing or singing mournfully.  Contrary to popular belief, banshees do not shriek.

**Battlefield Ghosts**- places with violence, trauma and intense emotion are typically subject to hauntings.  There are no places more violent than battlefields, and it is rare to hear of a battlefield that isn't haunted.  Most battlefield hauntings are residual hauntings where fragments of the battle are replayed over and over again.  Other hauntings are from spirits who have not crossed over, most likely because they feel they can't due to the nature of their death. Some believe retro cognition is also an element in battlefield hauntings.

**Calling Ghosts**- Ghosts that call out the names of the living to get their attention and lure them to their death. An example would be sirens of mythology.

**Clairvoyance**- paranormal vision of objects, events, places, and people not visible through normal sight.

**Crossroads**- The meeting and parting of ways has always been considered magical. In addition, crossroads are said to be haunted by various entities who lead confused travelers astray. It is also said that on All Hollow's Eve (Halloween), spirits of the dead appear at a crossroad.

**Ectoplasm**- Vaporous substance, often white in appearance, sometimes forms into faces, limbs, or entire bodies of ghosts.

**Electronic Voice Phenomenon**- (EVP) recording on audiotape, videotape, film, or digital recorder for which there is no physical source. Most often, these voices are difficult to understand.

**Elemental**- an angry or malicious spirit, also referred to as "earth spirits". Elementals are considered to be ancient.

**EMF**- electromagnetic frequency. EMF meters measure the amount of electromagnetic frequencies or forces in a specific location. You can get a "hit" off of wall outlets, electronic equipment, etc. so natural or man-made indicators must be ruled out in order to get a true paranormal reading.

**Exorcism**- Expulsion of ghosts, spirits, demons or other entities believed to be disturbing or possessing a human being or place that humans frequent. Exorcism can range from friendly conversations to rituals commanding the entity to leave.

**Extra**- A shape or face that appears in a photograph supernaturally and cannot be explained away as fraud, developing flaws, or faulty film.

**Extra Sensory Perception (ESP)**- Paranormal sensing of sight, sound, smell, taste, and touch separated into three categories: telepathy, clairvoyance, and precognition.

**Ghost**- generic term used to describe many different types of supernatural entities.

**Ghost Hunting**- methods of investigating reports of ghosts and hauntings to determine their authenticity.

**Grey Ladies**- ghosts of women who supposedly died violently for the sake of love or pined away from loss of love. The name comes from their frequent appearance as ladies dressed in grey. Variations include ladies in white such as the one that frequents Spangler's Spring in Gettysburg, PA.

**Haunting**- repeated manifestation of strange and unexplained sensory events such as smells, sounds, tactile sensations, and hallucinations, said to be caused by ghosts or spirits attached to the locale.

**Intelligent Haunting**- Paranormal activity that takes place around a person or location that is caused by an intelligent or conscious spirit. Best described as the spirit of an individual who has passed away but not crossed over. The spirit interacts with people trying to make its presence known through repeated sights, sounds, smells, and the manipulation of objects.

**Orb**- Energy anomalies that are recorded on film, digital cameras, infrared monitors, and videotape. They have also been seen using night vision goggles. Considered the most basic form of a spirit. Orbs provide the best evidence of a haunting. Do be careful of photographing reflective surfaces as these can create orbs in a photo.

**Paranormal**- meaning beyond the normal, term is used to refer to unexplainable events.

**Poltergeist**- from the German word *poltern* "to knock" and *geist* "spirit" this term is used to define a mischievous or malevolent ghost characterized by noises, moving objects, and physical disturbances. It is sometimes attributed to emotionally charged people whose volatile energy impacts their surroundings. They are usually unconscious of the fact they are causing the phenomenon happening around them. Teenagers are usually targeted as the suspected antagonist.

**Reciprocal Apparition**- A rare type of sighting where the spirit and the witness see each other and react to one another.

**Reincarnation**- concept that the soul returns after death to a new body. Explanation of past lives.

**Retrocognition**- Displacement in time in which one apparently sees into the past

**Séance**- Sitting organized for the purpose of communicating with the dead or to witness paranormal manifestations via the services of a medium.

**Spirit**- Discarnate being, essence or supernatural force of nature.

**Spirit Photography**- Photos alleged to reveal ghosts, spirits, or spirits of the dead. The first spirit photo was taken in 1861.

**Supernatural**- Events that take place beyond, or in violation of, the laws of nature.

**Telepathy**- communication between minds by some means other than the normal sensory channels; transference of thought.

**Urban Legend**- A story too good to be true. Contains strange but supposedly

real event.

## Select Bibliography:

The following authors graciously contributed to this book. A heartfelt thank you to:

**Susan S. Davis**. Susan has been the Executive Director and Curator of the Stanley Museum, both in Kingfield, Maine, and in Estes Park, Colorado for many years. She is an expert on the subject of F.O. Stanley and his impact on Estes Park. Her books include:

Stanley Ghost Stories (2005 Stanley Museum)

A History and Tour of The Stanley Hotel, Estes Park, Colorado (1999, Stanley Museum)

Stanley Family Reunion (Editor of the transcription of the Stanley Family Gathering, 1981)

**Ron Lasky**. Ron is a talented gentleman who did a wealth of background research on the Stanley Hotel. He and his wife Celeste often appear in period costume at the Hotel, posing as the late F.O. and Flora Stanley. Ron bears a striking resemblance to Mr. Stanley and has been used in media productions as his stand-in.

A Concise History of The Stanley Hotel, Estes Park, Colorado, 2nd Edition (2001, 2005, Write On Publications)

**Celeste Lasky.** Celeste is a warm, talented woman who worked at the Stanley Hotel for several years. Her collection of ghost stories from the hotel and other areas in Estes Park has been a popular read since their publication in 1998. She, along with her husband, Ron often pose in period costume as Flora and F.O. Stanley.

Ghost Stories of the Estes Valley, Volume 1 (1998, Write On Publications)

**Bev Vincent**. Bev is a contributing editor with *Cemetery Dance* magazine, where he has been writing the column "News from the Dead Zone" since 2001. He is a two-time Bram Stoker Award nominee, once for his first book, *The Road to the Dark Tower*, and then again for *The Stephen King Illustrated Companion*, which also garnered an Edgar Allan Poe Award nomination from the Mystery Writers of America."
He co-edited *The Illustrated Stephen King Trivia Book* and has published over fifty short stories. His screenplay for the "dollar baby" film *Stephen King's Gotham Café*, co-written with two other writers, was named Best Adaptation at the international Horror and Sci-Fi Film Festival in 2004. His Web site is www.bevvincent.com.

*The Stephen King Illustrated Companion* (2009, Fall River Press, by arrangement with becker&mayer! LLC)

**Loyd Auerbach, M.S.** Loyd is the Director of the Office of Paranormal Investigations, and has been investigating cases of apparitions, hauntings and poltergeists for over 30 years. He is a professor at JFK University, the creator/instructor of the Parapsychological Studied Program at HCH Institute and on the advisory boards of three major organizations. He is also the author of several books on ghosts, ESP and other psychic phenomena. His first book, *"ESP, Hauntings and Poltergeists"* was named the "sacred text" on ghosts by *Newsweek* in August, 1996. His latest book *Haunted by Chocolate,* out late 2010, is a much-anticipated release. Interviews with Mr. Auerbach can be found in abundance both in print, on TV and online.

**George Beahm**. *The Stephen King Story: A Literary Profile*, Kansas City, Missouri: Andrews and McMeel, 1992.

**David Juliano**. David is the creator of *The Shadowlands: Ghosts and Hauntings,* an informative and well researched website that has everything, and I do mean *everything*, you could ever want to know about the realm of the supernatural. Whether you are interested in learning more about definitions of what goes bump in the night, or out to stage your own ghost hunt, Dave's website is one-stop shopping, including all the technical gear needed to record and classify those elusive spirits.

## Recommended Reading:

*A Concise History of The Stanley Hotel, Estes Park, Colorado (2ⁿᵈ Edition).* Ron Lasky, Write On Publications, Loveland, Colorado, 2005

*Stanley Ghost Stories.* Edited by Susan S. Davis, The Stanley Museum, Estes Park, Colorado, 2005

*A History and Tour of The Stanley Hotel, Estes Park, Colorado.* Susan S. Davis, The Stanley Museum, Kingfield, Maine and Estes Park, Colorado, 1999.

*Ghost Stories of the Estes Valley, Volume 1.* Celeste Lasky, Write On Publications, Loveland, Colorado, 1998.

*Tenderfoot in the Rockies.* Flora Stanley, circa 1903. The Stanley Museum, Estes Park, Colorado and Kingfield, Maine.

*Stanley Family Reunion.* Edited by Susan S. Davis, Kingfield, Maine, 1982.

*It's Ghost Time at the Stanley Hotel.* Billy Ward, Temporal Mechanical Press, 2010.

*The Stanley Steamer, America's Legendary Steam Car.* Kit Foster, Stanley Museum, publisher, 2004.

For historical information on the building of Estes Park, the early settlers, the building of the Stanley Hotel, etc., please check out the books by James Pickering.

## Recommended...Period:

The Estes Park Museum
200 4th Street
Estes Park, Colorado  80517


Stanley Museum
40 School Street
Kingfield, Maine 04947


Historic Fall River Hydroplant Museum
1754 Fish Hatchery Road
Estes Park, Colorado 80517


MacGregor Ranch Museum
180 MacGregor Lane
Estes Park, Colorado 80517


The Rocky Mountain Ghost Explorers
For paranormal investigations, lectures and information
Kris Tennant and Mike Coletta
www.rockymountainghostexplorers.com
email:  contact@rockymountainghostexplorers.com

# ABOUT THE AUTHOR

Rebecca F. Pittman is a paranormal historian who is thrilled to make her living going into the most-haunted venues in America—that just happen to be National Historic Landmarks.

"It is such a humbling experience to be given "the keys" to these places that have witnessed so much history. Going through newspaper archives, digging through Historic Society records, interviewing people, and discovering secrets is pure joy. When you come across that nugget that lights up the property owner's eyes, that is the real thrill! The ghosts are just a bonus."

*The History and Haunting of the Stanley Hotel, The History and Haunting of the Myrtles Plantation,* and *The History and Haunting of Lemp Mansion, and The History and Haunting of Lizzie Borden* are all best-selling books that act as a personal tour guide to these amazing venues. Ms. Pittman is also working on a series of murder mystery thrillers with a supernatural bent. She has also authored books on creative art businesses, a dating and relationship guide for women called *Troubleshooting Men*, and a popular children's novel called *T.J. Finnel and the Well of Ghosts*, which is finding just as many adults reading it as children.

Lately her attention has also turned to writing television docudramas after being approached by a large production company interested in optioning her book on Lemp Mansion.

Rebecca makes her home in the foothills of the Rocky Mountains, where she enjoys golf, boating and adventures with her family.

# Other books by Rebecca F. Pittman:

## Paranormal History:
The History and Haunting of the Stanley Hotel, 1st Edition
(23 House Publishing, 2011)
The History and Haunting of the Myrtles Plantation
(23 House Publishing, 2012)
The History and Haunting of Lemp Mansion
(Wonderland Productions, 2015)
The History and Haunting of the Myrtles Plantation, 2nd Edition
(Wonderland Productions, 2016)
The History and Haunting of Lizzie Borden House
(Wonderland Productions, 2017)

**Coming Soon**:
The History and Haunting of Salem

## Business Books for the Creative Arts:

How to Start a Faux Painting or Mural Business, 1st & 2nd
Editions
(Allworth Press, 2003, 2010)
Scrapbooking for Profit, 1st & 2nd Editions
(Allworth Press, 2005, 2014)

## Self-Help/Dating & Marriage Advice for Women:
Troubleshooting Men: What in the WORLD do they want?
(Wonderland Productions, 2014)

## Paranormal Fiction:

T. J. Finnel and the Well of Ghosts

**Coming Soon in Paranormal Thrillers**:

Don't Look Now!
The Diamond Peacock Club

## T.J. Finnel and the Well of Ghosts.
## Now on Sale!

An ancient well with secret symbols sitting in the center of the most-haunted woods in America; constellations coming to life; witches, ghosts and creatures from other dimensions—all in search of four things before the Dark Moon rises: Lunar Potion, an ancient map, the Dark Orb and the Crone's crystal eye.

Join T.J., Mandolin Brandy and a talking troll-head walking cane named Twicket as they take on the Spectre Lands…and to do that, they must enter the Well of Ghosts.